D0844789

PATTERNS OF LOVE AND COURTESY
Essays in Memory of C. S. Lewis

PATTERNS OF
LOVE AND COURTESY

Essays in Memory of C. S. Lewis

Edited by
JOHN LAWLOR

Northwestern University Press
Evanston
1966

First published in the U.S.A. 1966 by Northwestern University Press
under arrangement with Edward Arnold (Publishers) Ltd., London

Second printing, 1970
ISBN 0-8101-0280-3

Copyright © Edward Arnold (Publishers), Ltd. 1966
Printed in the United States of America
Library of Congress Catalog Card Number: 66-22582

Preface

These essays are all in a field which the late C. S. Lewis made very much his own. It is hoped they extend and vary some of the considerations advanced in his writings, notably *The Allegory of Love*.

That the present writers, who all enjoyed Lewis's friendship, should on occasion qualify or oppose his contentions would have afforded him the liveliest satisfaction. He once described himself, most aptly, as a man 'hungry for rational opposition'. It is our loss that we cannot now look to him to challenge, to re-order, and where necessary to confute, what we have written.

Our hope had been to present this book to Lewis in the year of his retirement. As it is, we can only repeat words he himself used on a comparably sad occasion. 'Death forestalled us; we now offer as a memorial what had been devised as a greeting'.

J. L.

84071

Contents

The granz biens *of Marie de France*

C. S. Lewis's interest in 'courtly love' stimulates reflection on a wide range of topics, among them the varying relations between an ostensible good and the matter of love. In the oft-quoted prologue to her *lais* Marie de France speaks about her vocation to write:

> Ki Deus ad duné escïence
> E de parler bon' eloquence
> Ne s'en deit taisir ne celer,
> Ainz se deit volunters mustrer (1)

and about the good which ought to come of it:

> Quant uns granz biens est mult oïz,
> Dunc a primes est il fluriz,
> E quant loëz est de plusurs,
> Dunc ad espandues ses flurs. (5)

What, we may ask, is the *granz biens*? It seems a simple question, but the answer is far from simple—or, at least, it is not always as simple as she implies. As with many authors, the moral she pretends to draw may differ from the actual moral which emerges from her way of treating her *mateire*. This present essay will be concerned more with the effects of her treatment than with considering abstract ideas with which she may or may not claim acquaintance.[1]

I

Three short *lais* out of the twelve which survive typify her art in its essence—*Chevrefoil, Laüstic* and *Les Deuz Amanz*. Of these the first has

---

[1] The text used in this essay is that of A. Ewert, *Marie de France, Lais* (Blackwell, 1960). I have also profited from the edition of Jeanne Lods, *Les Lais de Marie de France* (CFMA, 1959) and from the standard edition of K. Warnke (Halle, 1885).

been almost endlessly discussed: it tells, somewhat enigmatically, an episode from the Tristan story—Tristan contrives a secret rendezvous with Isolde by means of a branch of hazel laid in her path. The second is of special interest because the author of *The Owl and the Nightingale* knew and used it. The third is less well known to English readers. *Les Deuz Amanz*, Marie tells us, is a Norman tale, based on a Breton *lai*:

> On a mountain in Normandy lie the graves of two young people (*li dui enfant*). Nearby is the town of Pitre. The widowed King of Pitre had one daughter to whom he was deeply attached. His people wish him to arrange her marriage. He agrees that he will—but only to the man who can carry her in his arms to the summit of the mountain, a task so difficult that all who try it fail. The young maiden herself is in love with a squire at court. To ensure his success in the task she provides him with a magic potion through an aunt who practises *l'art de phisike*. On the appointed day they set off up the mountain. He exults in his own strength and neglects to take the potion which his sweetheart urges upon him. As he reaches the summit he collapses and dies. She throws the magic potion on the ground; and as it spreads out it causes a miraculous growth of plants (*meinte bone erbe*). Then the maiden falls on her lover's body and dies too. They are given a rich burial on the summit of the mountain.

What is this *lai* really 'about'? The authoress (it might be safer to say the narrator) says, just before the climax, that she is afraid that the potion will be of little use to the young man, because he lacks *mesure*, moderation, balance of character. *Mesure* is certainly a favourite concept in the courtly romance as it is in the epic. But to follow Marie in this is to take too moral a tone, surely? The element of reckless courage, of 'braverie' (as the Elizabethans might have said), of aspiring self-assurance which goes beyond the bounds of common sense, is an essential characteristic of 'the hero who serves for love'. The *Lai des Deuz Amanz* is a young-love myth. He aspires so high, he is so confident; it is not enough for him to climb the mountain, he must do it in his own strength. The girl's reactions, of course, represent the other side of the heroism of love—the timorous, nagging self-doubt that help-lessly tries to help itself in the grip of love. The world, the reality of their own human condition, symbolized by the mountain, prevents the fulfilment of their aspiration. What impresses us in this *lai* is not the hero's lack of common sense but the inner logic of his imaginative ecstasy. The lover is driven by a fate within him to an impossible challenge. With all the symbols changed, this is a *Romeo and Juliet* situation, but etched by a miniaturist. It ends not in tragedy but in an intensity of pathos.

This little story has some of the quintessential feeling of romance. In particular, it reveals an experience of romantic love—an experience beautiful, fragile, aspiring, thriving on difficulties and in this case ultimately defeated by them, but making the moment of defeat a triumph. The lovers, lying together in cold innocence on the top of their mountain, have defeated 'this preposterous, pragmatical pig of a world'. Jeanne Lods, in her perceptive comments on this *lai*, rightly stresses that it is not a moral tale about the foolishness of lacking *mesure*. But she perhaps goes too far in suggesting that Marie de France is interested in adolescent love as such—'la psychologie du conte est une psychologie de l'adolescence'.[1] She maintains also that the Young Man of *Les Deuz Amanz* is one of the only two individually conceived male characters in the *lais* (Lanval is the other). True indeed that Marie's interests are more psychological than moral. But perhaps they are not fundamentally either. The psychology, like the courtly doctrine (her 'morality' never extends beyond), is a means to an end.

The *granz biens* is an experience. Not a theory, not a moral lesson, not even an insight into character, but an experience of fine feeling. The experience is embodied in a narrative, but it comes over most forcefully in an image, or series of images. The story often seems only to exist for the sake of the image, which carries the weight of the feeling engendered; the action is secondary to moments of lyrical intensity. To be paradoxical—if a ballad is 'a song that tells a story', a *lai* is 'a story that tells a song'. (The useful scholarly distinction between narrative and lyrical *lais* needs rather careful critical handling if it is not to mislead us as we read Marie de France.)

How in this context are we to define the word 'image'? It is in the simplest cases a specific object, with or without traditional symbolic or emblematic value, that strikes the inner eye and serves as focus for the 'fine feeling' of the *lai*. In *Laüstic* it is the dead nightingale. The lady, keeping a rendezvous at the bedroom window with her lover in the

[1] Lods, *op. cit.,* Introduction, p. xxvii.

neighbouring garden, tells her exasperated and inquisitive husband:

> 'Il nen ad joïe en cest mund
> Ki n'ot le laüstic chanter.' (84)

The husband *de ire e (de) maltalent en rist* (a vivid dramatic touch). He gets his servants to trap the bird, brutally kills it in front of her eyes— 'From now on you will be able to sleep in peace!'—and throws the blood-stained corpse against her, *un poi desur le piz devant*. She sorrow-fully wraps the dead bird in precious samite, embroidered in gold, and *tut escrit* with the sad adventure, and sends it to her lover. He, full of courtliness (*ne fu pas vileins ne lenz*), enshrines the dead nightingale in a golden, jewelled casket and meditates upon it every day. Or rather—and this is typical of the poet's reticence—we are left to imagine what the lover did every day; the last line of her story says simply: *Tuz jurs l'ad fet od lui porter.* More important, she is totally reticent about the 'meaning' of the nightingale. She could have said, 'The nightingale signifies a beautiful, innocent love; the brutality of its death signifies the cruel misapprehension that the world always affords to beauty and innocence; the rich incarceration signifies the high value which ought to be set on such a precious thing.' But there is none of this.

The image of the nightingale has the more potency, too, because Marie does not allow herself to be drawn into discussions of feeling. This is striking, especially in a twelfth-century author who is so centrally concerned with fine feeling. It could be said generally of Marie that she distils or represents, scarcely ever discusses or analyses, feeling. This *lai* is a good example. There are six lines of typical introduction (it is one of the formulae of *lai*-writing to discuss the title and source of the *lai*—see *Chaitivel*, especially). Lines 7–22 introduce the three principal characters, tell us where they lived and describe the courtly qualities of the two lovers-to-be in conventional terms. Lines 23–28 narrate their meeting and successful courtship: then we have a comment from the narrator:

> Sagement e bien s'entr'amerent;
> Mut se covrirent e garderent
> Qu'il ne feussent aparceüz. . .

The next passage (up to l. 56) describes the happy arrangements that, being neighbours, they were able to make: even if they could not often meet, they could always talk and see each other and throw each other

presents. The story proper begins at l. 57. It is early summer; the birds
sing *par grant ducur*:

> Ki amur ad a sun talent
> N'est merveille s'il i entent. (63)

This is the only generalized comment, extrinsic comment, in the tale.
Immediately we are back in the narrative: we are told how the lady
and her lover used to look at one another on moonlight nights, with
one laconic remark—

> Delit aveient al veer
> Quant plus ne poeient aver. (77)

From then on the narrative is continuous, as I outlined it earlier, from
l. 79 to the end, 156, except for one line commenting on the husband's
brutal insensitivity—

> De ceo fist il que trop vileins (116)—

and two lines, only, describing the lover's feelings. The tone is kept
superficially cool, in addition, through the fact that when she has wept,
and cursed the bird-limers who have taken away her joy (125), the wife
must do something practical to let her lover know why she does not
come to the window any more. This *lai* is a marvel of economy. In
many ways it displays an art which has greater affinities with folk-
ballad than with courtly romance. The tendency to go straight to the
crisis of action is, of course, even more marked in folk-ballad, as we
see if we compare *Fair Annie* with *Le Fresne*;[1] but the absence of both
moralizing (Christian or courtly) and of intellectual analysis, is striking.
To envisage what Chrétien de Troyes might have made of such an
episode it is only necessary to recall the passage from *Le Chevalier de la
Charrete* where Lancelot in quest of the Queen comes across a comb
with some of her hair still clinging to it.[2] The trance into which
Lancelot is rapt is described explicitly, at length and with great subtlety.
The language is the language of religious adoration.

    Miss Anna G. Hatcher has observed that Marie de France's typical
procedure is to choose 'a specific, concrete object as the centre of her
lai which shall develop, within the poem, new varieties of symbolic

---

[1] Child, *The English and Scottish Popular Ballads* (abridged in one volume),
No. 62.

[2] *Le Chevalier de la Charrete*, ed. Mario Roques, ll. 1354 ff.

content'. *Les Deuz Amans* (from which my consideration of 'images' began) 'centers', she suggests, 'about the magic potion, which represents, supposedly, a means and a necessary means, to the fulfilment of the lovers' desire'.[1] I have chosen the word 'image' rather than 'object' so as to give a wider and (I think) a truer approach. 'Object' suits *Laüstic* and *Chevrefoil* well enough. In the latter case the hazel-rod, intertwined with honeysuckle, is clearly the imaginative focus of the poem. In this *lai* the 'object' is actually contrived by a character as part of the story in order that it may convey a significance. Hence, the rather unusual explicit comment and, indeed, explication, leading up to the 'proverb of love':

> 'Bele amie, si est de nus:
> Ne vus sanz mei, ne mei sanz vus.' (77)

A limiting preoccupation with 'objects' leads Miss Thatcher to suggest that in *Les Deuz Amanz*, the 'central object' is the magic potion, *li beivre*. I should say, rather, that the central image is the mountain itself, impassive and immobile in contrast to the young man, with the girl in his arms, boldly and blindly striding upwards:

> Ki en aventure se met
> De li porter en sum le munt. (160)

The mountain is the first thing that Marie mentions in the story:

> Verité est kë en Neustrie,
> Que nus apelum Normendie,
> Ad un haut munt merveilles grant:
> La sus gisent li dui enfant. (7)

And it is the last—

> Desur le munt les enfüirent,
> E puis atant se departirent. (239)

The mountain is the ever-present, enduring, insentient, ineluctable obstacle to the fulfilment of their love; it is their death; and, now miraculously fertile, it is their memorial. The potion, on the other hand, though a necessary part of the apparatus of the story, carries little or

---

[1] Anna G. Hatcher, 'Le Lai de Chievrefueil', *Romania* lxxi (1950), 339. On this point there are also some stimulating pages in Suheyla Bayrav, *Symbolisme Médiéval* (1957), ch. I.

no symbolic weight, until just at the climax when the maiden seems to be pouring the whole promise of their mutual love on to the barren ground. Their love, flowering despite the lovers' death, is indeed the *granz biens* which in this *lai* has (literally) *fluriz* and *espandues ses flurs*.

Already then in a still quite short poem (244 lines) the 'image' is more complex than a simple object. But it is still the essential vehicle for the 'fine feeling' involved. The narrator makes, and indeed needs to make, very few comments of her own. The most moving lines are almost bare—the girl kneels down by her lover as he collapses:

> Les lui se met en genuilluns,
> Sun beivre li voleit doner;
> Mes il ne pout od li parler.
> Issi murut cum jeo vus di. . . (208)
> Ilec murut la dameisele,
> Que tant ert pruz e sage e bele. (226)

How does this 'image' method work in longer and more complicated stories? *Yonec* tells the story of a young and beautiful wife, jealously guarded in a tower by a *viel gelus*:

> One day a great bird flies into her room and is transformed into the knight of her dreams. They fall in love; but the renewal of the lady's beauty makes her husband suspicious and he catches the bird with a cruel trap as he flies through the window. The knight escapes, mortally wounded, and the lady follows him by leaping, pregnant, through the narrow window twenty feet from the ground. She tracks him by bloodstains to his palace where he dies. Before the moment of death he sends her away with a ring which will magically allay her husband's jealous suspicions and a sword with which their yet unborn son, Yonec, will one day avenge his father's death. This prophecy is fulfilled when Yonec, a grown man years later, finds himself with his stepfather and mother at his true father's tomb. Mother cries out that God has led them there: she gives Yonec his father's sword, swoons and dies. Yonec kills his stepfather and inherits the kingdom which has been waiting for him.

This is a complex narrative; and it is dominated not by a single but by a sequence of images. First there is the image of the *grant oisel*

which appears in answer to her prayers as a shadow in the narrow
window of her tower. This climactic moment is led up to with the
lady's long lament—

> 'Lasse,' fait ele, 'mar fui nee!
> Mut est dure ma destinee.' (67)

In this soliloquy the underlying fantasy of the *lais*, and of *Yonec* in
particular, is laid bare: 'I have often heard that in times past things
happened in this land—exciting things':

> 'Chevalers trovoënt puceles
> A lur talent gentes e beles,
> E dames truvoënt amanz
> Beaus e curteis, [pruz] e vaillanz. . .
> Deu, Ki de tut ad poësté,
> Il en face ma volenté!
> Quant ele ot faite pleinte issi,
> L'umbre d'un grant oisel choisi
> Par mi une estreite fenestre.' (95)

As befits a courtly tale, he is a courtly bird (*ostur sembla*: he looked
like a hawk) even before he turned into a *chevaler bel e gent*. The image
carries, then, associations not only of love and aspiration and sexual
desire but also of courtly *mores*—from the noble sport of falconry.

We need the imaginative impetus of this moment, which culminates
in the knight's declaration of love (129–30), to carry us through the
irrelevant, if not irreverent, episode which follows. The lady says that
she will make him her *dru* if he is a Christian. His *credo* is dignified and
satisfying (Marie could not write badly if she tried):

> Jeo crei mut bien al Creatur,
> Que nus geta de la tristur,
> U Adam nus mist, nostre pere,
> Par le mors de la pumme amere.
> Il est e ert e fu tuz jurs
> Vie e lumere as pecheürs. (149)

But then he proposes the Sacrament test, and in order to put this into
effect the lady has to hide him under the bed-clothes and pretend to be
ill. The chaplain brings her the *corpus domini* and *le vin de chalice* and
the knight successfully takes them. This part of the *lai* is unsatisfactory,

not primarily because we find it distasteful but because of the element of trickery involved. Marie de France's *lais* (unlike the *fabliaux*) are singularly free from *engin*; trickery is the sole prerogative of the baser characters, brutal husbands, *viel gelus* and their like. In *Guigemar* when the lady needs to escape she miraculously discovers the door of her prison is open (676); and in *Yonec* the lady leaps nimbly unhurt through an impossibly high and dangerous window.

The image of the bird is renewed at the fatal visit (309) when he is wounded to death. The first appearance conveyed the idea of the miraculous power of love to conquer all obstacles, as the *grant oisel* flew in to the inaccessible tower, and the feeling that you have only to wish hard enough for this miracle for it to be presented to you in its full glory; this last appearance tells us of the cruelly unpredictable power of fate to destroy what it had created. There is a clear statement that this was bound to happen. The *granz biens* of love so transforms its objects that they give themselves away. Love both must and cannot remain a secret. As the knight said, he knew *Vostre semblant nus ocireit* (322). There is stress, too, on the sacrificial quality of love: *Pur vostre amur perc jeo la vie*, says the knight (320).

The next telling image in the *lai* is the journey the lady makes after this leap, in pursuit of her wounded lover. Half-naked she follows the tracks of his blood along the road and through a *hoge* (evidently some kind of hollow hill, since there was *nule clarté* inside); thence, across a meadow into a city made all of silver. The city is apparently deserted; she enters the castle. In the first room is a knight asleep; in the second room another; in the third room she finds her *ami* on his richly ornate bed, wounded to death. No comment of any sort is made on this journey. In fact, it is more like a quest from a romance than anything else in the *lais*. It has what Marie's images seldom have, a quality of mystery. She is not generally a mysterious author; it is indeed an essential part of the definition of her elegant charm that they lack the numinous as they lack the spiritual. This passage is exceptional. The only comparable one, in my reading of the *lais*, is that in *Guigemar* where the hero finds a haven in which a mysteriously beautiful and deserted ship is waiting for him.

It is characteristic of the authoress that she devotes 450 lines to this part of the story and only 100 lines to the sequel (birth of Yonec, journey to father's land, discovery of father's tomb, etc.). In this sequel the most striking moment is the dramatic image of Yonec's mother calling on her son *a haute voiz* and giving him the sword to avenge her on *cist villarz*, her husband. Her mission accomplished, she dies at once on the tomb of her sweetheart. These 'images', as I have been calling them, whether single objects or simple actions, carry the message of the *lai*. There is very little 'thought', explicit comment, in *Yonec*. When the narrator makes her own presence felt, it is invariably to reinforce our sympathy for the lovers by a vivid engagement in the situation:—

> Unke si bel cuple ne vi. (192)
> Or li duinst Deus lunges joïr (224)
> Allas! cum ierent malbailli (254)
> Deus! qu'il ne sout la traïsun
> Quë aparaillot le felun. (295)

To urge the priority of 'dramatic images' is not, by the way, the same thing as to say she is simply a good story-teller. (Whether or not her audiences knew the stories is in any case irrelevant; they almost certainly did.) She does tell a story well; and if you have not read, for instance, *Eliduc* before, you long to know what will happen and how Eliduc can possibly resolve his tangle of 'two loves'. But usually the outcome is a foregone conclusion. The slightest experience of fairy-tales or Elizabethan comedies teaches us that the 'new bride' in *Le Fresne* must be the long-lost twin sister, and that they will all live happily ever after. Most significantly, there is no contrived suspense (except of the most obvious kind). Her climaxes are climaxes of the expected. There are no melodramatic surprises, no sudden twists. She does not want to catch us off our guard; she wants, rather, to meet our commonest and deepest expectations. *Of course* Guigemar will fall in love with the lady who finds him on the magic ship; *of course* the fairy-maiden will arrive in all her beauty to save Lanval from the consequences of his broken vow. She wants to meet our expectations on the level of the story because that is the way in which she can intensify and simplify emotions. The 'images' also have this intensifying and simplifying effect.

It can be admitted that few or none of the 'dramatic images' in Marie's *lais* are free inventions of her own. On the contrary, and in company with many greater writers, she ransacks the common store of fairy-tale and legendary motif. But this is neither here nor there. We misunderstand and underrate Marie de France when we deny her creative achievement, creative power, on the grounds that these images and stories are not new. A comparison of the motifs shared between two or more of the following *lais* might suggest that, if nothing else, the *conjointure* of her *lais* is her own—*Guigemar, Lanval, Yonec,* and the anonymous *lais, Guingamor, Graalant, Désiré.* A proper understanding of Marie's achievement depends, I think, on our response to the way in which she 'conjoins' the images in any one *lai.* The question is bound up with the relationship between thought and feeling in her art. In the second part of this paper I shall try to describe the unusual nature of this relationship through an analysis of some successful and some less successful *lais.*

II

A *lai* of Marie de France is commonly an imaginative whole. Not a flawless unity, granted, in every case; but *grasped.* There is no more vivid way of bringing this home than by considering one of the anonymous *lais* which are so closely related to her work that they have sometimes been thought part of it.

The purely haphazard character of a *lai* like *Doön* is not worth demonstrating. Let us take something better. *Guingamor* was, in fact, printed by P. Kusel in the third issue of K. Warnke's edition of Marie's *Lais*; it was described by G. Paris as 'le plus beau' of the group of *lais* which he published for the first time in 1879.[1] The attribution to Marie de France has been more seriously sustained than in the case of any, outside the twelve accepted ones. It has clear affinities with *Lanval* and the anonymous *Graalant.* The tale is an attractive one.

> Guingamor, nephew of the King and heir to the throne, rebuffs the advances of the Queen. In revenge the Queen issues a challenge to the court that no one will be so brave as to undertake *l'aventure de la forest*; she knows well that Guingamor will take it up. This he does, to the King's sorrow (though the latter seems as anxious at the prospect of losing his favourite *chaceor* and *brachet* as he does at the prospect of losing his heir). Guingamor, pursuing *li blans pors,* crosses *la riviére perilleuse* into *la lande aventureuse* where he finds a deserted palace. A little farther on he comes to a spring where he sees a beautiful naked maiden bathing. He takes her clothes away (*cf. Graalant*), but

[1] G. Paris, ed., in *Romania* viii (1879), 50 seq.

willingly returns them when asked. She tells him that he will never catch the white boar without her help and promises that in three days' time he shall return home successful in his quest. They love each other *de druerie* and return to the palace in the forest, now become a centre of courtly festivity. Three centuries pass without his knowing it. When he wants to go home, the lady tells him that it will be no use—everyone is dead. He decides to go and see for himself, and to come back to her if he finds it true. She lets him go, with the solemn warning that he must not eat anything the other side of the 'perilous river'. When he arrives in his own land, he talks to a wood-cutter in the forest and realizes that it is indeed three hundred years since he set out on his quest. He sets out back to the land of fairy, but on the way he succumbs to the temptation to eat from a wild apple tree. At once he becomes senile and feeble. The peasant thinks he is going to die; but two maidens ride up, reproach him for breaking the lady's commandment, and carry him back across the river (with his hound and his hunter).

The *matière* of this tale is most compelling; the motif of the *blans pors* (usually a hind—*Guigemar, Graalant* etc.) which leads the hero to his destined lady, the motif of the Land of Eternal Youth, the motif of the deserted city, and the 'Rip Van Winkle' return are of a kind to haunt the imagination. And there are several episodes which in addition proffer themselves for courtly development—the Queen's offer of her love to Guingamor; Guingamor's encounter with the fairy-maiden; their reception at the mysterious palace; her miraculous forgiveness; and the lovers' eventual reunion (the latter, by the way, is not even narrated in *Guingamor*). But the result is an imaginative and emotional jumble. If the tale has a climax, it is at the moment when we first are told what has really happened to Guingamor—quite different from what he hoped and expected: all that he has known and loved has died or been destroyed:

> N'i cuide que deus jors ester,
> Et au tierz s'en cuida raler: . . . (533)
> Autrement li fu trestorné:
> Car troiz cent ans i ot esté.
> Mors fu li rois et sa mesnie,
> Et toz iceus de sa lingnie,

> Et les citez qu'il ot veues
> Furent destruites et cheues. (539)

The subsequent meeting between Guingamor and the peasant renews the same sombre, all-flesh-is-but-grass, kind of reflection. This 'climax' is neither prepared for nor made use of. Marie de France, one imagines, would have given us a hint when Guingamor takes up the challenge in the first place. The anonymous author simply shows the King anxiously weighing the possibility of Guingamor not bringing back his favourite possessions on earth—his *brachet* and his *chaceor* (*N'avoit avoir qu'il amast tant*, 219). There is little suggestion of any deeper sense of impending loss; though some proper sentiment is introduced when town and court say a sad good-bye to him:

> Cil de la vile, li borjois,
> Et li vilain, et li cortois
> Le convoiérent autresi
> O grant dolor et o grant cri;
> Et nes les dames i aloient
> Merveillus duel por lui faisoient. (263)

If, on the other hand, the 'fruyt' of the tale was to have been in the proper handling of *courtly* sentiment (the triangle of Queen, Knight and fairy-mistress), the interest and skill of the opening conversation where the Queen reveals her love to Guingamor is never again approached. The 'gambit' is quite well handled, even if its 'indirection' is a bit obvious—

> 'Riche aventure vos atent;
> Amer pouez molt hautement,' (73)

says the Queen, in the tone of a week-end astrologer.

One could go on analysing this *lai*, and it would still remain a jumble. The scene with the beautiful maiden bathing in the fountain is simply thrown away; so is the hero's sudden dramatic ageing and his return to fairyland. I do not mean to say that the tale is without feeling. There is a moving 'sentimental' moment when the full realization comes to Guingamor that he will never see his uncle again—

> Merveilleuse pitié l'em prist
> Du roi qu'il ot ainsi perdu.

But it is for a moment only. The images of this *lai* are totally unco-ordin-ated; there is no fine feeling to hold them together. So far from its being 'worthy to rank with the best of (Marie's) *lais*',[1] I am convinced that she did not write it. She was (*pace* Bedier and others) an author in a fuller sense of the word.

The author of *Guingamor* simply wrote a fairy-tale, though with twelfth-century trappings. Marie de France wrote fairy-tales *for courtiers*. There is a difference. Unlike the anonymous authors, she was generally capable of a *conjointure*, capable of binding together the legendary 'images' (both objects and actions) to carry a significance. Let us return now to the 'dramatic image' of the lady in *Yonec*, pursuing her wounded bird-sweetheart by the tracks of his blood until she finds him in a deserted palace. This lonely journey is the perfect image of her desolation at the cruel loss of her lover. The point is delicately made. The first stage takes her through the hill (the *hoge*) of which we are told only two things—that the entry is covered in blood and that it was very dark:

> Ne pot nient avant veer. . . (349)
> El n'i trovat nule clarté. (353)

Contrasted with the dark *hoge* is the city made all of silver where her lover lies in his palace bleeding to death on his rich bed amid a blaze of light and unattended except for two sleeping knights in the ante-chambers:

> Le lit sun ami ad trové.
> Li pecul sunt de or esmeré;
> Ne sai mie les dras preisier;
> Li cirgë e li chandelier,
> Que nuit e jur sunt alumé,
> Valent tut d'or d'une cité. (387)

A comparable image, much more consciously conceived and used, is the deserted palace of Criseyde in *Troilus and Criseyde*, Book V. But here the emotional point is made in a different way. We do not need Marie de France to tell us (she probably never told herself) that they have 'bought the mansion of a love' and not (or only partly) possessed it; that there is a contrast between the illuminated gorgeousness of the

---

[1] Ewert, *op. cit.*, Introduction, p. xvi, continuing '. . . but one may argue that the whole story is too similar to that of *Lanval*.'

palace and the lonely death of its owner (too literally a hunted bird);
the candles are all alight, but

> Sempres murai devant le jur. (403)

And she will die, too, if she stays.[1] The fitness of the *narrative* conclusion
of the *lai* to this central image need not be laboured. Yonec, the son of
their true love, kills the *felun* husband, his stepfather, with the sword
of true love which his mother gives him, at the tomb where his father
lies. It is not a tragedy; it is a triumph, a triumph of love. Even the ring
which the bird-prince gives his sweetheart to preserve her from her
husband's malignancy has an obvious symbolic-emotional meaning. At
the end she is laid *a grant onur* in the coffin (it must be the same one,
though we are left to infer this—only the definite article tells us so:
al sarcu) and Yonec, the fruit of their love, inherits the kingdom. With
the exception of the passage I have already mentioned (the Sacrament
test), *Yonec* is an imaginative whole; it realizes the *granz biens* of fine
feeling through a coherent sequence of images.

Lanval, another representative of this group of folk-tales, shows as
surely as *Yonec* Marie de France's sureness of touch in handling traditional motifs and her power of achieving an emotional synthesis of
elements which other narrators leave disparate. The *lai* has been much
discussed, in relation to its French analogues and English derivatives. I
need only make one point which I hope will illuminate the relationship
between her thought and her feeling.

A. J. Bliss, contrasting *Lanval* with its English counterparts, amid
many helpful comments, makes the following observation:

> *Lanval* is civilised, discreet, even intellectual—as the interest
> in legal technicalities shows; *Landevale* is primitive, extravagant
> and emotional.[2]

I should rephrase this to say that *Lanval* is 'civilized, discreet *and emotional*
—only superficially intellectual'. One can be grateful to the learned
commentators for their help in elucidating the legal technicalities, in
making us realize what is there. We have learnt something about the
taste of the courtly audience and about Marie's ability to satisfy it.

---

[1] The central portion of *Yonec* powerfully recalls the atmosphere of the
Corpus Christi Carol.
[2] A. J. Bliss, ed., *Sir Launfal*, Introduction, p. 23.

But whether we have learnt anything essential about her art or about *Lanval* I am not so sure.

The legal procedures in *Lanval* may be interesting to lawyers, but to us (and, one suspects, to the courtly ladies who seem to have constituted Marie's main audience) they are rather tedious. In the hands of a lesser writer they could have been a serious blemish. Fortunately, Marie has the art to subordinate them to her real purposes. The function of the legal procedure is, surely, threefold—to increase the narrative tension and thereby intensify the climax (the appearance of the first pair of *puceles* is led up to by the Count of Cornwall's speech; and between each arrival we are taken back to the court of indecisive barons): to provide an imaginative foil, a dry contrast to the warmth and glamour of ideal courtliness (the description of the fairy-mistress is one of the longest set-pieces in all the *lais*): and, finally, to enhance the value of Love by showing its triumph over Law (the processes of law are emotionally in harmony with the angry, vengeful Queen and the offended King). Lanval's sureties, friends though they are, speak of his *fol'amur*; but this same mad lover rises to his lady's appearance, to her deliverance, with a grand gesture of his own:

> 'Par fei,' fet il, 'ceo est m'amie!
> Or m'en est gueres ki m'ocie,
> Si ele n'ad merci de mei;
> Kar gariz sui, quant jeo la vei.' (597)

He is restored to the only 'life' that has meaning, and can face even death with equanimity. Love triumphs not only over the laws of society but also over its own 'laws'. The obligation of secrecy imposed by the fairy-mistress provides a perfect example of Marie de France's art in synthesizing a legendary motif and a courtly 'law' (*Qui non celat amare non potest*).

The 'thought' in *Lanval* is, then, used as an artistic counter. The real issues (and here the authoress remains true to her proper genius) are never intellectualized, never discussed. The 'intellectual', courtly way of dealing with the violation of an oath of secrecy can be studied in such a poem as *La Chastelaine de Vergi*, where both intellectual and moral problems as well as emotional realities are embodied in an action; it is not only highly wrought, but deeply thought—as, for example, in the impassioned argument of the lady's speech before she dies. None of Marie de France's *lais* are deeply thought.

Equitan, to me, shows the kind of muddle that Marie gets into when she attempts to deal intellectually with a problem. It is worth observing in general that although her lovers always have difficulties, they scarcely ever have problems. They are 'up against it', usually, because something has gone wrong from outside (the *viel gelus* discovers what is going on; the people demand marriage for their king; feudal loyalty intervenes). This sense of obstacles to be overcome by loyal endurance is essential to the creation of her imaginative world; conscious intellectual, or intellectualized moral, problems are not.

> *Equitan* tells the story of a king who falls in love with the wife of his seneschal. He hesitates because such a love betrays the feudal bond between king and vassal; she hesitates because such a love is bound to be unequal. They plight their troth, nevertheless. After some time the king is urged by his subjects to take a wife. His mistress, who could be his queen, if only she were free, plots with him to kill her husband. They arrange for him to be scalded to death in a bath. The plot miscarries; the husband catches them making love, the king himself falls into the boiling bath, and his mistress is thrown in after him.

The 'moral' is as banal as in a *fabliau*:

> Tel purcace le mal d'altrui
> Dunt le mals [tut] revert sur lui. (309)

It seems likely on many counts that there was a demand among Marie's audience for 'problems of love', *questions d'amour*. These could range from sheer casuistry to the serious discussion of genuine moral issues. The first 180 lines of *Equitan* raise several 'problems' about the nature of true love:

> Cil metent lur vie en nuncure
> Que d'amur n'unt sen e mesure;
> Tels est la mesure de amer
> Que nul n'i deit reisun garder. (17)

(You cannot be happy in love unless you are moderate; but Love admits of no moderation.)

> E si jo l'aim, jeo ferai mal:
> Ceo est la femme al seneschal.
> Garder li dei amur e fei,
> Si cum jeo voil k'il face a mei. (71)

(A king cannot honourably love the wife of one of his subjects, any more than the subject can love the king's wife [*cf. Lanval*]. This is not a condemnation of adultery but of breaking a feudal loyalty.)

> Que devendreit sa curteisie,
> S'ele n'amast de drüerie? (81)

(Passionate love is essential to a woman's womanhood.)

> Ne sereit pas üel partie
> Entre nus deux la drüerie. . . (131)
> Quidereiez, a mun espeir,
> Le danger de l'amur aveir.
> Amur n'est pruz se n'est egals. (135)

(There is no possibility of love where there is no equality.)

Marie seems to have an attitude to the last problem raised—indeed, an answer to it: a prince can love a pauper, provided he has *lëauté en sei* (155–62; 142). The only obstacle to true love is 'lightness' (*Cil ki de amur sunt novellier*, 163). This is good courtly doctrine and we seem to hear Marie's authentic voice at the end of this long discussion, when she says of Equitan and the seneschal's wife,

> Bien les [lur fiaunces] tiendrent, mut s'entr' amerent,
> Puis en mururent e finirent. (183)

The trouble is that the second part of the *lai* shows their 'death' and 'end' without any emotional logic. There is no connexion between the only problem which has been eloquently discussed (*Amur n'est pruz se n'est egals*) and the sordid death of the King, Equitan, by scalding. They were, in fact, true and equal lovers and Marie approved of them. The nature of *desmesure* in love; the problem of to what extremes lovers may go to preserve the entity of their love—these are never discussed. The lovers are clearly not punished for adultery as such; they are being punished for transgressing a feudal obligation and the moral law. But it is hard to feel that this has any imaginative connexion with the true love of the earlier part.

Perhaps the least memorable of Marie's *lais* is the one called *Chaitivel*; its other name, she tells us, was *Quatre Dols*:

There was once a lady of Nantes, so beautiful and so accomplished that every knight in the land loved her. Four Breton lords loved her equally, and were equally encouraged by her. She could not bear the thought of losing the other three if she accepted one. At Easter there was a tournament at which all four jousted magnificently, but exposing themselves *trop folement* towards the evening, three were killed and one seriously wounded. The lady is deeply sorrowful and tells the survivor she wishes to make a *lai* about them all, called *Four Sorrows*. He replies that it should be re-written, and named after him, *The Wretched One*, because he has to suffer the misery of loving her, seeing her every day and having no reward from her except talk; he would rather be dead. She agrees that this re-writing would be a good idea.

The narrator adds her comment that either name is suitable, and the *lai* ends, in a curious, non-committal tone:

> Le Chaitivel ad nun en us.
> Ici finist, [il] n'i ad plus;
> Plus n'en oi, ne plus n'en sai,
> Ne plus ne vus en cunterai. (237)

The *lai* improves on re-reading, because we realize where the emotion is focused—on the plight of the surviving knight, the sorrow of the lady, and (most curious of all) on her outstanding courtly achievement. We no longer expect a narrative, or emotional, resolution of the tension. Marie presents it as a tension; but one suspects that it started as, or had been mooted as, a 'love problem': 'Suppose that a lady has four lovers, all equally noble . . . should she accept the single survivor as her *dru*, or should she remain faithful to her ideal?' In the hands of most other poets of the courtly tradition this would have been developed as a debate between the lady and the surviving lover—and would have remained as sterile as such debates usually are. Marie, in accordance with her usual method, seizes the emotional points. But she cannot afford to have two opposed emotional states, *both good in themselves*. In her tales the emotion normally surges strongly in one direction; with this emotion others may be contrasted, but not balanced (the husbands in *Yonec* and *Laüstic*, the Queen in *Lanval*—these are merely foils). *Le Chaitivel* is charged in two directions. On the one hand, the lady

> Ces quatre chevalers amoue
> E chescun par sei coveitoue;

> Mut par aveit en eus granz biens;
> Il m'amoënt sur tute riens
> Pur lur beauté, pur lur prüesce,
> Pur lur valur, pur lur largesce
> Les fis d'amer a mei entendre;
> Nes voil tuz perdre pur l'un prendre. (149)

On the other hand, we are made to feel the plight of *le chaitivel* himself:

> Li autre sunt pieça finé
> E tut le seclë unt usé,
> La grant peine k'il en suffreient
> De l'amur qu'il vers vus aveient;
> Mes jo ki sui eschapé vif,
> Tut esgaré e tut cheitif,
> Ceo que al secle puis plus amer
> Vei sovent venir e aler,
> Parler od mei matin e seir,
> Si n'nen puis nule joie aveir
> Ne de baisier ne d'acoler
> Ne d'autre bien fors de parler. (211)

The *lai* opens with a passage of love-doctrine which all the editors find obscure. Its general purpose seems to be 'a defence of love and its service, which yields rewards or is its own reward'.[1] This fits in well enough with the lady's conscious pride in her high achievement:

> Jamés dame de mun parage—
> [Ja] tant n'iert bele, pruz ne sage—
> Teus quatre ensemble n'amera
> N[ë] en un jur si nes perdra
> Fors vus. . . .
> Voil que mis doels seit remembrez. (195)

The 'love' that she wishes to celebrate (*De vus quatre ferai un lai*) is not a personal thing; it is, rather, a style, a way of life. (The Chaucerian parallel to it is, surely, to be found in *The Knight's Tale*.) But the love that the miserable survivor feels is the idealized personal relationship to which we are already accustomed in the *lais*. Marie does not take up the challenge, but drops it abruptly and disappears with a toss of the head.

Marie de France, I would argue, can neither develop an argument

---

[1] Ewert, *op. cit.*, p. 182.

nor resolve an emotional tension. Her great talent is to concentrate, to crystallize emotion in a single image or in a sequence of dramatic images. *Le Chaitivel* is imageless and unmemorable. *Eliduc* should provide us with the final and the decisive test. It is by far the longest of the *lais*—nearly 1,200 lines—and it is, I believe, among the best. Briefly, the story is this:

> Eliduc, a Breton lord, falsely accused by his own king, leaves home and country and offers his services as a mercenary to the king of some lands in Devon. Through his prowess and skill his king's enemies are completely vanquished. Soon afterwards he falls deeply in love with the king's daughter, Guilliadun, and she with him. She does not know that he is married, and he for his part is troubled by the vow of fidelity which he made to his wife when he left her. When his period of service has expired, he goes home, now reconciled to his former lord, but he soon returns to see Guilliadun as he had promised. Guilliadun asks only that he will take her with him. This with great secrecy he arranges. During the voyage a storm arises, and a sailor cries out that it is Guilliadun's presence which is endangering them—he already has a *femme leale* at home. At this disclosure Guilliadun goes into a deep swoon and is taken for dead. Eliduc lays her out in front of the altar in a hermit's chapel deep in the forest. Eliduc's wife noticing his extreme melancholy, finds out his secret; but when she visits the chapel with a squire she is completely overcome with Guilliadun's beauty. By observing the behaviour of two weasels, she hits on a miraculous flower-cure for Guilliadun. The latter, joyfully restored to life and to love, is united to Eliduc, whose wife equally joyfully surrenders her claims and retires to a nunnery. Many years later Guilliadun joins her; Eliduc finishes his days as a monk.

A lengthy analysis of this *lai* is not called for. The first 270 lines are preliminary and, I think, to a large extent redundant. They are not tedious only because the story of Eliduc's military exploits is well told. (It is amusing to see Marie reproducing, in miniature, an epic note; Eliduc's faithful warriors say:

> 'Sire', funt il, 'od vus irum
> E ceo que vus ferez ferum.') (163)

Although these 270 lines could be drastically shortened without loss
to the *granz biens* of the *lai*, Marie is careful at least not to introduce any
false note. Eliduc's parting from, and his oath to, his wife are narrated
with restraint and brevity. From 271 onwards, when the narrator
pauses to take stock of Eliduc—

> Eliduc fu curteis e sage,
> Beau chevaler [e] pruz e large—

and to introduce the heroine Guilliadun, the *lai* is of one piece. The
four observations which I wish to make about it will serve to sum up
what I have tried to say in this essay. They concern the characterization;
the 'morality'; the dramatic images; and the relationship between
thought and feeling.

There are some finely observed psychological passages in *Eliduc*,
the kind of passages which have led commentators to remark on her
skill in characterization. One might single out the passage where
Guilliadun, having sent her chamberlain to Eliduc with the gift of a
ring and a girdle, almost calls him back:

> Ele remeint en teu manere,
> Pur poi ne l'apelet arere;
> E nekedent le lait aler. . . (383)

(Chrétien de Troyes would surely have introduced a *débat* between
Amor and *Raison* here); the passage where the chamberlain returns
and she is impatient to know the truth (416–42: we recall Juliet and
her Nurse); the passage where the King tells his daughter, Guilliadun,
to entertain Eliduc hospitably and they sit in shy silence—

> Amdui erent de amur espris
> El ne l'osot areisuner. . . (502)

Such passages as these have led commentators to speak of her 'skill in
characterization', her ability to make her characters 'come alive'. Such
phrases are valid provided only that 'characterization' is not thought
to have been an aim in itself. The characters live only sufficiently to
create the fine feeling of *l'amur leale e fine*; not for their own sake.
They are not individualized, be it noted. All her heroes are one hero;
all her heroines, one heroine. If they appear to differ the one from the
other, it is because they exist to celebrate slightly different aspects of
the *granz biens* which Marie wishes to perpetuate in her tales.

The 'morality' of *Eliduc*, despite its length, is little more complicated than the 'morality' of *Laüstic*. Romantic love is the supreme good and *lëaute en sei* is its only prerequisite, the ground of its continuance and its reward. Conflicts of loyalty arise in Eliduc's mind—between his vow to his wife and his love for Guilliadun, between the demands of his contract to Guilliadun's father and his desire to carry her off. But there are no deep conflicts of feeling. Other ties must be respected if possible, but his heart is set on his only love; she will have his ultimate loyalty:

> Mes ki k'il turt a mesprisun,
> Vers li ferai tuz jurs raisun;
> Tute sa volenté ferai
> E par sun cunseil errerai. (605)

So he resolves when the moment of parting has arrived.

Such is the power of *amur leale e fine* that it will subdue all courtly and 'gentil' hearts to its purpose. Eliduc's wife's action is not to be understood as a moral one in any ordinary sense. Her decision to help the lovers (her husband and his mistress) is neither a victory over herself, a magnificent gesture of renunciation, nor a sign of her true and deep love for her husband ('I only desire his happiness'). It is a triumphant assent to the *granz biens*, which she recognizes and responds to as soon as she sees Guilliadun in all the beauty of her deathlike trance:

> E vit le lit a la pucele
> Que resemblot rose nuvele. . . .
> Par fei, jeo ne me merveil mie,
> Quant si bele femme est perie.
> Tant par pité, tant par amur,
> Jamés n'avrai joie nul jur. (1011; 1025)

Eliduc's wife gives him to Guilliadun (*Cele prenge qu'il eime tant*) for the sake of the *parfit amur* (1150) which she, as well as they, knows to be the supreme good. Her generous and noble gesture is suitably acknowledged, but it is never discussed and never questioned.

Eliduc contains fewer 'images', static or dynamic, than, for example, *Yonec* or *Lanval*. In the first half of the *lai*, the fine feeling is concentrated in the delicately observed dialogues which I have already mentioned. To these may be added the monologue in which Eliduc considers his impossible position. It is by no means a stock 'complaint'; there is a psychological accuracy in his rebellious line

Mar vi unkes ceste cuntree! (587)

But in the last 300 lines of the *lai* the feeling is once again embodied in a series of images. The central one is that of Guilliadun lying in her bed of state, as if dead, before the altar of the chapel where, a little before, the holy hermit had died. It is in this holy spot that Eliduc pours out his lament:

'Bele', fet il, 'ja Deu ne place
Que jamés puisse armes porter
Ne al secle vivre ne durer!
Bele amie, mar me veïstes!
Duce chere, mar me siwistes!
Bele, ja fuissiez vus reïne,
Ne fust l'amur leale e fine.' (938)

It is here also that Eliduc's wife is struck by the marvel of Guilliadun's beauty and where the miracle of the flower-healing is achieved.

It is indeed a striking climactic scene. One would expect it to be at one moment offensively religiose (it goes without saying that the 'religion' of the end of the tale is entirely at the service of love), and, at another, prosaic and bathetic ('Don't let the weasel get away!'). In fact, the 'fine feeling' invoked is strong enough to make one believe for the moment that death can only apparently, and not really, conquer love; and that every natural creature contributes in its way to the *granz biens* of love.

Marie de France concentrates her feeling into these dramatic 'images', whether they are simple objects (the nightingale in *Laüstic*), simple actions (the descent of *grant oisel* in *Yonec*), or more complex objects and actions (the entranced maiden of *Eliduc*; the voyages of the magic ship in *Guigemar*). The 'images' are the vehicle for her feeling, her one feeling (Love is Truth, Truth is Love). The relationship between thought and feeling is consequently a simple one. Feeling is everything; thought is nothing.

The *granz biens*, I have argued, is an experience—an experience offered for complete and unqualified sharing. Marie could fairly be called a 'popular' writer. One would feel, even without the testimony of her contemporary, Denis Piramus,[1] that she was giving her public what it wanted, without reservation or complication. A greater writer gives us what we want and also extends us and our experience in a way that haunts and stimulates the imagination. He gives us the experience and he puts a 'frame' around it, as Chaucer does; or he gives us the experience and makes it mysteriously more meaningful in unexpected dimensions, as Chrétien de Troyes. Marie de France is, it seems to me, totally without a framing irony, in the broadest sense (there are no contrary, unspoken meanings), and largely without suggestiveness[2] (she is reticent, but that is a different matter). Her sophistication (awareness of complexity) is all on the surface—in her technique, in the elegance of her rhythms and the clarity of her narrative art. She is able only, and wishes only, to conceive one thing at a time. In this one thing, her *granz biens*, she seems to be absolutely in sympathy with her audience. If she has an intention, as she says she has, towards her hearers, it is simply to make them feel more intensely what she knows they want to feel.

[1] Denis Piramus, *La Vie Seint Edmund le Rei* (ed. J. Kjellman), ll. 35 seq:
> Les lais solent as dames plaire,
> De joie les oient e de gré
> Qu'il sunt sulum lur volenté. (They are, indeed!)

[2] Despite the mysteriousness of an occasional passage like the pursuit of Yonec by his lady, which I have analysed above, I do not find myself in agreement with Mlle Wathelet-Willem's interesting reflections in 'Le Mystère chez Marie de France', *Revue Belge de Philologie et Historie* 39 (1961), 661 seq. She adapts Frappier's phrases about Chrétien to Marie: 'Elle n'a pas tout dit ni tout formulé . . .' Marie is never finally enigmatic, and does not wish to leave us guessing.

II

Dante and the Tradition of Courtly Love

The Allegory of Love (1936) marked an epoch in the study of courtly love and made Lewis's reputation as a scholar. The section on Andreas Capellanus's *Tractatus de Amore, libri tres,* or *De Arte Honeste Amandi,* was particularly striking to me, though I possessed no copy of it until S. Battaglia produced his new edition in 1947. My interest in Dante had at the time only just begun, and I was prepared to accept what Lewis said about him. But now nearly thirty years later I would like to look back on the problem of Dante's relations with the tradition of courtly love, beginning with Lewis's account of the matter.

I

After describing the *Concilium in Monte Romarici,* to illustrate the religion of the God Amor, Lewis comments:

> The Ovidian tradition, operated upon by the medieval taste for humorous blasphemy, is apparently quite sufficient to produce a love religion, and even in a sense a Christianized love religion, without any aid from the new seriousness of romantic passion. As against any theory which would derive medieval *Frauendienst* from Christianity and the worship of the Blessed Virgin, we must insist that the love religion often begins as a parody of the real religion. This does not mean that it may not soon become something more serious than a parody, nor even that it may not, as in Dante, find a *modus vivendi* with Christianity and produce a noble fusion of sexual and religious experience. . . . The distance between the 'lord of terrible aspect' in the *Vita Nuova* and the god of lovers in the *Council of Remiremont* is a measure of the tradition's width and complexity. Dante is as serious as a man can be; the French poet is not serious at all.[1]

[1] *Allegory of Love,* pp. 20–21.

Dante as 'at one extreme of the Courtly Love tradition' (Index, p. 370) is cited again:

> When *Frauendienst* succeeds in fusing with religion, as in Dante, unity is restored to the mind, and love can be treated with a solemnity that is whole-hearted. But where it is not so fused, it can never, under the shadow of its tremendous rival, be more than a temporary truancy.[1]

Lewis goes on to speak of Ovid's, the Chaplain's, Chaucer's and Malory's palinodes, and implies that Dante never recanted. He had the *Vita Nuova* chiefly in mind when he spoke of Dante *simpliciter*, but he implies that the *Comedy* exemplifies and continues without a break the same 'noble fusion' of sexual and religious experience. But if there is a fusion in both *Vita Nuova* and *Comedy*, we must ask whether it is the *same* fusion.

In his next chapter, on Allegory, Lewis quotes the famous Chapter XXV of the *Vita Nuova*:

> It seems chilling to be told that *Amor* in the *Vita Nuova* is only a personification; we would willingly believe that Dante, like a modern romantic, feels himself to be reaching after some transcendental reality which the forms of discursive thought cannot contain. It is quite certain, however, that Dante feels nothing of the kind; and to put an end to such misconceptions once and for all, we had better turn to Dante's own words. . . . 'You may be surprised', says Dante, 'that I speak of love as if it were a thing that could exist by itself; and not only as if it were an intelligent substance, but even as if it were a corporeal substance. Now this, according to the truth, is false. For love has not, like a substance, an existence of its own, but is only an accident occurring *in* a substance.' However the personification is to be defended, it is clear that Dante has no thought of pretending that it is more than a personification. It is, as he says himself a moment later, *figura o colore rettorico*, a piece of technique, a weapon in the armoury of ῥητορική . . . 'It would be a great disgrace', Dante adds, 'to a man, if he should rime matters under figure and rhetorical

---

[1] *ibid.*, p. 42.

colouring, and then, when he was asked, could not strip off that vesture and show the true sense.'[1]

In a note, p. 48, 2, Lewis accepts *Epistle* X (XIII) to Cangrande della Scala as genuine, though commenting sharply: 'Dante himself, while parading four senses (*Conv.* II, i, and *Ep.* xiii), makes singularly little use of them to explain his own work.' This implies the continuity of allegorical doctrine in the *Vita Nuova* and the *Comedy* as well as the continuity of the 'noble fusion' in the two.

Now, I want to suggest that between the *Vita Nuova* and the *Comedy* Dante makes his recantation of courtly love as he had expressed it in the *Vita Nuova*. Further, when in the *Comedy* he recants his recantation and goes back to the *Vita Nuova* to fulfil by means of the *Comedy* the promise made in the last chapter of the *Vita Nuova*, he goes back with a difference. The 'noble fusion of sexual and religious experience' in the *Comedy* is a different fusion from that of the *Vita Nuova*; in the *Vita Nuova* the religious element has in it elements of parody, even of blasphemy, that are wholly absent in the *Comedy*. The *Vita Nuova* exhibits a *modus vivendi*, not a real fusion and reconciliation, but rather a superimposition and juxtaposition of the two kinds of experience, covering up 'the irremediable rift between the two worlds'.[2] The difference between the *Vita Nuova* and the *Comedy* can be seen in the fact that the *Comedy* contains in the episode of Paolo and Francesca a recantation of courtly love. This recantation might seem to imply the total removal from the *Comedy* of any sexual element. It has been said that the division between courtly love and Christian morals ended in Germany by drawing married love into courtly *Minne* (Hartmann, Wolfram) and was bridged over in Italy by its absolute spiritualizing ('dolce stil nuovo').[3] The supposed allegorization by Dante of Beatrice in the *Comedy* lends support to this notion of an absolute spiritualization, which I reject or at least modify.[4] Nor do I accept the authenticity

[1] *Allegory of Love*, p. 121. cf. 'When a poet wrote about *Amor* he knew that he was merely personifying an "accident", which personification, as Dante says, "according to the truth is false". But he could not be so sure about Venus. Perhaps Venus was only an "accident"; but then, again, perhaps Venus was the name of a real force in nature, or even the name of the intelligence of the third heaven.'

[2] *Allegory*, p. 40.

[3] August Vezin, *Dante* (1949), p. 369.

[4] See my 'Beatrice's Chariot in Dante's Earthly Paradise' in *Deutsches Dante Jahrbuch* 39 (1961), 137–72.

of the Epistle to Cangrande,[1] because the *Comedy* itself, especially *Purg.* xxxiii, 72 ('*moralmente*'), and *Par.* iv, 40–48, contradicts it. As for *Vita Nuova* XXV, I shall argue that it destroys the whole plot of the *Vita Nuova* and is entirely inadequate as an account of the 'lord of terrible aspect' in ch. III, and that Dante came to see this clearly in the *Canzone Montanina* and its accompanying Letter IV, and in the *Comedy*, when his middle, rationalist, period came to an abrupt end. *Vita Nuova* XXV is for me a last-minute insertion into the 'libello', and belongs to the rationalistic recantation of it under the influence of the Averroism of Guido Cavalcanti, for whom the chapter was written.

II

It has often been thought that once Dante had written the famous promise of a great poem for Beatrice in the last chapter of the *Vita Nuova* he could never have lost sight of it and was always more or less consciously preparing himself to fulfil it. Some who see that Dante turned away from Beatrice between the *Vita Nuova* and the *Comedy* suppose that the *Vita Nuova* as we have it is not the original work of 1292–3, but that the present ending belongs to a second edition, written just after the *Comedy* was conceived in order to serve as a preface to the *Comedy*. What Dante says of the *Vita Nuova* in the *Convivio* has seemed incompatible with what we have in the *Vita Nuova*. The difficulties are indeed great, and cannot be discussed here, but I am convinced that the *Convivio* implies the *Vita Nuova* as we have it. Why, then, is there in the *Convivio* no reference to the promise in ch. XLII, and the defeat, even if it was only temporary, of the Donna Gentile in ch. XXXIX–XLI?

He wished not to 'derogate' (*Conv.* I, i, 16) in any way from the *Vita Nuova*, but to link his second, philosophical, post-Beatrician, phase of poetry to his first Beatrician, exhibiting the transition as natural from a 'fervid and passionate' poetry appropriate to adolescence, to that which, being 'virile and temperate', was appropriate to maturity. But this wish not to derogate in fact means the reversal of the meaning of the two ladies. In the *Vita Nuova*, his love for Beatrice, even if sensitive, is never contrary to Reason (ch. II, 9; IV, 2); but his love for the Donna Gentile is merely sensitive, and an 'adversary of reason' (ch. XXXIX, 1, 2). In the *Convivio*, love for Beatrice belongs to his passionate adolescence before reason was fully awakened in him,

[1] See 'The Epistle to Cangrande again', *DDJ* 38 (1961), 51–74.

and his love for the Donna Gentile purely rational, since the apparently sensitive element in it was merely the vestment of allegory. In the *Convivio*, Dante wished to build on his reputation as the poet of the *Vita Nuova*, and so he ignores his failure to keep his promise to Beatrice. But elsewhere, outside his careful self-stylization in the *Convivio*, he does not hesitate to boast that he has written a poem such as had never before been written for any lady, and this not for Beatrice but for the Donna Pietra. This is in the canzone *Amor, tu vedi ben che questa donna* Canz. 11; 45 in Contini's *Rime*), a *doppia sestina* that goes beyond the *sestina* of Arnaud Daniel; and it ends (64–66):

> Sì ch' io ardisco a far per questo freddo
> la novità che per tua forma luce,
> che non fu mai pensata in alcun tempo

(*cf. Vita Nuova* XLII, 2: 'io spero di dicer di lei quello che mai non fue detto d'alcuna'). It is precisely this poem that he quotes in *De vulgari Eloquentia* II, xiii, 12, as the exploit which made him a knight of poetry, gave him a patent of nobility:

> nisi forte novum aliquid atque intentatum artis hoc sibi preroget; ut nascentis militiae dies, qui cum nulla prerogativa suam indignatur preterire dietam; hoc etenim nos facere nisi sumus ibi, *Amor, tu vedi ben che questa donna*.

Again, outside the *Convivio*, and about the same time, Dante is much more explicit about his love for Beatrice, namely in his sonnet (CXI; 50A Contini) to Cino da Pistoia, *Io sono stato con amore insieme*, with its clear reference to his ninth year ('da la circolazion del sol mia nona'). The accompanying Letter III is even clearer, and it is Dante's famous experience of love for Beatrice that Cino appeals to and Dante draws upon.[1]

Dante treats his love for Beatrice as a passion of the sensitive soul. There is nothing unique about it; she is one of any number of similar possible objects of love:

---

[1] In Cino's sonnet *Dante, quando per caso*, in which he puts his *quaestio*, l. 13 'da te, che sei stato dentro ed extra' is interpreted by Contini (*Rime*, 188) as 'nella tua patria e fuori in esilio': but despite the political reference to the *nero* and *bianco* of the previous line, exile has no relevance to Dante's capacity to answer the question; so I prefer to explain l. 13 as 'from you who have been in and out (of love)'.

The soul can pass from one passion to another, while the nature of the passion remains the same but the objects vary, not in kind, but in number . . . Love for one object may subside and eventually perish, and again love for a second may be remade in the soul, since the corruption of one thing is the generation of another . . . every faculty which is not destroyed after the consummation (*corruptio*) of one act is naturally reserved for another. Consequently, the faculties of sense, if the organ survives, are not destroyed by the consummation of one act, but are naturally reserved for another. Since, then, the appetitive faculty, which is the seat of love, is a faculty of sense, it is manifest that after the exhaustion of the passion by which it was brought into operation it is reserved for another.

This translation (largely Toynbee's) perhaps stresses the sexual meaning where Dante's Latin is more coldly Aristotelian. Dante then cites the 'authority' of Ovid, and concludes by advising Cino to patience, just as in the other Sonnets of the same series (*Degno fa voi* and *Io mi credea*) he advises him not to be so susceptible and variable, but to follow Dante on another path, the pursuit of philosophy evidently, the cultivation of the *potentia rationalis*, in the spirit of the *Convivio*. At this time, Dante evidently had no thought of writing any further poems, even if he was engaged in a commentary on his poetry:

> io mi credea del tutto esser partito
> da queste nostre rime, messer Cino,

he says and applies his 'tired finger' for the moment to write a sonnet. This view of love, as an overindulgence of the passionate soul and an impediment to the exercise of reason, with the sharp separation of the 'souls', is the same as that of Guido Cavalcanti in the famous doctrinal canzone, *Donna me prega*. It is far from the doctrine of Guinizelli that the *Vita Nuova* makes its own in ch. XX:

> Amore e il cor gentil sono una cosa,
> sì come il saggio in suo dittare pone

(*i.e.* in his famous canzone, *Al cor gentil rempaira sempre, Amore*). This raises the question how the recantation in *Inf.* v is related to the two preceding conceptions of love, the Cavalcantian and the Guinizellian.

III

But the question of *Vita Nuova* XXV must be raised first. Professor Charles Singleton, in his *Essay on the Vita Nuova*,[1] has argued that the chapter marks the transition from *Amor* to *Caritas*, the liquidation of courtly love in the interest of Christian charity, and forms part of the subtle strategy of the *libello*, so subtle that it already anticipates the *Comedy*, and too advanced to allow of such a falling-off as we have just seen in the correspondence with Cino. Singleton's interpretation has not carried conviction with the reviewers.[2] My own view could not be farther removed. Dante in my opinion inserted the chapter (and prepared the way for it too, in ch. XII, 17), perhaps under the influence of the recent appearance of *Donna me prega*,[3] without seeing how inadequate to his whole story, indeed how destructive of it, his rather elementary piece on the rhetorical doctrine of personification (not yet allegory as in *Conv.* II, i) was. The plot of the *Vita Nuova* turns on the genuine prophecy of Beatrice's death contained in his vision of the lord of terrible aspect in ch. III: 'lo verace giudicio del detto sogno non fue veduto allora per alcuno, ma ora è manifestissimo a li piu semplici'. Now, if Amor utters a true prophecy of an event which comes true after seven years, namely Beatrice's death, he cannot be 'an accident in a substance', a mere personification of the fact that Dante is in love. He must be in some sense divine, and in the *Convivio* II, viii, 13, such divinatory dreams are cited as proof of the immortality of the soul. The soul that is informed must have some 'proportion' to what informs it. The informer is immortal, and therefore the informed must be also. In passing, too, we may note that the reduction of the giver of the oracle in *Aeneid* III, 94, *Dardanidae duri*, to an 'inanimate object' in ch. XXV, even if Dante was thinking of the cauldron as the source of the voice, is no less destructive of the plot of the *Aeneid*. If Apollo, Jupiter's mouthpiece, is an inanimate thing, the providence that guided Roman history, the predestination of Rome, to which Dante so wholly subscribes in the *Monarchy*, is a mere fancy of Virgil's.

---

[1] Harvard (1949).

[2] See also E. R. Vincent in *Centenary Essays* (Oxford, 1965).

[3] *Donna me prega* 'is no celebration of the courtly experience, but on the contrary a brilliant, largely hostile, critique of it' (Peter Dronke, *Medieval Latin and the Rise of European Love-Lyric,* Oxford (1965), I, 137, following Bruno Nardi's interpretation).

But, if I am right in my interpretation of the Canzone Montanina, *Amor, da che convien ch' io mi doglia*,[1] and of the Letter IV, which accompanied it, Dante's view of Amor there as 'amor terribilis et imperiosus' and 'ferox tanquam dominus pulsus a patria post longum exilium sola in sua repatrians' (words which surely echo 'ecce deus fortior me, qui veniens dominabitur mihi', *Vita Nuova* II, 5, and 'ego dominus tuus' *ibid*. III, 3) was not of an inanimate object to which he chose to apply the figure of personification, but the numinous command of a personal agent, a command not to continue with philosophy and politics, not to accept even an offer from Florence of return to her from exile. Here, it seems to me, is something that Dante could not rationalize or intellectualize away, strip of its vesture and explain in bald prose, but a 'transcendental reality', 'a real force', though not 'in nature' but beyond it. I would take issue with Lewis when he says:

> It would be a misunderstanding to suggest that there is another and better way of representing the inner world [than allegory], and that we have found it in the novel and the drama. . . That unitary 'soul' or 'personality' which interests the novelist is for him [the ordinary man] merely the arena in which the combatants meet: it is to the combatants—those 'accidents occurring in a substance'—that he must attend.[2]

Or again:

> For Claudian, just as for the religious poet [Prudentius], allegorical conflict is the natural method of dealing with psychology,

and where he says of the vision of an English monk, in the seventh or eighth century, that the story of his sins as persons whom he recognized by their voices as they cried out, 'Ego sum cupiditas tua, Ego sum vana gloria', and the like, and of his 'parvae virtutes' as offering him aid, 'may well recall an actual dream'.[3] I find it impossible to believe that such abstractions ever appear in real dreams. The 'natural method of dealing with psychology' is the method of dreams which present us with real people whom we have known or imagined, and it is on this 'method' that Dante's *Comedy* is built, and not on allegory. There

---

[1] See *Modern Language Review* 55 (1960), 359–70.
[2] *Allegory*, p. 61.
[3] *Allegory*, pp. 73; 86–87.

is, in my opinion, hardly any allegory or deliberate personification in the *Comedy* at all, not even the three beasts of *Inf.* i, but only the personified books of the Bible around Beatrice's chariot in *Purg.* xxix. Dante's self-analysis and purgation proceeds by his successive confrontations with individuals who have meant much to him, and he sees this meaning in a new light, when, for instance, Francesca as the type and representative of courtly love is shown to him inexorably in Hell.

In the *Comedy* the figure of Amor can scarcely be dismissed as a personified 'accident in a substance'. Amor is the divine and therefore personal power which drew Dante to Beatrice and thus ultimately, through her, to his vision of God, in which he found his true self as the poet of the *Comedy*. The three passages, *Purg.* xxxi, 117, *Par.* xxvi, 13–18, and xxviii, 12, might be treated as simply examples of the rhetorical figure, but *Purg.* xxiv, 52, the famous 'Io mi son un che quando Amor mi spira, noto', describes poetic inspiration in the same terms of an autonomous personal source as *Vita Nuova* XII, 8; XIX, 2, etc. Amor in the *Comedy* is as it were the holy spirit of poetry, and his story is of how the lost pilgrim of *Inf.* i achieved salvation as the poet of the *Comedy*. The *Comedy* takes the figure of Amor from the *Vita Nuova* and puts it in a theological framework. There is a curious and clear illustration of this. When Dante wrote the sonnet *A ciascun' alma presa e gentil core, Vita Nuova* III, 10, describing the dream of Amor with Beatrice in his arms, one of the many replies (III, 14) was the sonnet beginning 'Vedeste, al mio parere, ogni valore'. Now, this verse is adapted in *Par.* xxvi, 42: 'io ti farò veder ogni valore', where it translates God's reply (to Moses' request 'Ostende mihi gloriam tuam') 'ego ostendam omne bonum tibi', from Exod. xxxiii 18–19 (for 'valore' as God *cf. Par.* xxxiii, 81: 'valore infinito'). The author of the sonnet was, curiously, Guido Cavalcanti. So, though his famous 'disdegno' prevented his accompanying Dante on the supernatural journey, he the 'Epicurean' and Averroist who had so devalued courtly love in *Donna me prega*, had seen at once what Dante understood only much later in the *Comedy*, the immense significance of Amor in Dante's first dream. The status of Amor had troubled Dante in the period between *Vita Nuova* and *Comedy*; in the *Convivio* he gives a psychological definition, *Conv.* III, ii, 3; IV, i, 1, and alludes to personification in II, v, 14, but the Canzone Pietrosa, *Amor, tu vedi ben*, addressed as the first line shows to Amor, rather surprisingly in ll. 49–50 calls Amor

> vertù che sei prima che tempo,
> prima che moto o che sensibil luce.

Of Amor in this canzone Contini says: 'e su tutto spazia un Amore astratto, fatto dio, quasi un dio filosofico da inno neoplatonico'; and of these two lines he notes:

> Amore è una vertù, dunque non propriamente una sostanza; e si è d'accordo con la *Vita Nuova* XXV, 1: *Amore non è per sè sì come sustanzia, ma è uno accidente in sustanzia.* In quale sostanza? Risponde a questa domanda Virgilio in *Purg.* xvii, 91–3: *Nè creator nè creatura mai . . . fu sanza amore, O naturale o d'animo.* Se Amore è nell' eternità, è dunque anteriore al tempo al movimento e alla luce, che sono dei creati.[1]

But Virgil's words imply that Amor is a property, not an accident, of all created things, while in the Creator Amor belongs to His essence; and such an uncreated Love is not a substance within the naturalistic world of the Aristotelian concepts, but supernatural, before time, movement and light. Dante's neoplatonic hypostasis of Amor agrees neither with *Vita Nuova* XXV nor with the *Comedy*. The sonnet *Molti volendo dir* (XXIX: Contini 79), if it is Dante's, affirms that 'Amor non è sustanza Nè cosa corporal ch' abbia figura, Anzi è passione in disianza'. But if a personal Amor chooses to appear, like an Angel (*cf. Par.* iv, 43–48) in a vision in corporeal form, what can one say? If one 'denudes' him of his 'vesture' of human form, nothing is left.

IV

But it is time to turn away from these too-deep waters of metaphysics and theology to consider the recantation implied in *Inf.* v. The recent discussion by Contini[2] admirably illustrates how Dante concentrates in splendid and false rhetoric the essence of courtly love as he had learnt it from Guinizelli (and even Guittone) and, directly or indirectly, from Andreas Capellanus. 'Amor ch' al cor gentil ratto s'apprende' is a fusion of the first lines of the first two stanzas of Guinizelli's canzone, 'Al cor gentil rempara sempre Amore' and 'Foco

---

[1] Contini, *Rime* (1946), 160–1, note on l. 49.
[2] 'Dante Personaggio—Poeta', in *Secoli Vari* (*'300—'400—'500*), Sansoni, Florence (1958), 23–48, espec. 31–36.

d'amore in gentil cor s'aprende', with the addition of 'ratto', the *coup de foudre* that dissolves doubt ('dubbiosi disiri') into certainty of love returned. Contini has occasion to quote Andreas's Rules IX, XV, XVI, XVIII, XX, XXVI, with the discussion of nobility of which Rule XVIII is the compendium, and raises the question whether Dante knew Andreas's book, 'Il Gualtieri' (as it was then called, by the name of its addressee), only to answer 'domanda retorica, per quanto egli avvolga quel nome nel manto della più totale preterizione, e, certo, disistima'. But the answer is clear enough, since Guido Cavalcanti and Gianni Alfani had swapped references to Gualtieri and Andrea, and Cino studies

> sol nel libro di Gualtieri
> per trarne vero e novo intendimento

This and other evidence was already cited by P. Raina,[1] but declared inconclusive for Dante as also for Guittone d'Arezzo. Raina finds traces of Andreas in Italy as early as 1238 in the *Liber de amore et dilectione Dei* ('de quo Gualterius tractavit') which quotes sixteen of the Rules, and Contini in his *Poeti del Duecento* (1960) frequently adduces Andreas to illustrate poets from Giacomo da Lentini and Pier della Vigna onwards. In Carnino Ghiberti di Firenze he notes the Andrean (ch. 3, p. 13, Battaglia) derivation of 'amore' from 'amo' (*hamus*, hook) without, however, quoting Dante's reference to it in the sonnet to Cino *Io mi credea*, 6:

> che pigliar vi lasciate a ogni uncino.

The Florentine translation of 'Gualtieri', quoted by Contini (*P del D* II, 524) uses 'uncini' to translate Andreas' 'cupidinis vinculis'. It seems safe to assume Dante's acquaintance with Andreas. But his 'disistima' for him seems less certain. Contini rightly says 'L'Inferno (e il Purgatorio) di Dante è anche il luogo dei suoi peccati vinti, la sede delle sue tentazioni superate . . . vuol dire che è oltrepassato lo stadio dell' amor cortese, della mera *probitas*, dell' etica mondana, che perdura nello Stil Nuovo e si prolunga nella *Vita Nuova*. La sublimazione di Beatrice è attuata mediante l'analogia. Francesca è insomma una tappa, una tappa inferiore simpatica (voglio dire simpatetica) e respinta, dell' itinerario dantesco.' (On 'etica mondana' compare what Lewis says, pp. 41–42

---

[1] *Studi de filologia romanza* V (1889), 205–24: 'Il libro di Andrea Capellano in Italia nei secoli XIII e XIV.'

and note 1, on 'worldliness' and the ideal of the *gentleman*.) But this self-transcendence and passage beyond courtly love costs Dante great pain. He is so divided between sympathy with Francesca and horror at finding her in Hell that he cannot endure the tension, but faints:

> io venni men così com' io morisse;
> e caddi come corpo morto cade.

This faint and fall to the ground is the dream-expression of his 'mystical death', the death of this aspect of the Old Adam in him. The disesteem of the *Comedy* implies a high esteem before it. At least, in writing *Inf.* v, his own recantation, Dante must have felt more esteem for Andreas's recantation in his Book III! Andreas was generally esteemed: Pieraccio Tedaldi in a sonnet on Dante's death describes him as 'più copioso in iscienza che Catone Donato o ver Gualtieri'!

Inf. v is, then, the recantation of the courtly love that underlies the *Vita Nuova*, Dante's Guinizellian phase. Does he in the *Comedy* also recant his next Cavalcantian phase, the phase that already obtrudes itself into *Vita Nuova* XXV, and shatters the charming Guinizellian idealization? *Ep.* III treats Beatrice as one among many possible 'objecta diversa numero sed non specie'; and declares 'amorem hujus posse torpescere atque denique interire, nec non huius (quod corruptio unius generatio sit alterius) in anima reformari'. Beatrice disappears behind 'huius' and 'unius'. But in *Purg.* xxxi, 60, Dante makes her allude to this plurality of possible (and indeed actual) loves in one scathing line:

> o altra vanità con sì breve uso.

When Beatrice died, Dante's love for her should not have been 'corrupted' and died away, because she became more beautiful and stronger to save him, *Purg.* xxx, 128: 'e bellezza e virtù cresciuta m' era.' Beatrice dates Dante's unfaithfulness (126: 'questi si tolse a me, e diessi altrui') from her death and not from his failure to fulfil the promise of *Vita Nuova* XLII, 42, though 115 ('questi fu tal ne la sua vita nova') is a reference to the 'libello'. Dante's love for Beatrice was a unique experience (in life and in poetry), and she could have no successor, as Dante recognizes in *Purg.* xxxiii, 91–92:

> non mi ricorda
> che io straniassi me già mai da voi.

Her image had continued to live in his soul, 'che vive . . . in terra con la mia anima', *Conv.* II, ii, 1 (despite the past tense 'de la quale *fu* l'anima mia innamorata', *Conv.* II, viii, 16, and despite his attempt in the *Convivio* to represent his philosophical poetry as better than that which Beatrice had inspired). Dante had tried to degrade his poetry for Beatrice as merely the poetry of the sensitive soul in isolation, and elevate his philosophical poetry as that of the rational soul. The most absurd application of the doctrine of the tripartite soul is in the *De vulgari Eloquentia* II, ii, 6–10, where he divides poetry into three classes, *Salus, Venus* and *Virtus,* corresponding to the vegetative soul which pursues the useful, the sensitive which pursues the pleasurable, and the rational which pursues the 'honestum'. But this sharp separation is abandoned in the *Comedy* for a much more unified view of the soul, *Purg.* iv, 5–6, and xxv, 55 ff., so that in the *Comedy* Beatrice is, like Amor in *Vita Nuova* II, 9, and IV, 2, above reason and not below. She was not one of a series of possible objects of passion, but unique in her claim on Dante as her poet. There are then two or rather three recantations in the *Comedy*: that of courtly love in *Inf.* v; that of the Cavalcantian reduction of courtly love to an aberrant excess of sensuous passion; and finally that of a purely rational love for the Donna Gentile, the Lady Philosophy, which in the *Convivio* was expressed allegorically in terms of courtly love. It is often repeated that the symbol of the Donna Gentile, as it is found in the *Convivio*, is in the *Comedy* divided into Virgil, as the symbol of Reason, and Beatrice, the symbol of Grace, Revelation, the Church. I have elsewhere[1] argued that on the contrary the Donna Gentile is to be recognized in the Siren of *Purg.* xix.

V

We can now turn to consider the blend of sex and religion in the *Vita Nuova.* Except for ch. XXV, it moves in a very rarefied and sublimated world. The physical instinct is etherized into the finest of 'fine amore'. Nevertheless, in the recantation of the courtly love that Dante learnt from Guinizelli, the physical element is prominent in Francesca's reference to her 'bella persona' and in the adultery which leads to 'una morte', the death which makes the two lovers one for ever. Moreover, the sonnet *Guido, io vorrei che tu e Lapo ed io* shows that Dante had indulged such erotic fantasies, even if he excluded the sonnet from the *Vita Nuova* as unsuitable in tone and in any case not about Beatrice (who came ninth in the lost *sirventese* about the sixty fair ladies of Florence)

[1] *Letture del* 'Purgatorio', ed. Vittorio Vettori, Lect. Dant. Internaz. Marzorati (Milan, 1965).

but about Lady No. Thirty. Now Francesca alludes to the Arthurian cycle in 'Galeotto fu il libro', and the sonnet, too, is clearly derived from Arthurian romance, with the enchanted boat of Merlin, probably from the story of Tristan. Contini (*Rime*, pp. 52–54) quotes many parallels, in particular another sonnet of escape from all social pressures (except the company of the 'chorus' of like-minded devotees of love), *Io vorria in mezzo mar una montagna*, in which the knights errant of Brittany are expressly mentioned. The occupation of such an earthly paradise would be, Dante says, *ragionar sempre d' amore*. In her rebukes of Dante in the Earthly Paradise (also 'una montagna in mezzo mar') she, no less than Francesca, refers to her 'carne' and 'belle membra' and the 'piacer' that they presented to him, 'il sommo piacer'. Sexual love is the presupposition of the *Vita Nuova*, 'ma molto sottinteso', and the religious element is much more prominent. But how is the latter to be understood?

In this controversy Michele Barbi showed his usual balance and sanity, even if he did not say the last word, in discussing Pietrobono's views of 'Razionalismo e misticismo in Dante'.[1] Dante's ideal at the time of the *Vita Nuova* was the 'worldly' (in Lewis's sense) one of *donneare a guisa di leggiadro*, of being the perfect *cavaliere* or *gentilumo* (pp. 60–61). Dante learnt from Beatrice *leggiadria*, not the way to heaven:

> È amore che spinge il Poeta a pensare la sua donna là dov' è; è immaginazione d' amante che non sa staccare il pensiero dalla donna amata, e non desiderio di levarsi dalle cose terrene alle celesti, per immergersi in Dio. Il Poeta non cerca Dio nella creatura, nè la Santa come santa; non si sforza di salire per mezzo della creatura al creatore (p. 63).

If the *Vita Nuova* is regarded as simply the vestibule and preface to the *Comedy* and all that lay between them in Dante's life is ignored, the religious and mystical element of the *Vita Nuova* can be treated as the same as that which we find in the *Comedy*. Many critics besides Singleton still think that after the *Vita Nuova* all Dante's thought went to prepare himself for the *Comedy*.[2] But in *Vita Nuova* XLII, Dante had in mind

---

[1] *St. Dant.* 17 (1933) = *Problemi di critica dantesca*, seconda serie, Sansoni (Florence, 1941), 1–86.

[2] *e.g.* Piero Bigongiari, 'La Poesia di Guido Cavalcanti' in *Secoli Va i ('300—'400—'500)* (Florence, 1958), p. 4.

a grand 'tragic' canzone, not a comedy, and he fulfilled the promise
with the canzone *Amor, tu vedi ben*—but, as we have seen, for the wrong
lady. Since Dante could so easily strip his love for Beatrice of its
mystical and religious trappings and reduce it to sensuous passion, we
may suspect that there was no integration or fusion of sex and religion,
but only a borrowing of Biblical plumes to heighten the effect of his
story. The religious language of the *Vita Nuova* is then essentially 'colore
rettorico'. In the second stanza of *Donne ch' avete* (*Vita Nuova* XIX, 7–8),
the scene in heaven is unorthodox, if not slightly blasphemous, in
substituting for Christian salvation a rival salvation through Beatrice's
beauty. This is as much a defiance of religion as the scene in Guinizelli's
canzone from which it is developed, though Guinizelli is franker, in
Al cor gentil rempaira sempre Amore, stanza 6, 57–60, about his own
'presumption' and 'idolatry' in giving to his lady praises 'ch' a Me
[*sc.* God] conven . . . e a la reina del regname degno'. Dante knew
very well what he was about in making Amor speak half-biblical Latin
phrases and in quoting Jeremiah, *videte si est dolor ut dolor meus* (*Vita
Nuova* VII 3 and 7) and *quomodo sedet sola civitas* (*Vita Nuova* XXVIII),
and in the elaborate parallel of Giovanna-Primavera with St. John the
Baptist as forerunner (*Vita Nuova* XXIV). Later, too, in the *Monarchy*
and Political *Letters* that go with it (V, VI and VII) he was to clothe his
Emperor in Messianic robes. Examples are so frequent that critics are
no longer shocked when in *Mon.* III, x, 6, the *tunica inconsutilis* is the
Empire, not the Church; nor even when in *Ep.* VII, 7 and 10, Henry
VII has the words of the forerunner *Tu es qui venturus es?* and actually
Ecce Agnus Dei, ecce qui tollit peccata mundi applied to him (*cf. Ep.* VI, 25,
vere languores nostros ipse tulit, where, however, Dante apologizes by
adding *tanquam ad ipsum post Christum*). In the *Comedy*, on the contrary,
no Emperor is decked with these improper colours, and in the *Comedy*
Beatrice herself has to educate Dante slowly and persistently out of his
idolatry of her.[1] The supreme vision comes only when she has stepped
aside and become his equal (*Par.* xxxi, 85, 'Tu', no longer 'voi'), not his
superior.

If I am right in my interpretation of *Vita Nuova* XXV, Dante's
incipient rationalism had already blown away with its chill wind the

---

[1] *cf. Par.* xviii, 21: 'che *non* pur nei miei occhi è paradiso,' correcting *Par.* xiv
132 and xv, 36. I have tried to trace this process of education in *Centenary
Essays on Dante* (Oxford Dante Society), Clarendon Press (1965), 'The Symbol
of the Gryphon in *Purg.* xxix', pp. 123–6.

whole aura of religion, in declaring Amor to be a rhetorical fiction. In the brief mood of exaltation in which otherwise all the *Vita Nuova* was written, Dante believed in Amor's prophecy of Beatrice's death. He was quite right, in my opinion, to disbelieve it, but not therefore to reject his whole vision and to ignore what later, in *Purg.* xxxiii, 72, he was to call the 'moral' meaning of such dreams and visions, that is their revelation not of the future but of his present state. In the 'moral' interpretation which Richard of St. Victor gives the Book of Daniel, the 'prophecies' of that book are ignored, and instead all the figures are taken to be aspects of a single soul. On this interpretation the figure of Beatrice in Amor's arms in *Vita Nuova* III, 4, gives no information about the physical Beatrice outside Dante (still less about her death seven years hence), but only about her image within Dante's soul, her meaning for him. Dante makes no attempt to explain why Beatrice in the dream so dislikes the taste of Dante's flaming heart; for him the meaning of the dream is exhausted when he recognizes its prophecy of the future. In the *Comedy*, then, Dante had learnt to apply to himself, and to himself only, the products of his visions, dreams and more conscious 'forti imaginazioni' (*Vita Nuova* XXXIX, 1), and did not think that if he 'saw' Francesca or Farinata or Brunetto Latini in Hell, he had any objective information about the destiny of their souls. If, then, in the *Comedy* (*Par.* xxvi, 42, as we have seen above) he recalled the vision of *Vita Nuova* III, he gave it a new 'moral' interpretation, and recognized it as genuine religious experience such as went to the making of the *Comedy*. If so, the externals of religion in the *Vita Nuova* are *colori rettorici*, but the numinous quality with which Dante's dreams and visions invested Beatrice was genuine, even if Dante misinterpreted it and did not come to understand it until many years later. *Vita Nuova* XXV throws out the baby with the bath-water.

VI

Finally, is there a fusion of sex and religion in the *Comedy*, and, if so, of what kind? If in the *Comedy* Beatrice is an allegory of Grace, Revelation, the Church, it might appear that there was no more sex than, as he argued in the *Convivio*, in his purely rational love for the Lady Philosophy. The Donna Gentile was presented in the vesture of courtly love, but the 'verace intendimento' was quite other. But of the *Comedy* it is usually said (and the Letter to Cangrande quoted in support) that Dante's symbols are *both* literally and allegorically true.

Beatrice is both the Florentine girl and the Church in the mystic procession, as Virgil is both the author of *Aeneid* VI and Reason. Certainly Dante stresses the physical reality and death of Beatrice in *Purg.* xxx, 124–9, and xxxi, 50 and 82–84; certainly, too, Beatrice in the *Comedy* has a meaning beyond her physical existence; but I do not believe that she is an allegory of Grace, etc.[1] She means what she meant to Dante, the inspirer of his best poetry in the *Vita Nuova*, whose glorified image made him promise a poem in *Vita Nuova* XLII and in the *Canzone Montanina* recalled him peremptorily from philosophy and politics to his real vocation as a poet. Beatrice was thus Dante's Muse or, in Jungian parlance, his 'positive anima-figure' in all that concerned poetry. But he could not have recognized his 'anima' unless he had seen her incarnated in Beatrice Portinari, outside himself. Nevertheless, for full understanding, he had also to 'withdraw the projection' of himself on the outside world, and hold the two in equilibrium. But the understanding of dream-figures and the dramatic representation of aspects of oneself in more conscious exercises of imagination (in the 'natural' way in which dreams represent them) is not properly to be described as allegory, because one's 'unconscious' can present one with what one cannot understand (*Purg.* xxxiii, 64 and 74) and at first much dislikes.

Now in the *Comedy* Beatrice appears to Dante, not as a light or disembodied shade, but in the resurrection of her body (*cf. Par.* xxx, 96). But if in the other world 'in the resurrection they neither marry, nor are given in marriage, but are as the angels of God in heaven', how can we speak of any 'fusion of sexual and religious experience' at all in the *Comedy*, where sex is wholly sublimated even if it is not allegorized? Is Dante's love for Beatrice not contrasted, as wholly platonic, with the sexual errors of Francesca or Brunetto Latini in *Inferno*, or of Guinizelli and Arnaud Daniel in *Purg.* xxvi? Is the refinement by fire of Arnaud Daniel's poetry and of Guinizelli's *rime d' amor . . . dolci e leggiadre*, like the fire which Dante has to pass through in the next canto, a catharsis of sexuality in the sense of a total removal, or of a reduction to right proportion and order? Surely, as with pity and fear, a reduction not a

[1] Geoffrey Bickersteth, in the preface to his translation of the *Comedy*, Blackwell, Oxford (1965), pp. xxxvii and xxxix, says that Beatrice made Dante a Christian as well as a poet, and that she was 'God-bearer to himself'. Although this was what Virgil did for Statius, *Purg.* xxii, 73, Dante speaks otherwise of himself, *Par.* xxx, 8–11: 'ne la fede . . . quivi (in sul fonte del mio battesmo) intrai io' (like his ancestor Cacciaguida, *Par.* xv, 134–5.)

removal, since Dante can say shortly after, *Purg.* xxx, 48: 'conosco i segni de l'antica fiamma', and he puts Cunizza da Romano in Paradise, *Par.* ix, espec. 34–36. Certainly Dante's love for Beatrice is spiritualized[1]; but not in the way that so many critics imply, as thereby made incorporeal, but rather more corporeal. This paradox in Dante's *Comedy* needs to be emphasized, instead of being obscured by the widespread belief that the philosophy of the *Convivio* is continued in the *Comedy* with at most trivial changes. On the contrary, nothing is more striking than the reversal of Dante's attitude to matter and the body and to the part played by the vegetative and sensitive souls in the human experience of the unitary soul. The *Convivio* is marked by a strong neoplatonic tendency to exalt the rational soul in separation from the other two which are its basis: Dante even speaks of the soul as 'imprisoned' in the body, *Conv.* II, iv, 17. This is not the place to argue so complex and controversial a thesis (complicated because Dante is confused and self-contradictory in the *Convivio*, in a way that his admirers are loath to recognize). The *Comedy*, in my opinion, corrects the errors of the *Convivio* and does not continue them. I have quoted the discourse of Statius in *Purg.* xxv in which the vegetative and sensitive souls are not left behind at death but, taken up as they are into the rational soul, are made immortal. Individuation no longer is due to the matter of the body (*Conv.* III, vi, 6, and IV, xxi, 4–5) but to formal principles (*Par.* ii, 71 and 147) and the resurrection of the body is celebrated in *Par.* vii, 145 ff., and xiv, 43–66. Nothing is lost or made in vain, and therefore sexuality continues, recognizable if changed. In this connexion, an aspect of Dante's symbolism may be mentioned. In opposition to tradition (and to himself previously, in *Tre Donne*) Dante puts the Earthly Paradise in the Antipodes instead of the Far East or at the sources of the Nile, and makes the Antipodes inaccessible except through Hell. Before Dante can ascend into the heavens from the Mount of Purgatory, he has to descend into the lowest and most material part of the Universe, the centre of the Earth (where, paradoxically again, he finds the most spiritual of all created beings, Lucifer, to be incarcerated). He has to accept all that is most material in himself, before he can become spiritualized. Spiritualization is not, then, the escape from matter, but its acceptance and transformation. A tree is the symbol of

---

[1] Dante likes to compare Beatrice's relation to himself with that of a mother to her child: *Purg.* xxx, 79; *Par.* i, 101–2; *Par.* xxii, 1–6. He uses the same image of himself and Virgil, *Purg.* xxx, 44; *cf.* also *Par.* xxiii, 121; xxx, 82; xxxiii, 107–8.

vegetative life, and the heavens are a tree (*Par.* xviii, 29: 'albero che vive de la cima')—upside down, but then we on this side of the earth are standing on our heads! The tree has purple leaves (*Purg.* xxxii, 58) and its mode of growth is the opposite of the normal (*Purg.* xxii, 133–4), but it is a tree, and Dante insists on his symbolism (*Purg.* xxiv, 104, and xxvii, 115). The significance of the Antipodes is usually obscured by the belief that the 'dilettoso monte' or 'bel colle' of *Inf.* i and ii is an anticipation (on this side of the earth) of the mountain in the Antipodes; but I would argue that it is the delusive exterior of Mount Ida in Crete, inside of which the Old Man is to be found, secreting all the rivers of Hell.

When so much in the *Comedy* is still disputed—or not even disputed as it should be, but dumbly accepted in the traditional way—it is clear that no simple answer can be given to Lewis's questions about the fusion of sex and religion in Dante's two Beatrician works. I have tried to sketch my sort of answer to them, and found that they involve the interpretation of Dante's whole life and development, and the major questions still at issue in the *Comedy*. Dante might have helped us by placing Andreas Capellanus explicitly in one setting or another of the three realms of the *Comedy*—with Priscian perhaps 'con quella turba grama', for writing a grammar of courtly love; or with Cunizza in the heaven of Venus?

Ideals of Friendship

It has been suggested that there was a necessary conflict between standards of conduct presupposed in the medieval knightly class and the ethics of medieval scholasticism; sometimes, indeed, this has been cited almost as an axiom. It should therefore be of value to take representative texts from the vernacular and from scholastic Latin and to analyse the ideals that they teach. In this essay I will choose as my subject the ideal of romantic friendship.

Amis and Amiloun was the medieval English classic on such friendship. Although the first known Anglo-Norman version, *Amis e Amilon*, was composed about the year 1200, manuscript evidence shows that it maintained its appeal until the fifteenth century. It is essentially a didactic poem, but it is not by a learned writer. The Anglo-Norman version has survived in three manuscripts; the first is thirteenth century, the second probably mid-fourteenth century, and third late fourteenth. Even in the latest manuscript the story is still growing; there are fresh interpolations and a new character, Florentyn.

But there is also an English version, *Amis and Amiloun*, which is first found in the Auchinleck MS., of which the most likely date is possibly about 1360; in MS. Egerton 2862 (perhaps about 1390); in the fifteenth-century Douce MS. 326; and in Harleian MS. 2386. Compared to the single manuscript in which *Pearl* and *Gawayn* were transmitted this suggests that *Amis and Amiloun* possessed a considerable public. The story was popular throughout Europe; there were Welsh and Norse translations and parallel French and German versions. It is this that makes it so representative.

The Anglo-Norman poem begins by promising that it will be a song of love, of loyalty and of great sweetness ('d'amour, de leaute, et de grand doucour') and that it is to be about two youths ('de dous juvenceus'). Their physical beauty is described. Their mutual love is shown as transcending the love of women. But there is no suggestion of any homosexual element in their relationship. The idea of sodomy was, of course, very familiar in thirteenth- and fourteenth-century England; it formed a most damaging political charge. But in theory it was conceived as the antithesis of romantic friendship. For friendship was essentially an equal relationship ('per a per'); according to a familiar Latin adage, it found men equal or made them so.

Throughout all the versions of the poem the emphasis is laid on the union between the two friends, a union so close as to lead to unity. The plot consists in the successful testing of their mutual love. Amiloun chooses leprosy and poverty rather than desert Amis in an unjust quarrel. Amis kills his two small sons in order to heal Amiloun; and he could not know when he killed them that they would be restored to him by an angel. It had been an essential element in friendship that they were

> to hold to gider in everi nede
> in word, in werk, in wille, in dede.[1]

This high-wrought conception of friendship seems characteristic of didactic Anglo-Norman literature. It is notoriously difficult to distinguish between advice to friends and advice to lovers at a time when love between man and woman was expressed in terms of friendship, and friendship between man and man was expressed in terms of love. But it seems clear that in the early fourteenth-century poem 'La Lessoun a leals amantz'[2] the loyal lovers are two men who are friends even though their friendship is described as 'fyne amour'. The poem teaches that loyalty is the first requisite in friendship, but there should also be mutual equality, good sense and good manners. A late thirteenth-century treatise in the Bodleian[3] asserted that friendship implied not only mutual defence but a common sharing of secrets and of property. This suggests a parallel to a passage by Aquinas in the first Lectio of his Commentary on the eighth book of the Ethics.[4] 'Between friends there is no need of justice properly so called. They share everything in common. A friend is an alter ego and a man does not have justice towards himself.' It is significant that Digby MS. 86 is reinforced by a passage in a commentary on the Ethics of Aristotle.

[1] *Amis and Amiloun*, Middle English version, ll. 151–2.
[2] Edited by T. Wright in *Specimens of Lyric Poetry*, Percy Society 19 (1842), pp. 18–22.
[3] Digby MS. 86 (2).
[4] Here, as so often, I am using the translation of my friend Thomas Gilby.

Like so much else in medieval culture, the strength of the conception of friendship was derived from its double origins in Rome and in the Heroic Age. In the twelfth century the classical Ciceronian conception of 'Amicitia' as the central virtue in social relations had gained a quite new emotional content from the memory of the duties of blood-brotherhood and of the mutual obligations of fellow members of a war-band. The *De Amicitia* of Cicero had already been christened in the fourth and fifth centuries. It could be supported by appropriate citations from St. Ambrose, St. Augustine and St. Jerome. The twelfth-century Church accepted the new amalgam and expounded it in its treatises. The movement was at its strongest in England; no one in the twelfth century wrote more poignantly of friendship than Aelred of Rievaulx or more didactically than Peter of Blois.

Cicero's 'Friendship' had been Hellenistic Greek in origin; it was therefore not superseded but reinforced when Aristotelianism made its impact on thirteenth-century speculation. By the time of the death of St. Thomas Aquinas in 1274 it had been synthesized with Aristotle's Ethics. But it was an essentially thirteenth-century synthesis. The medieval Cicero was as markedly divorced from the last century of the Roman Republic as the medieval Ovid from the Augustan Age. It is significant to note the resemblances between the presuppositions of vernacular poetry and the analyses of the meaning of friendship in the treatises of Aquinas. The first is the emphasis on union. Aquinas wrote in the Prima Secundae of his *Summa*:

> the union of lover and beloved is twofold, real union when the beloved is present, and union of affection . . . love alike of desire and of friendship results from a perception of the oneness of the beloved with the lover. When we love a thing by desiring it we apprehend it as demanded by our well-being; when we love another in friendship we wish good to him just as we wish it to ourselves, we apprehend our friend as our other self. Augustine remarks that well did a man say to his friend 'Thou half of my soul'.[1]

Thus such a union implies that the friendship must be mutual. Aquinas writes in the Secunda Secundae of the *Summa*:

> Not every love has the quality of friendship. In the first place it is reserved to that love for another which wills his well

[1] Question 28, article 1.

being . . . neither does benevolence suffice for friendship: in addition a mutual loving is required, for a friend is a friend to a friend. This interplay of well-wishing is founded on companionship.[1]

'Amicus est amicus amico.' This is consonant with the memories of the war-band; with the echo from the song of Roland ('for love of thee here will I take my stand; together we endure things good or bad. I leave thee not for all incarnate man'); with the echo from the song of Maldon ('Aelfwin, remember your vows over the mead'). But it sharply differentiates the conception of friendship from that of unrequited love for a woman. Loyalty in true friendship was irrevocable and necessarily reciprocal; loyalty in true love was equally irrevocable even when that love was not returned. This had been recognized since twelfth-century Provence. It was the fashion to stress it at the court of Richard the Second, perhaps under the influence of the court of Paris. Chaucer wrote in the most characteristic of his court poems:

> 'Nay, God forbede a lovere shulde chaunge!'
> The turtel seyde, and wex for shame al red,
> 'Though that his lady everemore be straunge,
> Yit lat hym serve hire ever, til he be ded.'[2]

It was the lesson Troilus was to be taught:

> many a man hath love ful deere ybought
> Twenty wynter that his lady wiste,
> That nevere yet his lady mouth he kiste.
>
> What? sholde he therefore fallen in dispayr,
> Or be recreant for his owne tene,
> Or slen hymself, al be his lady fair?
> Nay, nay, but evere in oon be fressh and grene
> To serve and love his deere hertes queene,
> And thynk it is a guerdon, hire to serve,
> A thousand fold moore than he kan deserve.[3]

But this antithesis should not be overstressed. In the first place, it is significant that this was not the kind of loyalty in love which the

[1] Question 23, article I.
[2] *Parlement of Foules*, l. 582 seq.
[3] *Troilus and Criseyde*, i, 810 seq.

audience of the metrical romances cared to hear about. Their favourite plot centred upon a reciprocated love where mutual loyalty was tested by separation and by improbable adventures, and was then rewarded by a magnificent marriage feast and by the birth of many children. The mutual love of man and woman came to be described predominantly as 'Amistie'. For John Gower the ideal of marriage is expressed in the line 'Loiale amie avec loial amis',[1] and for him a marriage should be founded on love.[2]

Again, the possibility of a completely disinterested love is explicit enough in the scholastic treatment of 'Amicitia'. In the fourth article of the sixteenth question of the Prima Secundae of his Summa, Aquinas distinguishes the love of friendship from the love of concupiscence:

> We are said to love certain things because we desire them; thus a man is said to love wine because of its sweetness which he desires. But we have no friendship for wine and for such-like things. Therefore love of concupiscence is distinct from love of friendship . . . That which is loved with the love of friendship is loved simply and for itself whereas that which is loved with the love of concupiscence is loved not simply for itself but for something else.

The love of concupiscence is essentially self-love: it finds its expression in getting, not in giving; the other is loved for the lover's sake. But the love of friendship is of its nature unselfish: it finds its expression in giving not in getting; the other is loved for the other's sake. Aquinas was analysing the concept of love in the abstract; clearly, 'amor amicitiae' and 'amor concupiscentiae' can co-exist and interpenetrate in one concrete human relationship.

In the same article Aquinas had begun with a citation from Aristotle: 'love is a passion while a friendship is a habit, according to the Philosopher in the eighth book of the Ethics'. A habit, 'habitus', is a permanent disposition of the will. Here again the authority of Aristotle supported medieval preconceptions. Constancy was already held to be the test of a true friendship. St. Jerome was quoted: 'a friendship that can be broken was never a friendship'. Aelred of Rievaulx had added, 'I would have you believe that he was never a friend who could hurt one whom

---

[1] 'Traitie selonc les auctours pour essampler les amantz marietz.' French works of John Gower, ed. G. C. Macaulay, pp. 379–92.

[2] *ibid.*, pp. 338–42.

he had received in friendship'. This was a concept that was only strengthened by the New Learning of the fourteenth century. Petrarch wrote to Francesco Nelli, 'Friendship, that Divine Thing, is for ever; there is within it no room for suspicion, no possibility of error.'

From at least the twelfth century it had been assumed in vernacular literature that the betrayal of a friend was the ultimate villainy. It was this that made Ganelon horrifying to the audiences of the Song of Roland; Ganelon was an Iscariot. It was noted in the Anglo-Norman *Amis and Amilun* that 'nothing worse can come to pass than when one friend is ready to betray another'.[1]

Like its antithesis, betrayal, friendship found its expression in action. Aquinas noted in his commentary on the Gospel according to St. John, 'It is of the nature of friendship not to be hidden; otherwise it would only be a kind of well-wishing.'[2] The acts that flow from the habit of friendship presuppose the quality of friendliness. Aquinas in the sixth Lectio of his commentary on the eighth book of the Ethics observes:

> You cannot make friends with those whose company and con-
> versation you do not enjoy—with those for instance who are
> harsh, quarrelsome, and addicted to backbiting. Crusty old men
> may be benevolent in that they wish well and will do well if
> necessary; but they are not truly friendly, for they do not share
> their lives and rejoice together in the company of friends.

This quality of friendliness, as distinct from the habit of friendship, seems to be represented in the vernacular by the qualities of 'Franchise' and 'Bel Accuiel'. 'Franchise' slowly took the place of the 'debonneirete' of the early *roman courtois*. In the *Romaunt of the Rose* it is the arrow winged by courtesy and by courage.[3] It implied a freedom and natural-ness in manner and in form of approach. For the Chandos Herald it was an example of Edward of Woodstock's 'fraunchyse' that, on meeting his wife and son during his triumphal entry into Bordeaux, he dismount-ed and walked into the city holding their hands.[4] It was the mark of the well-bred, the 'frely fode', the antithesis of 'wrecced churlishness', as in

---

[1] *Amis and Amilun*, ll. 151–2.
[2] *In Ioannem*, 13.3.
[3] ll. 955–7; *cf.* l. 1211 seq. (The Middle English version is referred to here and throughout.)
[4] Chandos Herald, f. 53, l. 3769 seq.

the Franklin's Tale. A form of generosity of spirit, it was closely linked with fellowship, as in *Sir Gawain and the Green Knight*.[1] It was controlled by courtesy.

'Bel Accuiel', the art of welcome, was described in the *Romaunt of the Rose* as courtesy's son.[2] It was derived from the virtue of 'Bel Aculhir' much prized in twelfth-century Provence.[3] It was associated with a quality of youthfulness which could survive into age; Rigout de Barbezieux writes, 'You are old in renown, you are youthful in your fine welcome.'[4] As an ideal it was acclimatized early in the north; Galeran and Fresne are first praised because they are beautiful and welcoming.[5] Since it implied the readiness to greet others frankly,[6] it was associated with the custom of 'Le Baiser'.[7]

It would seem that such friendliness was based on the recognition of the essential connaturality of all men. Aquinas describes it as the kind of friendship which is termed 'affabilitas'.[8] He considers that it is a special virtue[9] and a part of justice,[10] since man has a debt of nature to live with others 'delectabiliter'. It is characteristic of the continuity of tradition that Aquinas was able to cite in his support not only the fifth Lectio of the eighth book of the Ethics but also Macrobius in the eighth chapter of his first book on the Dream of Scipio.

A closer connaturality knit two friends together as personalities. In the *Romaunt of the Rose*, Reason taught the lover 'Certys, he shulde ay freendly be', but that 'Love of freendshipp' was 'Of wille knytt bitwixe two'.[11] Aquinas recurred sporadically to the problem 'Utrum similitudo sit causa amoris'.[12] He summarized his conclusion in the third article of the twenty-seventh question of the Prima Secundae of the *Summa*. There he takes as his text 'every animal loveth his like'. 'The very fact

[1] l. 652.
[2] ll. 2934–5.
[3] *cf*. Peire Vidal 34.2.
[4] Rigout de Barbezieux 2.6.
[5] *Galeran*, v. 1152.
[6] *Eric et Enide*, v. 3143.
[7] *cf*. Continuation of *Perceval*, vv. 1265, 2652, 4724.
[8] *Summa*: Secunda secundae, question 114, article i.
[9] *loc cit.*, article 1, 'ad primum'.
[10] *loc. cit.*, article 2, *loc. cit.*, article 2 'ad primum'.
[11] ll. 5381, 5203.
[12] Commentary on the Third Book of the Sentences, Distinction 27, question 1; Commentary In Ioannem cap. 15 lection 4; Commentary on the Ethics 8.1.

that two men are alike, having as it were one form, makes them to be
in a manner one in that form . . . hence the affections of one tend to
the other as being one with him.' This connaturality may be due to the
possession of the same qualities or to the possession of quite different
qualities in the same proportion. As he notes in the answer to the
Second Objection in the article: 'if a good singer loves a good writer
the similitude of proportion is to be noted there'. Possibly this might be
best expressed in terms of rhythm and of music. It is the antithesis of
the discordant. The emphasis on 'fair harmony' was a legacy to medieval
thought from Boethius and Isidore and Bede.

This conception could be used to explain sudden friendship, like
sudden love. In the *Romaunt of the Rose* the friendship that implies
perfect trust comes after mutual testing:

> whanne that he hath founden oon
> That trusty is and trewe as ston[1]

a man may share his secrets and his goods with him. But then, the
doctrine in the *Romaunt of the Rose* is explicitly Ciceronian.[2] In either
case, friendship results from mutual choice. It accords with Reason.[3] It
is 'amour voulu' not 'amour fol'.

In its origins, whether in Aristotle or in Cicero or in the war-band,
it is essentially a relationship between men. It could on occasion be
contrasted with the love of woman. The primary plot of the Knight's
Tale is the conflict between loyalties of love and friendship.[4] But from
the twelfth century it was also applied to the relationship between man
and woman and it provided the framework for the new analyses of love.
It did much to humanize the medieval conception of marriage. William
the Marshal in the verses by John of Erleigh, and Edward of Woodstock
in those of the Chandos Herald, both call their wives 'fair friend'. In
the third book of his 'Contra Gentes' Aquinas bases his argument
against polygamy on the fact that marriage is a friendship.

In fact, there seems very little divergence between the theories of
friendship current in vernacular and in Latin; perhaps precisely because
vernacular and Latin texts interpenetrate and derive from the same

---

[1] ll. 5247–8.
[2] *op. cit.*, ll. 5285–6.
[3] *op. cit.*, ll. 5305–6.
[4] *Knight's Tale*, l. 270 seq.

sources. The medieval culture of which we have literary record seems homogeneous. In terms of social structure the division was not perhaps vertical but horizontal. It may have lain not between knights and clerks but beneath both, dividing them from a peasant culture with its own pre-Christian, prehistoric roots.

IV

Courtesy and the Gawain-*Poet*

All viable societies necessarily practise some forms of self-control and mutual help among their members, some forms of decency and gracefulness in daily social intercourse. This necessity in part took the form, in medieval European feudal society, of courtesy. Courtesy, the virtue of courts, as such, is a medieval European invention, like universities and nation-states and other notable institutions. 'Courtesy' came to be a characteristic of much medieval literature. Modern literature has seriously attacked concepts like courtesy, and the generalizing words which denote them, and modern life, has tended to follow literature. The favourable connotations quite recently given to the word 'aggressive' suggest our different set of values. So the first justification of the present subject is historical and analytical. Here is a concept which was once very important in literature, and of which many traces still survive in our general culture. It deserves investigation.

We soon find a bewildering variety of interpretations of the word, though not, alas, that full and general history the word and concept deserve. It is clear that 'courtesy' really contains a whole family of meanings, each related to others, but, as with other families, in some cases not necessarily in harmony with each other. It is first necessary to see what are the specific structures of meaning attributed to the word in individual instances. In English, apart from Spenser, the word has been most significantly used by the great poet—or poets— who wrote the group of late fourteenth-century poems in British Museum Manuscript Cotton Nero A X. Lewis himself knew these poems well, and courtesy was a quality he loved. One of these poems, *Sir Gawain and the Green Knight*, is now widely known as one of the great achievements of English literature. *Pearl*, another of the group, is in the opinion of those who know it as great as *Sir Gawain*. The two others, *Patience* and *Cleanness*, still almost unknown, are very delightful and interesting poems. So that an account, even if inadequate, of courtesy in these poems, however objectionable or antiquated the concept may seem, is justified on grounds of cultural history and analysis. But I should be deceiving the reader if I did not also confess that I find courtesy as a quality in itself attractive and desirable. I do not mean I hanker after medieval ways of life and thought. The present, besides being all we have, is much to be preferred. No do I think we can take over meanings from the past without both conscious and unconscious translation. But the actual quality and content of thought and feeling in these poems, of which courtesy is an important part, seem to me to be of high value in themselves, so far as we can understand them, and to be worth preserving because they enhance the pleasure and value of life now. It goes without saying that 'what the poems say' is the product of a verbal art of a most sophisticated kind which deserves elaborate commentary.[1] But my chief aim in this essay is to explore part of the pattern that the poet's art has created, rather than to make an analytical technical criticism of the poetic processes.

Perhaps I may be forgiven by those who know all these poems well if a few words of explanation come first. It is a paradox that four of the most splendid poems in English should exist in a single rather scruffy manuscript with some poor-quality illustrations. So slender are the physical threads which bind the literary culture of the past to us. It is still not proved that all four poems are by one author, though most of those who have worked on them think they are.[2] I do not propose to rehearse the arguments, which are detailed and technical, and to which reference can be found in the editions. *Gawain* and *Pearl* have been edited several times, *Patience* twice, and *Cleanness* thrice, one of which editions entitled it *Purity*.[3] The title *Purity* was chosen because the

[1] *Sir Gawain* has received some: see M. Borroff's *Sir Gawain and the Green Knight: a stylistic and metrical study* (New Haven, 1962). Mr. J. A. Burrow's *A Reading of Sir Gawain and the Green Knight* is announced but not available at the time of writing.

[2] Professor Morton Bloomfield, in an important article surveying *Gawain* studies, PMLA LXXVI (1961), reminds us that the question is still not settled.

[3] The following editions are used in this essay: *Sir Gawain and the Green Knight*, ed. Gollancz, Day and Serjeantson, Early English Text Society 210 (1940); *Pearl*, ed. E. V. Gordon (Oxford, 1953); *Patience*, ed. I. Gollancz (London, 1913) and H. Bateson (Manchester, 2nd. ed., 1918); *Cleanness*, ed. I. Gollancz, 2 vols. (Oxford, 1921 and 1933); *Purity*, ed. R. J. Menner, Yale Studies in English LXI (New Haven, Conn., 1920). *Pearl, Cleanness, Patience* were edited together; R. Morris, *Early English Alliterative Poems*, E.E.T.S., O.S.1, 1864.

metaphorical implications seemed clearer (and, of course, all these titles are editorial). But the poet takes 'cleanness' in its simplest most physical sense as the basis of his metaphor, and uses the word as often in the poem in this as in the metaphorical sense. The word 'purity' has to my feeling an air of urban refinement and delicacy alien to the aristocratic courtesy of the poet, who is plain-spoken in these matters, so that *Cleanness* is the title I prefer.

For convenience I assume that the same poet, whom I refer to as the *Gawain*-poet, wrote all four poems. They were certainly all written about the same time and place. They group themselves together in various similarities not only of phrase and reference but in quality of mind. Although they are part of the same alliterative tradition as *Winner and Waster* and *The Parlement of the Three Ages* and numerous other poems, they are clearly by a different author. Only *St. Erkenwald*[1] is now sometimes attributed to him in addition to the main four, but it is not a poem in which courtesy as a word or a concept is significant, and I express no opinion about its authorship. It would not damage my arguments if it could be proved that more than one author wrote the Cotton Nero A X poems, but it does seem easier to suppose only one. Since he was a great poet, his poems differ from each other and he did not materially repeat himself. It is natural to suppose the simpler poems are the earlier. The simplest and shortest, the most bookish, with least apparent experience of the courtly life, is *Patience*. It is strongly personal in its conclusions, as if the poet were exhorting himself to keep his courage up. *Cleanness* is longer, a little more complex, still with a certain tension as of a personal inner problem to solve. *Pearl* is, at least ostensibly, highly personal, in that the poet, as most but not all critics think, represents himself as a father mourning his dead daughter. It has a complexity and a certain detachment of treatment which make it very moving, and which can only be the product of a mature mind and art. *Sir Gawain* is the least personal and the most complex, and has the widest general appeal. It may or may not have been written after *Pearl*, but it will be convenient to consider it last.

How does the poet portray courtesy in these poems? We should consider his actual usages before imposing our own ideas of what courtesy was upon him.

Patience, after sixty lines of prelude on the need for patience, which

[1] ed. H. L. Savage, Yale Studies in English LXXII (New Haven, Conn., 1926).

take in the Beatitudes on the way, paraphrases the story of Jonah, as a rather surprising *exemplum*. The point is that God was patient both with Jonah and the city of Nineveh, and the poet takes the lesson to himself, to encourage himself to be patient in bearing poverty, and to do the will of God; that is, to act in accordance with reality, with 'how things are'. *Courtesy* as a word at first sight comes in oddly here. Jonah, pitched on to the shore of Nineveh with great reluctance by God's agency, via the whale's noisome belly, has to preach God's wrath. He is so successful that the people repent and God forgives them. Jonah is furious. God has let him down. So yet again he remonstrates with the Lord. 'Well knew I thy courtesy,' he says bitterly—I knew well you were soft, and *that's* why I didn't want to come. The words that go with 'courtesy' are interesting here; they are part synonyms, part members of the associative field of the word.

> Wel knew I þi cortaysye, þy quoynt soffraunce,
> Þy bounté of debonerté, & þy bene grace,
> Þy longe abydyng with lur, þy late vengaunce;
> & ay þy mercy is mete, be mysse neuer so huge.

417–20

'Wise sufferance', 'kindly grace', 'long endurance with loss', 'delayed retribution', are all, of course, aspects of patience, conceived in rather theological terms as attributes of a long-suffering God of mercy. 'Wisdom' is also important. On the other hand, 'Bounty of debonerté', words frequently applied to God in the fourteenth century, have also more courtly associations. Ladies are asked for 'bounty', and have 'debonerté' attributed to them; and both ladies and God are frequently asked for 'mercy'. 'Cortaysye' in this passage actually refers to the biblical Latin *clemens*, which the contemporary Wycliffite version translates *meke and merciful*. Thus *cortaysye* is a word describing a relationship between persons, here God and mankind. The relationship is not between equals; it is from high to low. Yet it is marked by warmth which may be greater than the merit of him who receives it, even though it must be earned. In one sense, courtesy is undiscriminating, since it is not exclusive to one person. It is not, in fact, to be equated with romantic love, settled upon one object, though it is close to love. As applied to God in these few lines it is very much like Grace. Yet it is conceived in terms of secular relationship. A reinforcement of these characteristics of the word is found in the parallel words of the king

of Nineveh who repented, though for obvious reasons he is not so
irritated with God as Jonah is: 'Who can know if the sound of our
repentance may please the Being', he says,

> Þat is hende in þe hyȝt of his gentryse?
>
> 397–8

—'who is *hende* in the height of his nobility?' *Hende* is a curious word,[1]
but here, from the context and on empirical grounds, one can see its
equivalence to 'courteous'. The king continues,

> I wot his myȝt is so much, þaȝ he be mysse-payed,
> Þat in his mylde amesyng he mercy may fynde.
>
> 399–400

God has nobility, power, mild gentleness, mercy—he has power to hurt,
yet will do none—this is what it is, for the poet, to be *hende*. The word
is the English equivalent of the French-derived 'courteous'. In this poem
the poet seems to use the English word *hende* for the more concrete
adjective, and the French word *cortaysye* for the more abstract noun—
a situation that is still in general not unfamiliar. But the associations of
power, nobility, graciousness, of both *hende* and 'courteous', are the
same. And in each case the poet makes the general meaning of the words
'drift' towards the concept of patience.

In *Cleanness* the idea of courtesy is used more consciously by the poet
to give force to the special concept of the poem. *Cleanness* is much
longer than *Patience* and consists of a series of stories, told at very varying length. The poem illustrates that associative principle of literary
and linguistic construction which is so important in both language and
literature, and which has been almost totally neglected by modern
critical theory and criticism.[2] The stories illustrate various aspects of
cleanness, or rather, of uncleanness and its destruction in the Flood,
Sodom, and the death of Belshazzar. The poet in his preliminaries presents God very clearly as a king in his court, and in so doing strikes, perhaps for the first time, the major image that underlies all his poetry—the
court. The court may be good, like Arthur's in *Sir Gawain*, or the

---

[1] See note on *Hende*, pp. 84–85, below.
[2] As a principle of language, see R. Jakobson, 'Two Aspects of Language' in
R. Jakobson and M. Halle, *Fundamentals of Language*, The Hague, 1956. The
only critic who has used the principle in literary studies appears to be A. M. F.
Gunn, *The Mirror of Love* (Texas, 1951).

instrument of evil, like Belshazzar's: it may be the image of secular society, or of the Kingdom (significant word) of Heaven. It is always hierarchical, festival, splendid:

> (God) is so clene in his courte, þe kyng þat al weldeʒ
> & honeste in his hous-holde, & hagherlych serued
> With angeleʒ enourled in alle þat is clene,
> Boþe wyth-inne & wyth-outen, in wedeʒ ful bryʒt.
>
> 17–20

Again, in the parable of the Wedding Feast, which the poet proceeds to relate with zest, and where the lord, is, of course, a figure for God, the lord is seen as a king or great baron who gives a courtly banquet complete with roast swan and crane in the most liberal fourteenth-century style. Those who are brought to his court from the highways and byways are placed according to their degree by the marshal in hall, and served with meat and noble minstrelsy. The 'great lord' of the feast comes out like a cheerful fourteenth-century baron to welcome his guests 'and bid them be merry'. When he finds the thrall who has not put on his 'festival frock', but is wearing clothes stained with work—which must be the mucky toil of the farmyard—he changes his mood terrifyingly, like a fiercely jovial sergeant-major who finds an improperly dressed soldier. The lord calls his tormentors, the man is put in stocks, and set deep in a dungeon. One recalls those dark dungeons, full of the castle sewage, which even now, as they may be seen open and dry by twentieth-century tourists, strike chill on a summer's day, and shadow the mind with the knowledge of suffering. This is the dark underside of glory and praise. The possibility of Heaven creates the possibility of Hell. God in this poem is felt very much as a noble, just, warm-hearted, but therefore also passionate and indeed hot-tempered, feudal lord.

The poet, however, does not use the court as a simple image of the good life, natural or supernatural. He is better grounded in the particularity and actuality of experience than that, as is shown in the description of Belshazzar's court. The court shines with idealized splendour, but it is the court of a tyrant and blasphemer. The associations of festival splendour, reverence, proper hierarchy, are still there, but described with a touch of sarcasm. The feast is held so that dukes and 'other dear lords' should come to acknowledge their allegiance and pay reverence, and to revel, and also to look on Belshazzar's concubines, his 'lemmans', and 'call them ladies' (1365–72). (Lemman, like 'wenches' (1423), is almost always a contemptuous word with this poet, as with Chaucer.) The feast is prepared 'gluttons to serve' (1505) and there are around many a 'boaster on bench', who bib till they are as drunk as the devil (1499–1500). Belshazzar himself gets drunk. Yet the misuse of riches and power is not necessarily a condemnation of them. There is nothing in the poet's description to suggest any condemnation of courtly splendour as such: in itself it is a good, and the poet's natural image of good in this life and the next.

Of course, we today cannot so easily take the medieval feudal court as a type of earthly good life and heavenly splendour, with God as king. It implies many elements of medieval Christian belief that no one can now take to be true. But we are well used to disentangling, say, the literary greatness of Yeats and D. H. Lawrence from much of what they thought true, but which now seems nonsense or an abominable proto-Fascism. We have a well-known doctrine of the symbolic image, and we need find no difficulty in accepting as a singularly potent and valuable image of God, or at least of certain aspects of 'reality', the personal splendour and power of the medieval king or magnate and his court. 'All these', as the poet says, 'are signs and tokens', though he goes on, as we cannot, 'to believe in yet'.

The court in itself, as an image of splendour and power, the greatest that the poet knows, if it were no more, would be only the place of 'courtesy'. In addition, the court demands a standard of behaviour which is central to the poet's concept. That is, although the social grouping, represented by the court, with its external standards and all its ties and obligations between persons, is important, it must be related to inward, subjective, standards. Thus, while, in *Cleanness*, the poet associates the court with simple and literal external cleanliness (a secular and courtly virtue which the poor could not afford and which monks repudiated), he thinks equally of metaphorical cleanness, which is an internal value, and which is indeed superior. Early in the poem he speaks of priests, who ought to be 'clean'; immediately he builds multifold significances into his imagery of courtesy:

> Bot if þay conterfete crafte, & cortaysye wont,
> As be honest vtwyth, & in-with alle fylþeȝ,
> Þen ar þay synful hemself, sulpe(n) altogeder
> Boþe God and his gere, & hym to greme cachen.

13–16

Courtesy, that is, implies lack of 'inward filth'; it is 'courteous' for inner values to correspond to outer. In courtesy external cleanliness signifies inner purity, good manners are a sign of moral goodness, appearance *is* reality. No hypocrite can be courteous. (This contrasts with complaints in courtly poetry, and repeated in Chaucer, of the flattery and lies found in courts.) The poet's high view of courtesy is reinforced by the imposing list of sins that can cause one to 'miss the Creator's court' (177 ff.). But the special sin is 'uncleanness', generally conceived, in that it includes Belshazzar's sacrilege, but seen at its most gross in sexual perversion. The virtue of cleanness is in this poem made synonymous with 'courtesy'. When Christ is born he is known by his cleanness to be king of nature (1087), which again establishes the royal power of the concept.

There are yet further associations, only lightly touched on. There is an association of courtesy with moderation, or 'mesure', always implicit perhaps, but explicit where God 'knit a covenant courteously with mankind', in 'the mesure of his mode'—the moderation of his mind (564–5). Moderation also appears in the courtesy of Lot, when he tries to persuade the Sodomites who are besieging his gates to go away:

> Þenne he meled to þo men mesurable wordeȝ
> For harloteȝ wyth his hendelayk he hoped to chast
>
> 859–60

—he hoped his courtesy would correct them by his moderate words.

This, like other passages, shows how essential to the relationships demanded by courtesy is *speech*. Courteous words give comely comfort (512); 'hende' speech of the courteous one heals those who call on him (1098); not all speech is courteous, but one of the chief ways that courtesy is made known is with speech. The combination of social sensibility with inner virtue, on the secular plane, which is one major characteristic of courtesy, comes out especially clearly here. And it is associated with education. Courtesy is product of 'nobleye of nurture', though this is not completely dissociated from *nature*. Christ is known by his cleanness as king of nature, as already mentioned. 'And if cleanly he then came' (referring to his sinless conception) says the poet, 'full courteous thereafter': he hated evil and filth 'by nobleye of nurture' (1085–92). Gawain is later to be described as 'fine fader of nurture' (*Sir Gawain* 919). Medieval courtly life highly valued eloquent speech. The knight in Chaucer's *Squire's Tale* addresses the king 'as art of speech' had taught him. Heroines, like Chaucer's in *The Book of the Duchess* (919 ff.), were both soft of speech and supremely eloquent. The highest value was set on friendly, intelligent, lively, modest speech; courtly culture was a notably oral culture, though it had a manuscript base. All the same, speech is not the only, though it may be the chief, witness of manners. Gollancz notes a curious point of courteous manners attributed to Christ in the poem, though it is not peculiar to the author. In the fourteenth century it was considered impolite to *break* bread, which should only be cut: how should the 'king of nature', with his 'nobleye of nurture', break bread with his fingers? The answer is that when Christ broke bread it was divided more neatly than could have been done 'by all the blades of Toulouse' (1105-8).[1] Nothing illustrates more clearly the assimilation of biblical manners to those of the medieval court.

The 'nobility of nurture' retains its Christian quality in the emphasis in this poem on the willingness of Christ in his cleanness to be approached by and to heal the filthy. The poet typically thinks especially of the physically filthy, repulsive lepers, as well as all other sufferers of physical ills, who 'alle called on þat cortayse', at whose touch all filth fled, for

So (h)en(d)e watȝ his hondelyng, vche ordure hit schonied.

1101

The movement of courtesy is here from high to low; the internal quality of cleanness is shown in social action.

The cluster, or family, of meanings and relationships within the general concept of courtesy receives further additions and complications in *Pearl*, and the whole poem defines the extent of courtesy. It is difficult to speak temperately of the rich beauty of *Pearl* in thought, feeling and expression—its deep tenderness and pathos, its progressive transformation of pathos into acceptance and resolution, its intellectual force and metrical art. It is little known because of the difficulty of its language, and perhaps because its deepest appeal is to fathers of small daughters, who do not, as a rule, form a large class among the undergraduates on whom, in the last resort, dissemination of this kind of literary culture rests. Perhaps social change will change that, too. But it would be a gross error to think that literature depends for its effect on the audience having had direct experience of what is described. Words

---

[1] *cf. Early English Meals and Manners*, ed. F. J. Furnivall, Early English Text Society, O.S. 32, 1868.

themselves can generate experience, or all our studies are vain. Further-more, the patterns of events, thoughts and feelings conveyed in words, that constitute a work of art, can reflect, or suggest, other patterns, of which the writer may himself have been quite unaware. This considera-tion is important for *Pearl* because of the arguments about its 'real' meaning. The question essentially has been whether the 'real' meaning is centred in the ostensible subject, the primary pattern, of a father who is instructed and consoled in a vision by the glorified spirit of his dead daughter; or whether the 'real' meaning is centred in some other pattern, that is, in some symbolic meaning represented by but quite different from the ostensible subject. A great work of art is open to many interpretations. But *courtesy*, so important in the poem, is part of the ostensible, primary subject, and I leave arguments about general interpretation aside.[1]

After the poet has told how, in his misery, he fell asleep, we are transported to a land of shining splendour where we meet the girl in gleaming white at the foot of the crystal cliff with its 'royal' rays. Such description establishes a setting for courtesy; as soon as the poet sees the girl, his eyes eagerly 'question her fair face' (169 ff.), and a 'gladdening glory' glides into him, such as he has been little accustomed to. The vision 'stings his heart'; he is abashed and stands 'as hende as hawke in halle' (184). There is a special poignancy in this. A loving father might well, in those days of authority, expect his daughter to be obedient, quiet, a little in awe of *him*. A grown man naturally governs a little child, and courtesy tends to flow from superior to inferior. But here, though only partially (and the more poetically) sensed for the moment, a reversal of the flow of courtesy takes place. *Hende* can quite well be used of God, as in *Cleanness*; but here in familiar alliterative phrase, com-monplace, casual, expressing the tied-down docility of the well-trained bird of prey, it conveys the complementary aspect of *courtesy*, modesty, restraint, quietness, self-negation, receptivity. The situation, with the father in awe before the child, is tenderly ironic. The poem proceeds to create more fully the vision of the touchingly slight figure, regally dressed, her golden hair and long fashionable hanging sleeves, all gloriously adorned with pearls. She is splendidly crowned, a courtly heroine in a setting of unearthly brilliance. She is the pearl of great price, that was 'nearer to him than aunt or niece', whose finding again brings great joy. They speak, and the dialogue modulates with great

[1] Some of them are summarized in the edition by E. V. Gordon.

delicacy between his joyous, loving, half-reproachful words (a version of that strange mixture of feelings any parent will know, arising, in the recovery of a child, from anxiety and relief) and her unexpectedly reproachful, sober, though loving, response—a masterpiece of unusual narrative dialogue. It is she who instructs him, and indeed speaks sharply to him for his incomprehension. The dialogue is in itself wonderfully courteous; and yet again an ironic complexity is unfolded when she accuses him of discourtesy. He is

> much to blame and vncortayse
>
> 303

because he believes 'our Lord would make a lie', when our Lord promised he would raise us after death. The concept of courtesy here is centred on words, and discourtesy is the failure to believe a promise; but its special significance is internal, on the failure to regulate properly the mind and heart, lack of self-control. The father is not, in fact, being 'as hende as hawke in halle'. He acknowledges this in apologizing most courteously:

> Þaʒ cortaysly ʒe carp con
> I am bot mol and manereʒ mysse.
>
> 381–2

He uses the polite second person plural to the child to whom normally he would use the familiar, casual singular form (as he does sometimes later). *She* can speak courteously, he admits; *he* is as dust, he lacks manners. It is worth noticing that she can speak pretty sharply and yet courteously because she is in a superior position. Her courtesy is not lowliness now that she is a spirit enskied and sainted. As soon as he excuses himself in his misery she is warm and forgiving:

> For now þy speche is to me dere.
> Maysterful mod and hyʒe pryde
> I hete þe, arn heterly hated here.
>
> 400–2

An alternation between superiority and inferiority is established when he shows a proper humility, which, in his position, is an essential element in courtesy.

The interplay between the necessary inequalities of courteous relationships now becomes the motif of the section of the poem that

follows, but this interplay is also associated with the demand that
courtesy makes for a proper regard for others, and hence for a proper
equality before God. This paradox of equality within inequality that
courtesy requires is again developed in a marvellous piece of narrative
dialogue. The Pearl says she has been crowned queen, in blissful
marriage with the Lamb. But how, says the poet? He represents himself
as then, at that point, having been naïvely, almost comically, confused.[1]
Very apologetically he says, What about Mary, unique as the Phoenix,
whom we call 'Queen of cortaysye' (421–32)? *Cortaysye* then becomes
the link-word of the next group of linked stanzas and the concept is
part of their subject-matter. There are no supplanters in heaven, and
Mary is empress of heaven and earth and hell, for 'she is Queen of
Courtesy' (440–4). The mutual support the words 'Queen' and 'Courtesy'
give each other, each raising the other's power, is in the context clear
enough. Yet it is very difficult to give a precise meaning to the phrase
'of cortaysye'. As often with this poet, the aura of association does the
necessary work, without any precisely defined centre of meaning.
Perhaps *cortaysye* may be taken here to imply all the network of relationships in heaven, the mutual love and respect that all individuals
bear for each other; but since Mary is supreme, her courtesy is particularly the raining down of grace upon others. God's court has this
special quality, the Pearl continues, that all there are kings or queens,
all are equal, none is envious, none deprives others by his own merit;
and yet Mary has the empire over all. The paradoxical dual relationships
between persons, equality and hierarchy, apparently illogical, yet con-
veying a profound truth about human relationships on earth, not to
speak of heaven, is now further illustrated from St. Paul:

[1] It would be easy here to make what is now the familiar dichotomy between
the simple narrator inside the poem and the subtle poet who is writing the
poem but quite outside it, as Henry James in his late novels is outside the
internal narrator of his novel. It is a distinction familiar in Chaucer criticism
that has helped to clarify much. But the pleasure and poetry here, as actually
in Chaucer, comes from the *real* unity of the 'internal' narrator and 'external'
poet. A man recounting his past actions identifies himself, at least partially, with
his past self (because of the continuity), yet dissociates himself from his past self,
who is a character acting *then* whereas he is speaking *now*. Good raconteurs,
again, usually tell stories as if they were personal experience. The achievement
of such duality in unity is a rich effect that all the major fourteenth-century
European poets were fond of; Machaut, Deschamps, Froissart, Dante, Petrarch,
Langland, Gower, Chaucer, certainly practise it.

'Of courtaysye, as saytʒ Saynt Poule,
Al arn we membreʒ of Jesu Kryst:
As heued and arme and legg and naule
Temen to hys body ful trwe and tryste,
Ryʒt so is vch a Krysten sawle
A longande lym to þe Mayster of myste.
Þenne loke what hate oþer any gawle
Is tached oþer tyʒed þy lymmeʒ bytwyste.
Þy heued hat nauþer greme ne gryste,
On arme oþer fynger þaʒ þou ber byʒe.
So fare we alle wyth luf and lyste
To kyng and quene by cortaysye.'

457–68

This draws on the familiar teaching in I Corinthians xii, that we are all
members one of another, that each person has his necessary place, just as
the various parts of the body have their necessary parts to play in the
whole man. Once again, it is difficult to give a precise meaning to 'of
courtaysye'. It looks as if the poet is quoting St. Paul, and Gordon
indeed says that *courtaysye* here means theological *grace*. But there is, in
fact, no word in the biblical text that corresponds with *courtaysye*, and
Paul is discussing in this passage not divine grace but unity in diversity,
which might indeed be an aspect of courtesy. The poet agrees there
may well be courtesy and great charity (a reminiscence of the famous
following chapter, xiii, in I Corinthians) among the heavenly host; but
he goes on to distinguish, it seems, another aspect of courtesy, the
generosity or beneficence of God in making everyone king or queen in
heaven. This fairness is unfair; it is too generous, since it rewards equally
those who have not suffered on earth, and those who have suffered
much to win heaven. There follows in reply the parable of the labourers
in the vineyard, justifying the equality of reward. One may perhaps
detect here an underlying disregard for the asceticism which men were
accustomed to practise, punishing their bodies to attain a heavenly
reward, a disregard natural to the poet who celebrates marriage in *Cleanness* and the courtly life in *Gawain*. But essentially the retelling of the
parable is an exploration of relationships between individuals in a group.
The regulation of such relationships is supremely for this poet in this
poem the content and function of courtesy. Included in this, courtesy
means courteous speech (by which relationships are expressed and regu-

lated): courtly manners, which are the other expression of proper relationships, and which are, of course, in any case largely a matter of speech: and that internal virtue (here in its aspect of faith; in *Cleanness*, of purity; in *Patience*, of patience) which is the central *bien ordonnance* of the spirit, the virtue which the poet above all cherishes. Of this complex, the secular fourteenth-century court provides the physical image, but, as we have seen, there has so far been little or nothing to suggest that, for the poet, courtesy has anything to do with the service of ladies and what is usually, though misleadingly, called 'courtly love'.

Yet the relationships between men and women, if not of that all-usurping importance sometimes attributed to them now, are obviously of special piquancy, interest, pleasure, and difficulty, since their human variety is built upon the simplest and one of the most powerful biological drives. Much of the traditional literature of courtesy has been concerned with the relationships between men and women (see Historical Note, pp. 78–80, below).

When the poet of *Patience, Cleanness, Pearl*, or his twin brother, took up the subject of the Testing of Gawain, he brought to the very front of his mind that image of the secular court which in the other poems is only occasionally evoked, or which remains in the background as a conditioning factor. In the fourteenth-century court there were many ladies, and the poet has been shown to be no ascetic. He had a Spenserian love of virtue, and a Spenserian susceptibility to beauty. Like Spenser, and in accordance with the general trend of courtly literature of his day, he had an idealizing cast of mind, modified by that 'heightened realism' which Miss Everett has shown to be an important characteristic of medieval romance.[1] Courtly life, when treated by such a mind, becomes an elaborate embodiment of courtesy itself. Courtesy becomes both the general element of the poem, seen in the characters' every action, and also, paradoxically, a less generally moralized, more specific part of the courtly life.

The two courts of *Sir Gawain and the Green Knight*, Arthur's and Bertilak's, are each represented as the height of courtesy. The words denoting courtesy, *courteous, hende*, and their natural associates, *gentle, noble, good, comely, aþel*, chime throughout the poem. *Hende* (used of Mary queen of heaven, of Gawain, of the lady, of Arthur) and *cortays*, are especially frequent. Every action within these courts is *courteous*, except only for the Green Knight's uncouth lack of manners when he first enters Arthur's hall. In particular, the way in which Gawain is

[1] D. Everett, *Essays on Middle English Literature* (Oxford, 1955).

received at Bertilak's castle on Christmas Eve, with the salutations, and the extremely polite attention paid to his needs, is almost a summary of the romance-ideal of the courteous life, very reminiscent of passages from the Grail-romance *Perlesvaus*.[1] The poet's constant association of court with festival is even a heightening of the normal medieval literary presentation. The whole way of life, again, is thought of as the elaborate product of education, and Gawain, as already mentioned, is 'the fyne fader of nurture' (919)—the very origin of this way of life. Courtesy has, as usual, the aura of virtue. The Virgin Mary is 'hende' (647), the noble Jesus and St. Julian have 'courteously' shown Gawain the way to the castle (775), Gawain 'hendely' takes off his helmet to pray (773)— just as he does to thank the Green Knight, incidentally (2408); his 'hendelayk' goes coupled with his 'honour' according to the lady (1228). In particular, Gawain's courtesy is associated with his virtue in the symbolic device of the pentangle in his shield. The five virtues attributed to him, separate yet inextricably connected like the points of the pentangle, are *franchise*, fellowship, cleanness, courtesy, pity (652–5). Really, all these virtues might be said to be subsumed, in one way or another, under courtesy, as that concept has been built up through the other poems. All five are the socially oriented virtues of a close-knit society, economically assured, where some degree of internalization has developed the normal social need for self-control. The pentangle shows that the meanings of the words are not distinct. We are not to attribute the same kind of precision of meaning to part-oral poetry as we are to the poetry of print. Gawain's five moral virtues are doubtless not analytically set down, and they all mingle with each other.

Nevertheless, within the general *bien ordonnance* suggested by courtesy there does seem to be a more specific area of meaning attributed to courtesy in this poem. That meaning has to do with good manners, and as with *Pearl* the high point of good manners is found in courteous speech. Very early in the action, when Gawain asks to take over the adventure of the Beheading from Arthur, we see Gawain's good manners brilliantly made clear in perhaps the most courteous and elaborate speech in the whole poem.[2] Gawain's whole manner is a

---

[1] For a valuable summary of the courtly ideal of behaviour in French literature, which has many resemblances to *Sir Gawain*, see H. Dupin, *La Courtoisie au Moyen Age* (Picard, Paris, 1931).

[2] Admirably analysed by A. C. Spearing, *Criticism and Medieval Poetry* (London, 1964), p. 40.

vindication of the court where, as the Green Knight has sneered, 'courtesy is known' (263). Gawain's speech expresses his own self-control and 'mesure', his deference to Arthur and the Queen and the ways of the court, his boldness and defiance towards the 'aghlich mayster', all at once—a living expression of courtesy.

Gawain's supreme courtesy, and its special expression in speech, is further emphasized when he arrives at the castle. Everyone is delighted to know that it is Gawain himself who is come—the knight who possesses all excellence, prowess, refined manners, who is honoured above all others:

916 'Now shal we semlych se sleȝteȝ of þeweȝ
    & þe teccheles termes of talkyng noble;
    Wich spede is in speche, vnspurd may we lerne,
    Syn we haf fonged þat fyne fader of nurture;
    God hatȝ geuen vs his grace godly forsoþe,
    Þat such a gest as Gawan graunteȝ vs to haue,
    When burneȝ blyþe of his burþe schal sitte
      & synge.
    In menyng of mannereȝ mere
    Þis burne now schal vs bryng,
    I hope þat may hym here
    Schal lerne of luf-talkyng.'

The emphasis here is clearly upon speech. When Gawain finishes dinner he goes to chapel, meets the lord, and his beautiful wife and the ugly old lady with her, in a mutual display of exquisite manners, proceeds with them to take spices and play Christmas party games, and so to bed. The following day, being Christmas Day, the birth of our Lord was joyfully celebrated with meat and mirth and much joy at a rich and dainty banquet where the lord of the castle sat by the old lady and Gawain with the young. Gawain and she took great comfort of each other's company:

Þurȝ her dere dalyaunce of her derne wordeȝ
With clene cortays carp, closed fro fylþe,
[Þat] hor play watȝ passande vche prynce gomen
    in vayres.

1012–15

The spotless terms of noble talk, the profit of speech, the significance of pleasant manners, are the general aspects of courtesy: they are specifically shown in 'love-talking', the 'dear dalliance of private words, with clean courteous conversation, excluding filth'.

The deliberate emphasis on 'love-talking' is unmistakable. It is equally clear that the concept of courtesy here is narrowed from what it was in *Patience*, *Cleanness* and *Pearl*, and even from the earlier part of the poem, where it comes close to being identified with the whole chivalric way of life. Yet this narrowing is not an inconsistency. It is characteristic of the poet to emphasize some special element in the general structure of the word's meaning in each of the poems. Nothing in this 'love-talking', as both the teller and the tale assure us, was contrary to virtue. It was not the prelude to seduction on Gawain's part, and not indecent, but *very* delightful and *very* polite, and presumably about love, the favourite topic of medieval courtly conversation.

The specific, realistic, social context no doubt to some extent causes the poet to emphasize Gawain's courtly speech. It is that aspect of courtesy which is peculiarly appropriate to that situation, to a knight's social relationship to a lady. There is also a deeper reason. The plot itself depends on the nature of courtly speech. The plot is now to show how Gawain's virtue of courtesy is to be used against him. This is a more subtle parallel to the similar use made of Gawain's virtue of bravery by the lady's husband. The original challenge is an unfair trick, since the Green Knight can manage without his head rather more easily than a mortal man. By the challenge the Green Knight attempts to destroy Gawain, not to mention Guenever, through Gawain's own bravery. Were Gawain not brave he would not have been endangered by the Green Knight's challenge. Similarly, were Gawain not courteous he would not have been endangered by the lady's attempt at seduction. In neither case does it seem justified to think that the poet disapproves of Gawain's virtue.[1]

When Bertilak has gone hunting and the lady attempts to seduce Gawain the main weapon she employs is words. This is partly the mere effect of the medium, yet not only. The lady is beautiful, sits on his bed, leans over him to pin the bed-clothes down on each side. This might

[1] A *modern* view might well be different. It would be perfectly possible from a modern point of view to maintain that, for example, Sir Philip Sidney met his death through criminal folly, and that as a general he ought to have been ashamed of himself for wantonly risking his life. Thus, when the Green Knight turned up in his bullying way at Arthur's feast, if no one had taken any notice of him (!), his plan would have been foiled without all the trouble that was caused.

have been vividly and concretely described: imagine what a modern novelist would have made of it. In fact, it is only indirectly revealed by the dialogue. A more pictorial description would have placed the story at the level of bedroom farce—in medieval terms, of *fabliau*—and would have made Gawain look ridiculous.

Gawain is in exactly the same dilemma that another brave 'knight' of chastity, Britomart, found herself in. She, like Gawain, came to a luxurious castle where she was most courteously welcomed, Castle Joyous. It was full of comely glee, though all the inhabitants were 'swimming deep in sensuall desyres'. The lady of the castle, taking the armed Britomart for a handsome knight, fell in love with her and very soon

> she told her briefe
> That, but if she [Britomart] did lend her short reliefe
> And do her comfort, she mote algates dye.
>
> (III.1.53)

Britomart, like Gawain,

> For thy she would not in discourteise wise,
> Scorne the faire offer of good will profest;
> For great rebuke it is, loue to despise,
> Or rudely sdeigne a gentle harts request;
> But with faire countenaunce, as beseemed best,
> Her entertaynd; nath'lesse she inly deemd
> Her loue too light, to wooe a wandring guest.
>
> (III.1.55)

The very similar situation that Spenser portrays with explicit comment, and the very similar temper of Spenser to the *Gawain*-poet, are useful in helping us to see Gawain's situation and in confirming our sense of his dilemma. Puritan as Spenser is, he loves courtesy, and is not particularly shocked by, though he disapproves of, the lady's behaviour. Similarly, Gawain does not approve of the lady, but he is bound to be courteous towards her.

The lady's first assault is told with great relish for the comedy of Gawain's pretence of sleep, the lady's beauty, the innuendo of her words, and finally her bluntness (1178-1240). That Gawain was ashamed for her (1189), however, is a clear enough indication of what we should think about the situation, even if our own good sense and morality do not tell us. Gawain is 'the good man' (1179), but the lady flatters him to the top of his bent, particularly emphasizing his courtesy and that many ladies love him. At the end of her speech she quite bluntly offers him her body,

> ʒe ar welcum to my cors.
>
> 1237

It is always embarrassing to refuse a frank offer made with flattery. But Gawain must not be embarrassed or offensive, for that would be discourteous. Gawain cherishes his courtesy, and when a little later the lady hints he is less than courteous he responds quickly, 'afraid he had failed in form of his manners' (1295). At the same time, Gawain must not be complaisant, for that, as the story later shows, would be fatal. His reply steers beautifully between discourtesy and what the poet would probably have called, had he cared to specify, 'uncleanness'.

There are two levels of narration present in this seduction scene. One is that of surface realism. On this level, the lady is a wanton wife who follows, on the whole, normal social convention, but who wishes to evade it in one material particular. She makes pious reference to God (1256) and accepts the social conventions of courtesy that emphasize its verbal quality—the supreme joy of Gawain's company being 'to dally with dearly (his) dainty words' (1253). She also accepts as the norm, while trying to evade, the usual conventions of morality. Thus Gawain through his superior courtesy and ingenuity is able to pretend that she is just being very courteous herself; he praises her noble frankness! (1264). Gawain's verbal courtesy here is also the outward and visible sign of his inward invisible integrity, that prevents him betraying his host and also betraying himself. As such this narrative passage might come from a witty, sophisticated, and unusually decent Restoration comedy. The various motives and sanctions are those we might still recognize in ordinary social life.

There is another level, determined by the story structure. The general premise behind the story is the obligation to fulfil a bond, even to a demon. The demon, the Green Knight, wishes to destroy the hero, so he tricks him into a bargain, the Beheading Game. The hero does not know that the demon has a magical attribute: he can survive unimpaired when his head is cut off, as the hero cannot. But the hero, unknown to himself, also has a magical attribute. While he remains chaste the Green Knight cannot harm him. In consequence, the demon gets his wife to try to seduce the hero. In so far as she succeeds in getting him, for any reason, to accept a gift, a sign of love, the hero loses his invulnerability. (If he had accepted the gift of her body he would have become completely vulnerable.) As he accepted only a trivial gift, he received only a snick in the neck. Such is the logic of the story—whether put together by the *Gawain*-poet or not, does not matter. Such a story, like all the best stories, does not depend on realistic logic, psychological motivation, nor development of character (in the sense of personality). It uses role, not *personality* (young man, young woman, enemy, friend, etc.). By its bold non-realistic fantasy it presents human situations, truths, fears and desires, with a vividness and profundity which no realism, no purely abstract formulation, can attain of themselves. The story of Oedipus, in terms of myth, and the life of Christ, in historical actuality (and no doubt mythic formulation), are obvious examples. The story of Gawain at a less exalted level shows in its fantasies that if you keep your nerve you will probably survive. It says that promiscuous sexual intercourse (or perhaps just sex) leaves a man weak and defenceless. Far from associating sex with life it shows the ancient association (repeated daily in our newspapers) between sex and death. Life and all that makes it worth while, the story says, depends on the control of sexual desire. Such was the wisdom of our ancestors.

To put such a mythic story into even partly realistic terms almost always leads to minor inconsistencies, as Chaucer in *The Clerk's Tale* and Milton in *Paradise Lost* illustrate. There is always the possibility of a gap, as it were, between the logic of realism and the structure of fantasy, often leading to irrelevant questions, particularly psychological ones. The local realism of speech and behaviour in the seduction scenes of *Sir Gawain* may thus lead us to question the motivation of Bertilak and his lady—are they really evil; what was their real aim? There is no answer. The situation, the individual in relation to another, or to a group, controls the effects, and there is a fruitful, often ironic, tension between the 'surface' of the story and its underlying structure. The courtesy of Gawain is part of this poet's version of the goodness of the hero. The bridge between the profound but unrealistic fantasy of the story and the social high comedy of the surface-realism is created by the common situation, the testing of Gawain. On the social level, the test is one of morals: on the story level, one of survival.

It is also clear that the poet's main interest is in the social and moral level, rather than in the story-structure. One may well wonder whether, though he responded to a story whose moral implications were obviously sympathetic to him, he very clearly understood the structure. Surely, Bertilak ought to be more sinister, under his joviality?[1] The poet finds it hard to present evil at any extent, especially in a courtly environment, as *Cleanness* shows. Nevertheless, the underlying story gives a tension to the relationship between Gawain and the lady which it would lack—as Restoration comedy lacks tension—if the mythic structure were absent. And the mythic structure accounts for such a social breakdown as the lady's blunt offer of her body, which is so much at variance with the courteous tone of the rest of her speech.

At last, when the lady goes, she gets a kiss from him, by wondering if he is Gawain indeed, as he has not yet asked for a kiss. As already mentioned, he fears he has been discourteous. She says

> 'So god as Gawayn gaynly is halden,
> & cortaysye is closed so clene in hym-seluen,
> Couth not ly3tly haf lenged so long wyth a lady,
> Bot he had craued a cosse bi his courtaysye,
> Bi sum towch of summe tryfle at sum tale3 ende.'
>
>   1297–1302

Gawain most courteously says he will kiss at her commandment. What is noticeable here is that the appeal is made to Gawain's regard for his own ideal of behaviour: the kiss itself becomes paradoxically impersonal, as later kisses are that have to be begged. When the lady leaves him she has been defeated by the very courtesy she has invoked, by Gawain's humility conveyed by delightfully ingenious politeness.

On her next visit, after being made to ask for a kiss (which thus loses any amatory significance from Gawain, and which Gawain can thus easily give up at the Exchange of Winnings with Bertilak), the lady speaks of love again. Of all chivalry, she says, the chief thing that is praised is the 'loyal game of love' (presumably a transposed epithet—the game of loyal love), which is 'the learning of arms'; knowledge about love is the sort of knowledge good knights have (1512–13). She goes on to give a brief summary of the romances of adventure, how

[1] J. Speirs, in *Scrutiny*, 1949, repr. in *English Medieval Poetry: the non-Chaucerian Tradition*, 1957, interprets Bertilak as a fundamentally friendly, favourable person, which accords with the tone of presentation, but seems to deny the story-structure. In a valuable article, 'Magic, Fate and Providence in Medieval Narrative and *Sir Gawain and the Green Knight*', *Review of English Studies*, NS XVI (1965), T. McAlindon illuminates the tradition of jovial demons.

knights have endured hard experiences for their love. But from him that is so courteous she has heard nothing about love. He ought to teach 'a young thing', who is so anxious to learn! Or is he ignorant? Or does he think her too dull? Once again, however, she is defeated by her very appeal to his courtesy. His courtesy must compliment her. *She* knows far more than he about love—which is presumably true as well as complimentary. She has to accept the compliment like the fashionable lady she appears to be, and Gawain escapes again.

Perhaps the most interesting general consideration here is the lady's attempt to identify courtesy with love, and Gawain's successful refusal. In a sense the lady is endeavouring to fasten on Gawain the promiscuous sexuality of the Gawain of the late French romances (see note on the Character of Gawain, pp. 80–84, below). Gawain here, and in the later scene, where he says he has no beloved (1790–1), repudiates the French character. His courtesy is essentially that of the Gawain of the earliest stories.

On her third visit Gawain has had a bad night, anticipating fearfully the fate that apparently awaits him at the Beheading. The lady is much more pictorially described, for the more serious occasion, and the resistance made to the previous temptations, now allow the poet to increase the tension. She is beautifully but seductively dressed, with very low-cut gown. Gawain is more tempted sexually than ever before. She pressed him so hard, says the poet, that his usual dilemma was even sharper: he must either accept her love or rudely (*lodly*) refuse (1772). Yet the poet does not seem to make an absolute distinction even here between courtesy and chastity. True, he goes on

> He cared for his cortaysye, lest craþayn he were,
> & more for his meschef, ȝif he schulde make synne
> & be traytor to þat tolke þat þat telde aȝt.
>
> 1773–5

This certainly suggests a division between courtesy and chastity, and no doubt courtesy is thought of here for a moment in narrow terms of social politeness. But sharp distinctions are not characteristic of this poet's style, and it is not clear either whether the 'synne' of adultery is thought of separately, or whether it is merged into the consideration of loyalty to his host. As the narrative and dialogue continues, all three considerations, courtesy, chastity and loyalty, are all equally valued and preserved, as Gawain, 'with love-laughing' puts aside all the lady's 'speeches of speciality', and tells her he loves no one, and intends to love no one. This she accepts. The point is of some importance because this passage so far has defined Gawain's courtesy in terms of pleasant conversation with ladies, but has again specifically excluded from it any concept of *fine amour*. As the action has proceeded the lady herself, compelled by the demands of the plot, has become discourteous. It has been pointed out that the normal love-conventions, where the knight takes the initiative, have been reversed.[1] But such a reversal is not an attack on, or a rejection of, courtesy. Gawain's courtesy has remained unimpaired, for the humility that is part of it has allowed him to refuse to take the initiative himself, and the lady apparently accepts defeat in calling him 'hende of hyʒe honours' (1813). When, as if by afterthought and with much trouble, she eventually persuades him to accept the 'magic' girdle, it is clear that he takes it in the hope of saving his own life, though she pretends it is a 'love-gift', and the poet actually calls it a 'love lace' (1874). Even here, the real failing is not in accepting the girdle, but in failing to give it up according to his bargain with his host. In this respect he failed a little in loyalty, as the Green Knight later says (2366), though this is involved with his relationship with the lady, because he obviously would never have accepted the girdle if he had intended to surrender it later. Since he acted so to save his own life he can reasonably, from his own high standards, describe his failure to hand over the girdle as 'cowardice and covetousness', 'treachery and untruth' (2379–83). But nowhere does he accuse himself, or the poet accuse him, of discourtesy.

After Gawain has loyally and bravely fulfilled his year-old promise to meet the Green Knight, has withstood the three strokes and the nick in his flesh that pays for the trivial fault in accepting the girdle, the long explanation that follows takes place on the moral, social and realistic plane rather than on the mythic, and some questions, such as those about Bertilak's motivation and true status, are answered rapidly but not clearly. What *is* clear is that Gawain the brave, the good, the courteous, remains an exemplary figure. By all human standards his bravery is unimpaired; so are his chastity and loyalty, which in various ways are aspects of his bravery. So is his courtesy, inextricably connected, as in the pentangle, with his other virtues, but with a special quality of its own. He has maintained the somewhat paradoxical ideal of all medieval knights, as expressed in the lament for Launcelot in

[1] See J. F. Kiteley, *Anglia* 79 (1963).

Malory, in Chaucer's description of the Knight in the *General Prologue*, in the alliterative *Morte Arthure*, and which indeed goes back to *Beowulf*: the perfect knight is a lion on the field of battle, and a lamb in the hall. Gawain's performance in this poem is an unusually rich and subtle enactment of this familiar and noble ideal.

Yet it has been maintained by several critics that Gawain, and through him, the poet, rejects courtesy at the end of the poem. When the Green Knight explains he knew all the time about his wife's foisting of the girdle upon him, Gawain is shown with a fine dramatic realism condemning himself heartily for his slip. The very tones of exasperated mortification ring in his speech of self-reproach. He is furious with himself. He politely takes off his helmet and thanks the Green Knight— with what restrained bitterness—and commends himself to 'that cortays', the lady, and the old lady, too, 'mine honoured ladies that have thus cleverly tricked their knight' (2412-13). The undertone is bitter: the manner is irreproachably courteous. This might almost be Gawain's last test. He is exemplary still, even if we may permit ourselves a sympathetic smile at him. Then he goes on to say, 'but it is not surprising that a fool (i.e. himself) should go mad, and be brought to sorrow by the wiles of women, for Adam, and Solomon, and Samson and David, were all tricked' (2414-19). It is these six lines that have been taken to show the rejection of the whole courtly system based on devotion to women, and to show that Christianity in this poem is conceived of as an essentially ascetic life-denying system. Yet the immediately preceding half-dozen lines in the same stanza, when he sends his respects to the ladies, have been as courteous as anything, almost *more* courteous than anything, Gawain has ever uttered. The half-dozen lines of traditional anti-feminism would be a feeble denial of the whole elaborate and virtuous system of courtesy as evolved in the poem. In truth, they are dramatic and not without a touch of comedy as wrung from the knight of courtesy by his intense exasperation with himself. In the economy of the poem they bear much the same relationship to Gawain's courtesy as his acceptance of the girdle did to his bravery. They constitute the minute flaw that makes his virtue human. Any man, even as good as Gawain (and who is?), after all he had gone through might well be annoyed. We believe in Gawain's courtesy the more readily after this brief explosion. Nor should we exaggerate its discourtesy. After all, no ladies are present to be offended, and masculine society must be allowed some freedom of comment when it cannot give offence. Gawain continues his speech to say that as regards ladies it were a great delight 'to love them well and not to believe them' (2421). Now, there is nothing in any concept of courtesy that states that courteous knights should *believe* ladies who try to seduce them, or indeed, should believe ladies in general under any circumstances. To love them well and not to believe them is a courtly paradox, an ironic, half-comic, complexity of behaviour very characteristic of the *Gawain*-poet and, of course, of that fascinating culture which he represents. We do it, and ourselves, an injustice if we unduly neglect or oversimplify it. Courtesy is one of its major constituents and pleasures, and not the least complex. It is an ideal very variously explored and fully maintained throughout all these remarkable poems.[1]

An Historical Note

Courtesy is usually thought to be an offshoot of 'love', but this seems to be an oversimplification. A very early use of 'courteous' comes in *La Chanson de Roland*, where Oliver, who knows *mesure*, is *curteis*, while Roland fails in courtesy.[2] But there is no doubt that in those significant poems of the troubadours in the early twelfth century, where the new feeling of romantic self-abasing love begins to show itself most clearly, courtesy is understood to be one of the characteristics of love.[3] It would seem most likely that courtesy arose with the new courts of Europe, along with a new feeling about love, a new sense of personal identity, and consequently a different sense of the individual's relations to the group. This complex of new feelings underlay both secular and religious life, but may have started as a secular phenomenon, as the word *courtesy* itself suggests. Such complex changes have complex

[1] The view of the *Gawain*-poet's presentation of courtesy put forward here differs from that of other critics, who assume that courtesy is the same as *fine amour*. See in particular, besides the works of A. C. Spearing and J. F. Kiteley already cited, the important articles by M. W. Bloomfield, PMLA 76 (1961), and Professor G. V. Smithers, 'What *Sir Gawain and the Green Knight* is about', *Medium Aevum* XXXII (1964) (which has much other valuable material), and the brief, brilliant interpretation by E. T. Donaldson in *The Norton Anthology of English Literature* (New York, 1962).

[2] Pointed out by André Burger, in a review of *The ethos of the Song of Roland*, by G. F. Jones, *Medium Aevum* XXXIV (1965), p. 53. Burger points out traces of the influence of love and of ladies in *The Song of Roland*; but love and courtesy, though associated, are different things.

[3] A. J. Denomy, 'Courtly Love and Courtliness', *Speculum* XXVIII (1953).

causes, and to the several that have been already suggested—Classical influence, Arabic influence, economic improvement—I should add, lay literacy, changing the basis of courts from an oral culture to a manuscript culture, where individuality had more expression than in an oral culture, but was still in close *rapport* with the group, unlike the solitary author and reader in a print culture.[1]

By the end of the twelfth century the concept of courtesy was elaborate and widespread through France. According to Dupin it comprised a whole scale of internal and external values, and was most usually associated with love. 'One cannot be courteous unless one loves', says Marie de France.[2] There can be no doubt that for some reason there was a new influence of women in the lay secular courts of Europe, and that, as always, this influence had a civilizing effect, especially on that brutal military aristocracy. But the assumption that love and courtesy *are the same thing* is shown to be historically untrue from the beginning by the example of *La Chanson de Roland*. We can say no more than that there was a close association. This association was to some extent broken by the writers of the Arthurian Grail Romances, like *Perlezvaus*, who are, as Dupin shows, deeply conditioned by the ideal of courtesy, but hostile to secular love. Even in purely secular relationships and behaviour courtesy became very generalized.

Courtesy is indeed complex. I close this note with a quotation from the late twelfth-century poem *Guillaume de Palerne*, very popular in its day. A little boy is being taken to court, and he is instructed how he should behave there. It is a passage which could be matched in a good many French and English romances, but it is specially worth noting here, as this poem was translated into English in the middle of the fourteenth century as *William of Palerne*, the first of the poems of the Alliterative Revival. It expresses that sense of individual integrity in relation to the group, that sense of self-control and moderation, of active goodwill and kindness to others, which I take to be central to the concept of courtesy; but it has no word of love.

'Si ferés, fix', disit li preudon,
'Car grans biens vos en puet venir.
Si soiés prex du deservir
Et de faire tot son voloir,

(The cowherd) seide 'þou swete sone,
  seþþe þou schalt hennes wende
Whanne þou komest to kourt
  among þe kete lordes,

---

[1] *cf.* M. McLuhan, *The Gutenberg Galaxy* (Toronto, 1962).
[2] *Guigemar*, 59, quoted by H. Dupin, *La Courtoisie au Moyen Age*, p. 93.

Et quanques vos poés savoir
C'on doit a si haut cort faire;
Si soiés frans et debonaire
Et servicables et temprés.
Ne soiés pas desmesurés,
Ne outrageus, fel ne estous,
Et vos faites amer a tous;
Ne de ton droit ne te destort
Nus plus prisiés de toi en cort
Que vos si bien nel deteigniés,
Que tort ne blasme n'i aiés,
Ta parole garde et tes dis
Que tu ne soiés entrepris
Si que blasmer ne vos en sace
Nus hom en rue ne en place.
As povres vos humeliés,
Contre les riches or aidiés.
En cort si haute emperial
Mult i sont cointe cil vassal:
Mult voelent bien que lor paroles
Soient sages u soient foles,
Aient lor lieus, soient oies
Et chier tenues et joies
Nus ne vos i prenge a vo tort;
Mais de ton droit te truissent fort
Ne troveras qui li t'apreigne.'[1]

& knowest alle þe kuþþes
   þat to kourt langes
bere þe boxumly & bonure
   þat ich burn þe loue.
Be meke and mesurabul,
   nouȝt of many wordes,
be no tellere of talis
   but trewe to þi lord
& prestely for pore men
   profer þe euer,
For hem to rekene wiþ þe riche
   in riȝt & in skille.
Be feiȝtful & fre,
   euer of faire speche,
& seruisabul to þe simple,
   so as to þe riche,
& felawe in faire manere,
   as falles for þi state.
So schaltou gete Goddes loue,
   & alle gode mennes.'[2]

The Character of Gawain

'Character' in a work of literature can usually be placed somewhere on a line between two poles. The one pole is character as role. Using the word 'character' simply to denote the personage in the work of literature, we may say that the character appears as role when he (or she) has only generally defined characteristics, which are sufficient for the purpose in hand. Examples of roles are lecherous young students, like those in Chaucer's *Miller's* and *Reeve's Tales*, or brave and good knights, like Troilus, or beautiful and virtuous ladies, like Dorigen in the *Franklin's Tale*. Such characters have their main interest as performers in a series of events, or as part of the situational pattern. At the other extreme, character can be portrayed as personality for its own

[1] *Guillaume de Palerne*, ed. H. Michelant, Société des Anciens Textes Français (Paris, 1876), ll. 544–73.
[2] *William of Palerne*, ed. W. W. Skeat, Early English Text Society, Extra Series I (London, 1867), ll. 329–40.

sake, almost independent of the story or other characters: examples might be Fielding's Parson Adams, many of Dickens's characters, Hardy's Henshaw. The late nineteenth century saw the heyday of character as personality, often drawn with great psychological insight, and we still tend to value this literary achievement higher than almost all others. There is no strict dividing line, but the two types of portrayal are nevertheless usually distinct. Medieval literature very rarely created character as personality. Chaucer merged role with individual personality to some extent in *The General Prologue to the Canterbury Tales*, and with Pandarus, but much less so in the *Tales*. The important thing is to recognize that each type of character portrayal has its own advantages and then not to confuse them. It is pointless to demand personality from the portrayal of Gawain in *Sir Gawain and the Green Knight*. His role is presented with flashes of psychological insight (as is Chaucer's Troilus) but that is a different matter. Gawain is always exemplary in *Sir Gawain and the Green Knight*.

Gawain is not always presented quite as the *Gawain*-poet presents him, though he never becomes a unique person. B. J. Whiting has studied his various appearances in medieval literature, and finds that though he is called *courteous* on the whole more often than other knights, his courtesy is never insisted upon so much as in *Sir Gawain and the Green Knight*.[1] Whiting found his presentation fell into three main stages, corresponding with the three main stages of development of the Matter of Britain. First come the chronicle-like accounts of the life and death of Arthur, where Arthur is the central figure and Gawain is his chief knight, the ideal warrior, loyal and honourable. Second come the episodic verse romances, of which the poems of Chrétien de Troyes are an example. Arthur's court is the place of departure and return, but the interest is in the adventures of many different knights. Gawain is always prominent, and often the hero. He has many adventures, military and amorous. He is brave, charming and promiscuous, and consequently welcomed with enthusiasm by almost every maiden he meets. The stories are fantasies of prodigious military and sexual valour:

> Gawain as a lover followed a well-defined pattern: when he met an unattached girl he made love to her; if she rebuffed him he departed; if, as more often, she welcomed his attentions,

[1] B. J. Whiting, 'Gawain: His Reputation, His Courtesy', *Medieval Studies* IX, 1947.

he also departed, but not so soon. With him, too, out of sight was out of mind. For him a love affair was an exchange of verbal and physical courtesies, and he had no realization of his own unworthiness or the lady's supreme condescension in granting him her slightest favor. If we also remember that, for whatever reason, he did not make love to married women, we understand that Gawain could not be a participant in any game of love played by the rules of the code.[1]

In the third stage, when the verse romances were turned into prose and extended and added to, some authors, especially those of the Grail-legend who made virginity the supreme value, blackened Gawain's character. It is this darker character whom we are most familiar with in the middle part of Malory's *Morte Darthur*, and in later treatments like Tennyson's, though Malory cuts out much of Gawain's love-making.

To locate the *Gawain*-poet's treatment of Gawain historically we need to return to the first stage of Arthurian story. Whether or not he knew it, the most striking portrayal of Gawain in English before his own poem is in the alliterative *Morte Arthure*. This poem is based on the chronicle stories of early Arthurian romance, and so, though late fourteenth century in date, represents the first Arthurian stage.[2] It is a poem at the centre of the fourteenth-century alliterative revival, and like the others, though proudly provincial, is not ignorant of the king's court. *Morte Arthure* is a stern, pious, poem, with a vein of repellent brutality as well as a hearty enthusiasm for battle. Surely no minstrel wrote this, but a cleric of some great baron's court. The author is patriotic, historically minded, concerned with public affairs. Though Arthur is severely criticized, the author and the assumed audience are decidedly on his side, and one has very much the feeling that the presentation of Arthur has deliberate parallels with Edward III. For all the fantasy of such episodes as Arthur's fight with the giant, the poem gives an extraordinarily vivid sense of infantry war in general and the Hundred Years War in particular. It is a fascinating poem for any middle-aged soldiers and politicians who may be able to read a slightly difficult Middle English dialect: not much likely to attract women and undergraduates. Malory, it will be remembered, used the poem perhaps

[1] B. J. Whiting, *loc. cit.*, p. 215.

[2] *Morte Arthure*, ed. E. Brock, Early English Text Society (1871), O.S. 8; ed. E. Björkman (Heidelberg, 1915).

as the starting-point for his whole work,[1] but changed its tone somewhat, and by inventing episodes brought Sir Launcelot into prominence.

In *The Morte Arthure* Sir Gawain 'of the West Marches' (2953) is most
prominent, after the King. When the King and his chief knights withdraw to a chamber after the feast it is Gawain who takes in Queen
Guenever (233). He is the 'warden' of the knights, wins most glory in
battle, and is called 'father' as a term of respect by the younger knights.
When the 'good Gawain, gracious and noble' (2851) is outnumbered
by the enemy and advised not to fight, he makes a speech that reminds
one of Henry V's speech before Agincourt in Shakespeare's play, and
he finishes up with an appeal to Mary, 'that mild queen'. (All this was
cut by Malory.) He meets his end in a sortie that he himself recognizes
as suicidally reckless. When Arthur finds Gawain dead 'the sweet king
swoons', and sweetly kisses the corpse until his beard is as smeared with
blood as if he had been cutting up beasts (3969-72). He collects Gawain's
blood in a helmet, and vows to Messiah and 'Mary, the mild queen of
heaven', that he will never hunt at roe nor reindeer, nor handle a
hawk nor hold a Round Table, 'till thy death, my dear, be duly
revenged' (4006).

This poem without love is not without courtesy. *Courteous* itself is
used in such collocations as 'kind and courteous' (21), 'courteous and
gentle' (987). The apparatus of the courtly life is gloried in—for
example, the rich feast at Christmas-time at Caerleon, which calls for
comparison with the similar feast in *Sir Gawain and the Green Knight*.
Arthur arms himself in a set-piece description (900 ff.) that should also
be compared with the arming of Gawain in the later poem (566 ff.).
The poem creates a courtly context that is potentially similar to that in
Sir Gawain and the Green Knight. The highest reach comes with the
lament for Gawain's death spoken—and it is a fine touch—by no other
than Modred, the traitor who killed him. When a foreign king asks who
the mighty fighter was, Modred replies that he was matchless, 'Gawain
the good', 'the most gracious man', 'hardiest of hand', 'happiest in arms'

> And the hendeste in hawle vndire heuene riche;
> Þe lordelieste of ledinge qwhylles he lyffe myghte,
> ffore he was lyone allossede in londes i-newe.
>
> 3880-82

[1] See my remarks in *Essays on Malory*, ed. J. A. W. Bennett (Oxford, 1963),
pp. 46-47.

'Hendest in hall', a lamb in the hall; a lion in the field, like Launcelot and Beowulf and others. There is no mention of ladies in the poem, apart from Guenever, but there is no doubt of, if no emphasis on, Gawain's courtesy. Here is the basis for the *Gawain*-poet's portrayal of his exemplary knight.

But the lady in *Sir Gawain and the Green Knight* had clearly been reading the romances of chivalry very extensively, and it is from these that *she* takes Gawain's character. This character is not one, as Whiting points out, that cherishes *fine amour*, like Launcelot; it is the character of a man who simply cannot resist any young and pretty woman. The poet, however, leaves this version of Gawain's character entirely in the mouth of the lady. Gawain's courteous *speech* is a natural development of the virtuous earlier Gawain, and of late fourteenth-century ideals of courtly education. The existence of two views of Gawain, so to say, the lady's and the poet's, helps to increase the social tension in the scenes between them. Even in the light of the stories of the promiscuous Gawain, however, the poet is not entirely changing his character; for it seems, according to Whiting, that he never made love to married women.

Hende

Hende is the Middle English form of Old English *gehende*, meaning 'near, convenient, at hand.' Only rarely, in Scots, does it seem to retain something like this sense in later centuries. Early in the Middle English period in England it developed the further metaphorical senses of 'dexterous', hence 'clever', and came to be associated occasionally with learning. But at the same time (about 1200) it developed as a general epithet of praise of persons, and was so used extremely commonly, both of human beings and of God and Mary. As such it came into collocation with *courteous*, which had similarly developed a very wide general sense of approval. Although it is difficult to be certain from the necessarily limited number of quotations in OED, it does look as if *hende* was more current in the west and north. The abstract noun with an Old Norse suffix, *hendelayk*, is rare and certainly not found in the south.

(The noun *courtesy* is first recorded in *The Ancrene Wisse* about 1200, but towards the end of the thirteenth, and in the fourteenth century, together with its adjective and adverb, becomes very widespread and often generalized in meaning to mean simply 'the good'.)

Apart from his early translation, *The Romaunt of the Rose*, Chaucer uses *hende* to suggest an uneducated speaker, like the Host in *The General Prologue* (once), and the Wife of Bath, who uses the word once of 'jolly Jankin' the clerk. Chaucer uses it no less than eleven times in referring to 'hende Nicholas' of *The Miller's Tale*, in which old-fashioned love-language is used, to put it very simply, to satirize low-class persons aping the (courtly) manners of their betters.[1] Chaucer's aristocratic views clearly made him feel that *hende* was old-fashioned, provincial, low-class, hackneyed. It is also noticeable that, for whatever reason, *hende* had a strong association with the idea of a 'clerk', a student, for Chaucer. In this, as in other ways, he was very different from the *Gawain*-poet.

[1] E. T. Donaldson makes a close examination of Chaucer's use of *hende* in a valuable essay, 'Idiom of Popular Poetry in "The Miller's Tale"', *English Institute Essays 1950*, ed. A. S. Downer (New York, 1951).

GENERAL SUMMARY

No summary of characteristics can do justice to the poet's rich concept of courtesy, but some principal traits have been established. Essentially courtesy is for him an ideal of personal integrity (and therefore of mental and spiritual self-realization), but its quality can only be realized in benevolent *actions* or at least speech towards other people. Another way of putting it would be to say that courtesy consists in loving God and one's neighbour as oneself. The three persons, God, neighbour and self, are for the poet indissolubly linked, which is one reason why he is no ascetic. The general concept is fully realized in delightfully concrete fourteenth-century terms, physical, social and moral. It includes beauty, politeness, humour, self-control, bravery, cleanliness. For our poet it does *not* include *fine amour*, any more than it (apparently) includes, say, almsgiving.

V

'Troilus and Criseyde': a Reconsideration

Although many academic critics have expressed 'second thoughts' about C. S. Lewis's overall view of *Troilus and Criseyde*—'a great poem in praise of love'[1]—I suspect that most readers will continue to find him a precise and sensitive guide to Chaucer's meaning:

> It semed hire he wiste what she thoughte
> Withouten word, so that it was no nede
> To bidde hym ought to doon, or ought forbeede;
> For which she thought that love, al come it late,
> Of alle joie hadde opned hire the yate.[2]

It would be difficult, under the influence of *The Allegory of Love*, to miss the significance of those lines: original to Chaucer, they are offered as a tribute to the seriousness rather than to the fretting urgency of human love, which is poised at that moment in the poem between recognition and fulfilment. Criseyde surely refers back to 'such sober certainty' when she later tells Troilus

> Ne hadde I er now, my swete herte deere,
> Ben yold, ywis, I were now nought heere!
>
> (iii, 1210–11)

and it is an eccentric gloss which requires us to hear her words as an admission of connivance.[3]

In spite of the challenges thrown down by more recent criticism, the centrality, the 'passionate sanity'[4] of C. S. Lewis's writing on *Troilus*

[1] *The Allegory of Love* (Oxford, 1936), p. 197.

[2] *Troilus and Criseyde* iii, 465–9, ed. F. N. Robinson, *The Poetical Works of Chaucer* (Cambridge, Mass., 1961).

[3] See D. W. Robertson, *A Preface to Chaucer* (Princeton, 1963), p. 491.

[4] J. A. W. Bennett, 'The Humane Medievalist', An Inaugural Lecture (C.U.P., 1965), p. 27.

has not been obscured or outdated: there are few important works which are not indebted in some way to the comparative methods of study he advocated in 'What Chaucer really did to *Il Filostrato*'[1] or to the wider interpretative modes of the *Allegory of Love*. If there is still a need to 'reconsider' *Troilus and Criseyde*, it is not because his directions were substantially wrong, but because many of these directions have not been fully explored. Intensive studies of *Troilus*[2] and its sources have not mined ore of the same quality as his short and exemplary article in *Essays and Studies*, and learning quite as impressive as his has been misapplied to the understanding of the poem, since it could not draw on the same kind of literary responsiveness which distinguished and stabilized *The Allegory of Love*.[3]

It is still possible to see the main area of *Troilus* criticism divided between writers whose effort is simply to demonstrate more precisely the 'grete worthynesse' of Chaucer's work, and those who are set to disturb traditional attitudes by exercising ingenuity at the expense of common sense and sensibility. But close attention to the form and texture of Chaucer's verse—an attention which marked all of C. S. Lewis's commentary—makes either extreme reverence or extreme inventiveness unnecessary. Much remains to be said about *Troilus and Criseyde*, but I doubt whether we shall improve on his way of encountering the poem.

No real confidence, for instance, could now be placed in judgements of the poem which are not prepared to take into account Chaucer's dealings with his sources. Minute or major changes, redispositions of material, are crucial to our understanding of 'the poet at work', and, ultimately to our understanding of the work itself. A simple and yet immensely important example of this occurs at the end of Book III. Chaucer's refusal to conclude this Book with Boccaccio's ominous lines—

> Ma poco tempo durò cotal bene,
> Mercé della fortuna invidiosa,

---

[1] *Essays and Studies* XVII (1932), 56–75.
[2] For example, the study by Sanford B. Meech, *Design in Chaucer's Troilus* (Syracuse University Press, 1959).
[3] D. W. Robertson's treatment of the poem in his article 'Chaucerian Tragedy', *E.L.H.* XIX (1952), 1–37, and in *A Preface to Chaucer*, pp. 472–502, is often invalid for this reason.

... Crisëida gli tolse e'dolci frutti,
e' lieti amor rivolse in tristi lutti[1]

is the climax of a series of actions designed to seal off that section of the
narrative from its bleak hinterlands of violence and betrayal. So, too,
the whole of Book II, with its perplexing heroine and its uncertain
narrator, must first be seen as a struggle with materials only partially
tractable to the poet's emerging purposes. The logical conclusion of an
unbiased study of 'Chaucer at work' in *Troilus* may not yet have been
fairly represented. The acceptability of such statements as 'he achieves
a symmetry, a balance, in episode and detail', or 'he communicates to
us a view of the whole in which tolerance and critical perception are
harmoniously blended',[2] has still to be proved. For *Troilus and Criseyde*
shows unmistakable signs of conflicting purposes, unresolved difficulties.
And it is, above all, a striking example of a medieval poem which
forbids the easy use of terms such as 'unity', 'consistency'. It would be
possible to say that the very magnitude of what Chaucer attempted to
do in *Troilus* was the guarantee of some measure of failure, and that,
unless we allow for this, we minimize his imaginative strength,
demonstrated with such special triumph in Book III of the poem.

The situation in *Troilus* is similar to that in other major poems of
Chaucer's: given a narrative which cannot be *radically* altered, Chaucer
proceeds to treat that narrative in ways which demand, for the sake of
unity and consistency, just that radical action denied to him. And if the
text is given close scrutiny, it is hard to resist the conclusion that
Chaucer's dealings with his material were often arbitrary, and certainly
not always the result of premeditated design. The greatest problem of
Troilus and Criseyde is not the character of Criseyde, nor the adjustment
of Boethian philosophy with courtly love, but the poet Chaucer—for
his workings are, at times, most problematic.[3]

In brief outline, *Troilus* displays to us a poet whose gradually changing purposes involve him in greater and greater difficulty with his
sources. Warnings, in Book I, of possible clashes of substance and
interpretation are confirmed by Book II: this is perhaps the most con-

---

[1] *Il Filostrato*, ed. V. Pernicone (Bari, 1937), p. 94.

[2] Meech, *op. cit.*, pp. 424, 427.

[3] Two essential articles on Chaucer's methods of work are: D. S. Brewer,
'Love and Marriage in Chaucer's Poetry', *M.L.R.* XLIX (1954), 461–4, and E. T.
Donaldson, 'The Ending of Chaucer's *Troilus*', *Early English and Norse Studies
Presented to Hugh Smith*, ed. A. Brown and P. Foote (London, 1963), pp. 26–45.

fused and at the same time the most interesting of all five Books from the point of view of 'poet at work'. Out of its near-chaos comes the great resolution of Book III, which justifies, retrospectively, the uneven conflicts of Book II. And here I think Chaucer intended his readers to accept a break, a pause in the movement of the poem. Books IV and V can also be seen in terms of conflict: the poet's gradual—and at times extremely painful—accommodation to the dictates of his narrative. So the ending of *Troilus* has, indeed, been prepared for throughout the poem, but mainly in the sense that it is an urgent declaration of a pre-dicament in which Chaucer began to find himself as early, perhaps, as Book I: a predicament born of the decision to free his imagination, and to write about the love of Troilus and Criseyde not simply as a gay, sensual episode, nor as an ennobling example of 'amour courtois', nor indeed as a proof of 'worldes brotelnesse', but as an embodiment of 'the holiness of the heart's affections'.[1] For the unique excellence of *Troilus and Criseyde* is not, surely, to be counted the creation of 'characters' such as Pandarus and Criseyde, nor the weaving of a rich and many-stranded poetic fabric, but, more basically, the growth and release of a poet's imagination.

In *Troilus*, triumphing momentarily over both his story and his age, Chaucer is in his element—

> . . . for his bounty,
> There was no winter in it: an autumn 'twas
> That grew the more by reaping . . .

But the operative word is 'momentarily'. It should not, nowadays, be anything but a commonplace to say that a medieval poet's conception of 'unity' in a work of art could differ sharply from that of later writers. The 'unity' of Malory's *Morte D'Arthur*, of *The Canterbury Tales*, of a cycle of Miracle Plays is loose-knit, and not easily categorized in terms acceptable to post-Renaissance criticism. In *Troilus* certain kinds of unity can be recognized immediately: the narrative completes the curve described by Chaucer in Book I—

---

[1] This will not mean that the ending of the poem is 'not a part of the whole . . . is detachable at will . . . one need not of necessity consider it at all in an interpretation of the drama' (W. C. Curry, *Chaucer and the Mediaeval Sciences*, 2nd ed., New York, 1960, p. 298). It remains an integral part of the poem, not least because it focuses our attention on the pressing and largely unresolved artistic problems which Chaucer faced throughout his work.

> In which ye may the double sorwes here
> Of Troilus in lovynge of Criseyde,
> And how that she forsook hym er she deyde;
>
> (ll. 54–56)

there is a general unity of verisimilitude in the movement of the main characters in the context of the poem; and there is undoubted unity in the perfectly sustained quality of the verse over all five Books. But recognition of this need not make us anxious to press for a more comprehensive and thorough unity. Chaucer shows here and elsewhere that he is only too willing to work for local effectiveness at the expense of total consistency and continuity.[1] In a poem which still accepted oral recitation as a possible mode of delivery—'And red wherso thow be, or elles songe'—discrepancies of tone, of attitude, of reference would not appear to be of paramount importance. We should not, however, fail to notice that they exist.

To take one isolated example: Chaucer's references at the close of the poem to 'payens corsed olde rites', 'what alle hire goddes may availle', 'Jove, Appollo . . . Mars . . . swich rascaille' (v, 1849, 1850, 1853) depend for their effectiveness on the reader's consent not to range back meticulously over the length of the poem, inquiring whether the poet's strictures are supported by the evidence of his work. They depend on an inaccurate recollection of the whole substance of Book III, and on the poet's right to establish a local forcefulness without regard to total congruity. However ingenious our arguments, the relationship between the ending of *Troilus* and Book III remains uncertain: the elevation of Boccaccio's terrestrial passion to 'love, that his hestes hath in hevenes hye . . .', a process which occupies a good part of Books II and III, is not so much comprehended as misrepresented by the final judgements of Book V. The stanza in question is not only suspiciously vehement but careless,[2] and I doubt if we should spend much energy trying to justify what Chaucer himself preferred to ignore—or at most to notice cursorily.

Then also, we should allow for a considerable element of wilfulness in Chaucer's methods of procedure. The progress of his poem does not seem to have been controlled by steady consciousness of an overall plan. Book II, in particular, is a piece of writing in which sudden, happy

---

[1] *The Canterbury Tales* seem to me to illustrate this point most aptly.

[2] Curry, *op. cit.*, p. 295, noted some of its improprieties.

improvisation jostles with hesitation, and recklessness is followed by uncertainty. Here sometimes the poet's imagination is allowed to leap forward at a heedless pace, and the verse records the very uneasy commerce of creative invention with narrative discretion. But the vital point to make is that Chaucer assumes his right to take sudden decisions about the development of his work in mid-career. Book I gives only slight indication of what was soon to begin stirring his creative processes and setting his poem so decisively apart from Boccaccio.

Two factors must weigh in a fresh consideration of *Troilus and Criseyde*. There is a strong possibility that Chaucer's view of his poem allowed for discontinuity of attitude and mode of presentation as well as for the preservation of other kinds of continuity. There is the equally strong possibility that Chaucer's purposes were not entirely clear to him even when the poem was well under way: the graph of *Troilus* records sudden advances and recessions, as the poet realizes—and pauses to consider—where his independence is leading him. This is not to brush aside the significance of Chaucer's revisions of the poem, but simply to ask whether they do, in fact, argue his grasp of 'the parallels and the symmetry of the poem's structure'.[1] Such an approach need not seek to isolate *Troilus* from the rest of Chaucer's work. It is proper to recall *The House of Fame*, in which the tendency to sudden and arbitrary action is most freely—and perhaps disastrously—indulged: to recall also *The Canterbury Tales*, in which impromptu and disruptive episodes (the Canon's Yeoman episode is a brilliant example) are part of a complex pattern of continuities and discontinuities operated on narrative, dramatic and thematic levels.

Although Book I of the poem does not pose any very serious problems, it is clear, even as early as this, that Chaucer does not intend to allow his preordained narrative to keep him from ways of writing which may, ultimately, come into conflict with it. The narrator's advice to lovers is a case in point. The tone of the passage is not ironic: advice is plainly given, and it bases its argument on the power and the virtue of love:

> Now sith it may nat goodly ben withstonde,
> And is a thing so vertuous in kynde,
> Refuseth nat to Love for to ben bonde . . .
>
> (i, 253–5)

[1] C. A. Owen, 'The Significance of Chaucer's Revisions of *Troilus and Criseyde*', *Modern Philology* LV (1957–8), 5.

Boethian insights are already present:

> . . . Love is he that alle thing may bynde,
> For may no man fordon the lawe of kynde . . .
>
> (i, 237–8)

Already Chaucer shows his inclination to write for the moment: the disastrous outcome of love—'Swich fyn hath, lo, this Troilus for love!' —is not remotely in mind, as Chaucer invites his audience to honour the 'fall' of Troilus—

> Blissed be Love, that kan thus folk converte!
>
> (i, 308)

and his dedication to a life of love, service and 'vertu':

> Dede were his japes and his cruelte,
> His heighe port, and his manere estraunge,
> And ecch of tho gan for a vertu chaunge.
>
> (i, 1083–5)

This high valuation of human love, which the more prudent Boccaccio did not suggest, is confirmed by words given—incongruously, perhaps—to Pandarus. The Italian heroine's 'aptness' for love is turned by Chaucer from a cynical and slightly vulgar appraisal of woman's nature into a dignified statement about the proper sequential relationship of love 'Celestial, or elles love of kynde' (i, 979). This is the first time in the poem that earthly love is clearly set into some kind of cosmic pattern, and the significance of Chaucer's action cannot be overemphasized. For not only is he anxious (we may think) to protect Criseyde from the casual lash of Boccaccio's remark: he seems also to be eager to establish high status for the quality and import of love between creatures. The dramatic unlikeliness of the words, coming from Pandarus, is a sure sign of their *thematic* relevance:

> It sit hire naught to ben celestial
> As yet, *though that hire liste bothe and kowthe* . . .
>
> (i, 983–4)

The potentialities of Criseyde, and, through her, the potentialities of human kind, moving from terrestrial to heavenly love—these are the points at stake. If they have little to do either with the character of Pandarus or with the 'double sorwe' of Troilus, Chaucer is not greatly perturbed. It could be claimed that already there are signs of his reluctance to feel himself wholly committed by accepting the story in its main essentials. As Book I closes, we cannot forecast exactly what he intends: Troilus 'dryeth forth his aventure', but the line gives no distinct foreboding of ill fortune, and could be hinting at happiness which 'vertu' will come to deserve. We can forecast, however, that the dignifying and deepening of the concept of human love will make for a more complex poem, and that the handling of betrayal and disillusion may be correspondingly difficult. It would be impossible to say how far Chaucer anticipates, or, indeed, cares to consider this.

The Proem to Book II, which he apparently added to his first draft of the poem, raises questions for the reader. If the value of its opening stanzas as high-styled apostrophe is undebatable, its main function is not so easily described. It seems to spring from a need to say something about artistic responsibility; it may be read, in part, as Chaucer's (retrospective) admission of the problems inherent in his treatment of the story. The desire to shed some responsibility for the nature and conduct of the poem is clearly pressing him, and when we remember how Book II develops, it is hardly surprising that he felt bound to make some kind of comment. Direct discussion of artistic motive and predicament is rare in Chaucer's period: there is no real precedent for him. But in these words which preface Book II a strong sense of Chaucer's uneasiness about the progress of his poem makes itself felt:

> Wherfore I nyl have neither thank ne blame
> Of al this werk, but prey yow mekely,
> Disblameth me, if any word be lame,
> For as myn auctour seyde, so sey I . . .
>
> (ii, 15–18)

We need not deny that the stanzas are cast in the familiar rhetorical form of *dubitatio*, nor that their overt conclusion is 'In sondry londes, sondry ben usages'. What is crucial here is that Chaucer should return to enforce the point about 'myn auctour' (l. 49): his anxiety to invoke his sources can be interpreted as a recognition, not a solution, of the 'cas' he finds himself in as Book II moves erratically to its precipice of suspense—

> —O myghty God, what shal he seye?

For it is, surely, in Book II that Chaucer begins to put his powers of independent action to the test: the angle of divergence from Boccaccio widens, and the passages which convey the poet's increasing—and not always happy—awareness of the situation are more prominent. Although there have been intimations of change in Book I, Book II marks a quickening of the tempo of change: fresh energy is released to the business of adaptation, and the poetry swings dramatically between 'drede and sikernesse', showing doubt and confidence in the propriety of what is being done. This is particularly clear in the case of Criseyde: Chaucer's dealings with her in this Book are sometimes bold and imaginative, sometimes timorous in the extreme. She struggles to emerge from the poetry, but if she remains largely an enigma, this is less the result of subtle characterization than of an imperfect fusion of old and new material.

The nature of her reply to the first unmistakable suggestion that she should *love* Troilus is important here. The violence of her outburst is surprising in the immediate context; Pandarus has been calculating with her in terms of 'tendre wittes' (ii, 271): she has appeared demure, complaisant, a little playful and a little curious—'I shal felen what he meneth, ywis . . .'—and Chaucer has shown no great interest in developing the serious note he introduced in Book I. But the words she uses to Pandarus, in rebuke, are serious indeed—much too serious for the narrative as it has been forecast, and for the events which follow almost immediately. Her severe, intelligent complaint belongs to a narrative which might take a different course, to a woman who might either be steadfast in chastity, or prove worthy of a man's virtuous love, and faithful to him. At this point Chaucer does not resist the prompting of his imagination; the speech is magnificently inappropriate:

> What! is this al the joye and al the feste?
> Is this youre reed? Is this my blisful cas?
> Is this the verray mede of youre byheeste?
> Is al this paynted proces seyd, alas!
> Right for this fyn? . . .
>
> (ii, 421-5)

It is hardly relevant to debate whether Criseyde is genuinely outraged or not: the interesting fact is that Chaucer considered such language fitted to the occasion. The incisive quality of the verse is not so much a measure of his concern to save the reputation of Criseyde as a measure of his growing dissatisfaction with the nature of Boccaccio's narrative.

This dissatisfaction seems to centre more and more on the *status* of the love he is to celebrate in Book III. For it must be increasingly clear to him that if he is to write solemnly, even responsibly, about this love, the Italian heroine, who makes most of her decisions on the basis of expediency and desire, will not do. He has already revealed something of the context in which he wishes to set this 'love of kynde'; it is a commitment which is both exciting and perturbing him by Book II. His efforts to manipulate Criseyde, so that she may be a serious participant in his changing concept of the poem's theme, occupy a good part of Book II, but they are efforts often balked by the sheer weight of substance of the original. Chaucer may have felt free to deepen the reactions of this woman, to give her sharp protests of disillusioned wisdom: he did not feel free—nor, in all probability, did he feel obliged —to attempt a total recasting of her. The importance of the stanzas in question is thematic, rather than psychological: they belong as much to the poet and his readers as to Criseyde, and function as a warning that the gradient to love will be steep. By stating and then rejecting what his Italian source so patently deals in (a 'paynted proces'), Chaucer establishes his right to ask for a different valuation of the affair, even if he cannot re-order events.

So he proceeds, with a mixture of confidence and nervousness: his confident invention of the scene in which Criseyde sees Troilus riding back from battle 'so lik a man of armes and a knyght', and finds her fears about love assuaged by his sobriety as well as by his valour, is followed by a display of artistic misgivings. Suddenly he loses conviction about what is now superbly evident—that Criseyde is not approaching love easily, but with difficult self-adjustment. The comment by the narrator—

> Now myghte som envious jangle thus:
> This was a sodeyn love; how myght it be
> That she so lightly loved Troilus . . .
>
> (ii, 666 seq.)

is quite gratuitous from the dramatic point of view: it is highly significant, nevertheless, as a comment on Chaucer's creative battles, already partly over and won. That he feels it necessary is a gauge of the pressures constantly at work on him throughout this critical stage of the poem's development. For it is vital to his writing in the coming Book that some kind of transformation should be effected now: a transformation of values, since it cannot, in the medieval contract, be a total transformation of material.

And in all these dealings, it is surely on Book III, no further, that his vision rests. The conquests being won so hardly are for near objectives, and will require fresh campaigning as the poem turns to its conclusion. There is no evidence that in the restless manoeuvring of Book II Chaucer had anything more than Book III in sight:

> For for o fyn is al that evere I telle . . .
>
> (ii, 1596)

The 'fyn' he refers to here is certainly not that of Book V: it is closer, more immediate. This emerges again in the elaborate Deiphebus episode. No one could deny that here, in the busy intriguing of Pandarus, Chaucer allowed himself splendid opportunities for dramatic verse—'O verray God, so have I ronne!' He also, for very practical purposes, allowed the innocence of Criseyde to be enmeshed by Pandarus in his less endearing, slightly more sinister capacity—'But Pandarus thought, "It shal nought be so . . ."' (ii, 1296).

But the episode has another special claim on our attention as a preparation for Book III. It marks a decisive severing of allegiance to the standards and expectations of the original Italian. It comes as a sudden burst of free composition after a period of uneven progress, and demonstrates the imaginative strength of the poet, who is now so confidently at variance with his original that he can allow himself a major addition to the narrative—and, in some respects, a redirection of the narrative. For the Deiphebus episode begins to intimate to the reader how love will grow uncorrupted out of the centre of intrigue:

> Lo, hold the at thi triste cloos, and I
> Shal wel the deer unto thi bowe dryve . . .
>
> (ii, 1534-5)

The transformation of values has been achieved, and Criseyde goes to Troilus freed of responsibility for events, and untouched, except by compassion for a man she has begun to trust:

> Al innocent of Pandarus entente,
> Quod tho Criseyde, 'Go we uncle deere'.
>
> (ii, 1723-4)

It is significant that Pandarus conjures Criseyde to behave with pity towards Troilus

> On his half which that soule us alle sende,
> And in the vertu of corones tweyne . . .
>
> (ii, 1734–5)

Such language, with its particular Christian references and its nuptial imagery, is not only, of course, anachronistic, but uncharacteristic of the speaker: it is only appropriate to the developing theme of the poem. The general tone is right, if the dramatic context is not, and confirmation of this will not be long delayed. It says as clearly as it can that whatever *events* the narrative is destined to recount, the *theme* of the central part of the poem will be honourable and legitimate love. And if the breathless concluding line of the Book is not patently Christian in phrasing, it carries sufficient religious associations to act as a bridge to the Proem of Book III:

> . . . O myghty God, what shal he seye?

In this Proem, for the first time, religious language has an unambiguous part to play. Books I and II mingle pagan and Christian references in a way which is sometimes of obvious importance, and sometimes quite fortuitous. But now Chaucer takes the opportunity not only to reposition material from his Italian source, but to recast some of it in strongly Christian terms. The impulse towards change and the nature of the change are both notable. The first stanza of the Proem,

> O blisful light, of which the bemes clere
> Adorneth al the thridde heven faire . . .

could be dealing with the highest form of *amour courtois*: the second stanza could not. After translating Boccaccio's Boethian lines, 'Il ciel, la terra ed il mare e lo'nferno/ciascuno in sé la tua potenza sente . . .' (*op. cit.*, p. 90), Chaucer gives us plain words:

> *God loveth, and to love wol nought werne,*
> And in this world no lyves creature
> Withouten love is worth, or may endure.
>
> (iii, 12–15)

The passage in Boccaccio is quite differently set:

> e gli uomini e gl'iddii; né creatura
> sanza di te nel mondo vale o dura.
>
> (*loc. cit.*)

The substitution of 'God' for 'gods', and the assertion of heavenly benevolence in the matter of human love are both remarkable, and should not be passed over. In width of concept and precision of language the whole stanza bears comparison with many statements in orthodox religious treatises of Chaucer's own day:

> . . . from out the great ring which represents the Eternal Godhead, there flow forth little rings, which may be taken to signify the high nobility of natural creatures . . .[1]

> For this was showed: that our life is all grounded and rooted in love, and without love we may not live: and therefore . . . the soul . . . of his special grace seeth so far into the high marvellous goodness of God, and seeth that we are endlessly joined to him in love . . .[2]

The effect of this stanza is felt throughout the Proem and beyond. It lends warmth and seriousness to the poet's invocation—

> How I mot telle anonright the gladnesse
> Of Troilus, to Venus heryinge?
> To which gladnesse, who nede hath, *God hym bringe*!
>
> (iii, 47–49)

But it is particularly interesting as a deliberate—and, in all likelihood, later—declaration of progress and intent. There can be no doubt now about Chaucer's desire to clarify and confirm his position. The tentative, exploratory move in Book I towards a definition of love which could touch simultaneously human and celestial boundaries[3] is here followed through with assurance—'God loveth, and to love wol nought werne . . .' With these words Chaucer crowns his efforts to achieve a 'reformation of feeling' in his poem. For they define the outer limits of the love that is to be the subject of the coming Book, and they announce a new mood of reconciliation—not simply the reconciliation of pagan and Christian elements in that cosmic dance described in this and surrounding stanzas, but the reconciliation of Chaucer with his poetic materials and his inclinations. The words are a manifesto of intention about the conduct of the next stage of the story and, further, a manifesto

[1] Henry Suso, *Life*, tr. T. F. Knox (London, 1915), ch. lvi.
[2] Julian of Norwich, *Revelations of Divine Love*, ed. G. Warrack (London, 1923), p. 103.
[3] i. 977 ff.

of Chaucer's status as a creative artist. They establish his right to present his narrative according to his imaginative convictions, and not according to the dictates of his original or the narrower doctrines of his age. He will not be subject to Boccaccio, nor to the homilists, and, indeed, throughout this Book he demands from his readers an unqualified sympathy with 'the high nobility of natural creatures'. He has won for himself freedom of action in a situation where freedom was scarcely to be expected, and he has won it by widening the perspectives of his poetry[1] to a degree uncalled for, and even unjustified, by his given material, with its evanescent delight and its sombre outcome. Book III is dedicated, in defiance of the known ending of the story, to what Spenser described in his *Epithalamium* as 'the safety of our joy', and the strength of the poetry is directly related to Chaucer's new-found security: 'God loveth, and to love wol nought werne.'

For Book III has, in a special sense, an independent existence, and Chaucer must have expected his readers to accept this. Not that, even now, there is total consistency of attitude and subject-matter: it is typical—and, in the long run, unimportant—that Chaucer should allow the odd jarring note to be heard. The careful and delicate phrasing of Criseyde's promises to Troilus—

> Bysechyng hym, for Goddes love, that he
> Wolde, in honour of trouthe and gentilesse,
> As I wele mene, eke menen wel to me . . .
>
> (iii, 162–4)

and the equally fastidious account of her capitulation by Pandarus—

> For the have I my nece, of vices cleene,
> So fully maad thy gentilesse triste,
> That al shal ben right as thiselven liste . . .
>
> (iii, 257–9)

are followed by that jaunty passage in which Troilus offers

> . . . my faire suster Polixene,
> Cassandre, Eleyne, or any of the frape . . .
>
> (iii, 409–10)

---

[1] T. P. Dunning, in 'God and Man in *Troilus and Criseyde*', *English and Mediaeval Studies Presented to J. R. R. Tolkien* (London, 1962), holds that in Book III 'the narrator narrows the perspective . . .' (p. 179).

to Pandarus in return for his services. It is a careless adjustment of old and new.[1]

But much more noticeable is the confidence of the writing. It is confidence—based on persuasions of the goodness and legitimacy of this relationship—which allows Chaucer to take Book III at such a leisurely pace. The period between Criseyde's long-awaited words

> . . . I wol wel trewely
> . . . Receyven hym fully to my servyse . . .
>
> (iii, 159, 161)

and their fulfilment is slowly and compassionately charted: their love is proved first in service and companionship. It is no accident that some of the most moving poetry about human love in this Book comes well before that 'blisful nyght, of hem so longe isought', and that an atmosphere of 'concorde and quiete' announces the central act of the story—

> That to ben in his goode governaunce,
> So wis he was, she was namore afered . . .
>
> (iii, 481–2)

It is also no accident that the bitter outcry of Criseyde against the 'brotel wele of mannes joie unstable . . .'[2] cannot really disturb the sense of safety which pervades the Book. The movement between momentary 'drede' and 'sikernesse' is simple, and Criseyde's sadness is easily transformed into a positive desire to solace Troilus:

> 'Hadde I hym nevere lief? by God, I weene
> Ye hadde nevere thyng so lief!' quod she.
>
> (iii, 869–70)

From that point to the end of the Book the poem's development is one of expanding certainty: the setbacks experienced by the lovers are

---

[1] Chaucer deliberately refined Boccaccio's cruder language for ll. 257–9:

> 'i' ho dal cuor di Criseida rimosso
> ogni vergogna e ciaschedun pensiero
> che contra t'era, ed hol tanto percosso
> col ragionar del tuo amor sincero . . .' (op. cit., p. 71)

But he did not bother to refine Troilus's offer.

[2] It is, of course, an outcry provoked by false representation, and the poet knows that his audience will take it less seriously than they otherwise might.

minimal, their humorous setting acceptable, because so many serious assumptions have already been made. And seriousness grows in exact proportion to the sensuousness of the poetry: every new move is endorsed by religious language.[1] When Troilus takes the final step towards happiness, it is with a benediction:

> This Troilus, with blisse of that supprised,
> *Putte al in Goddes hand*,[2] as he that mente
> Nothyng but wel; and sodeynly avysed,
> He hire in armes faste to hym hente . . .
>
> (iii, 1184–7)

After this, it cannot seem inappropriate that Criseyde's generosity in love should be praised in devout words:

> For love of God, take every womman heede
> To werken thus, if it comth to the neede,[3]
>
> (iii, 1224–5)

nor that the excited description of her beauty should be followed by a fresh affirmation of the cosmic power of love:

> Benigne love, thow holy bond of thynges . . .

The poet writes, and the characters act, out of a deep assurance of propriety; for all its delighted 'concreteness'[4] the dominant mood of the poetry is 'pees' and 'suffisaunce', and the dominant movement is *andante cantabile*:

> . . . myn owen hertes list,
> My ground of ese, and al myn herte deere,
> Gramercy, for on that is al my trist!
>
> (iii, 1303–5)

Even at the very centre of misery, the moment of 'disseveraunce',

---

[1] See ll. 1052–3, 1165–6.

[2] The phrasing recalls that of Walter Hilton, in his *Scale of Perfection*, ed. E. Underhill (London, 1923), pp. 395–6: 'Other men that stand in the common way of charity, and are not yet so far forth in grace, but work under the bidding of reason . . . have not put themselves all fully in God's hand.'

[3] The point is even clearer in some MSS. of the poem which read 'whan it comth to the neede': see *The Book of Troilus and Criseyde*, ed. R. K. Root (Princeton, 1945), p. 201.

[4] Lewis, *The Allegory of Love*, p. 196.

reconciliation is suggested: the immediate pressure of pain is reduced by wide-ranging allusions to Creation, Order, Purpose:

> O blake nyght, as folk in bokes rede,
> That shapen art by God this world to hide
> At certeyn tymes wyth thi derke wede . . .
> Thow rakle nyght, ther God, maker of kynde . . .
> Ther God thi light so quenche, for his grace . . .
>
> (iii, 1429–31, 1437, 1456)

Criseyde comforts Troilus in an ascending series of passionate and religious statements, and it would be a perverse reading of the poetry at this stage which could find intended irony in her juxtaposition of

> by God and by my trouthe . . .
>
> (iii, 1512)

It is not surprising that the warnings of Pandarus, next day, about 'discretion', 'moderation' are, in the circumstances, not so much portentous as inadequate. In the lighter Italian text they had a significant part to play, but in this changed context their concern with

> Be naught to rakel . . .
> Bridle alwey wel thi speche and thi desir . . .
>
> (iii, 1630, 1635)

seems peripheral. Even the additions to the Italian—'For worldly joie halt nought but by a wir . . .' (iii, 1636) are not strong enough to shake the belief that 'hire hertes wel assured were'. They witness more to Chaucer's sense that the original words fall short of touching the new situation than to an anxious sense of approaching doom. For they come between the lovers' dedication to each other, and Troilus's total dedication not simply to love but to love as the divine principle of the universe. Only one line gives a hint that all may not ultimately be well, and this is so firmly embedded in the celebration of 'suffisaunce . . blisse . . . singynges . . .' (iii, 1716) that Chaucer cannot have intended that it should halt his readers for long:

> And thus Fortune a tyme ledde in joie
> Criseyde, and ek this kynges sone of Troie.
>
> (iii, 1714–15)

The last stanzas of the Book, by their additions and omissions, ratify all that has gone before. Writing his own *finis* to this part of the story,

Chaucer invokes religious philosophy of the highest and most solemn kind. By setting Troilus to associate (not, it must be noted, to identify) his love with

> Love, that of erthe and se hath governaunce,
> Love, that his hestes hath in hevenes hye,
> Love, that with an holsom alliaunce
> Halt peples joyned . . .
>
> (iii, 1744–7)

he makes his most moving case for 'the high nobility of natural creatures' and their 'holsom alliaunce'. No irony plays about his comprehensive statement of the interlocking of human and divine loves:

> So wolde God, that auctour is of kynde,
> That with his bond Love of his vertu liste
> To cerclen hertes alle, and faste bynde . . .
>
> (iii, 1765–7)

The spirit of the words is hardly different from that of Julian's 'we are endlessly joined to him in love'. After this, Boccaccio's summary announcement of impending disaster would have been completely out of tune: its omission, and transference to the Proem of Book IV, is of greatest importance to our understanding of Chaucer's intentions. His admission that he has deliberately altered Boccaccio's ending is candid but unrepentant:

> My thridde bok now ende I in this wyse . . .
>
> (iii, 1818)

And so it is in 'lust and in quiete' that the Book fulfils its promise. Giving religious sanction to a love which originally asked and needed none, Chaucer gave sanction to a freedom of imaginative movement hard to equal in any work of his age which dealt with 'love of kynde'. It is both a sad and a triumphant fact that the only medieval writings on love which rival the grace and intensity of Chaucer's language in Book III of *Troilus* are religious treatises, and Chaucer had to win the release of his full imaginative powers for this difficult subject by religious means. The word to stress is 'full': medieval literature abounds in descriptions of human love—sensual, casual, refined, ritualized, practical and brutal—but few artists found ways to take full imaginative grasp of this complex human condition, to admit its dignity as well as its vulnerability, and to give serious status to bodily as well as spiritual compassion.

But the cost of this to Chaucer in *Troilus and Criseyde* should not be underestimated. If Book II records, by a series of surface disturbances, a deep turmoil of decisions, and if Book III records the confident outcome of decisions taken, the two remaining Books record a gradual, difficult readjustment to authority in the shape of the original narrative. By the end of Book III, Chaucer has worked certain transmutations: the rest of the poem must be a process of disenchantment. Expectations encouraged by Book III must be refused to the reader, and the divergence of narrative and presentation, by now wide and serious, must be reduced. With the beginning of Book IV, Chaucer tackles fresh problems: problems which he has, to a large extent, created for himself by energetic development of unsuspected potential in his sources. The admirable recklessness of his actions has to be paid for.

The unpalatable nature of what lies before him is the real subject of his Proem to Book IV, and we should see in it not only regret for the tarnishing of his bright image of Criseyde,

> Allas! that they sholde evere cause fynde
> To speke hire harm . . .
>
> (iv, 19–20)

but also his reluctance to begin the closing-down of the great imaginative vistas of Book III. From now on the story will lay strongest claims to his allegiance, and he will have only a small area for freedom of operation. The deepest 'drede' which fills him at this point is fear of imaginative restriction by the events henceforth to be 'matere of my book'.

The poem is, indeed, entering a new phase, and Chaucer warns his readers to look for decisive changes—not only in the way his characters must behave, but also in the attitudes he and they must begin to adopt towards such behaviour. Nothing he has so brilliantly evoked in Book III can be any help towards *understanding* what will happen: he has ensured that the rift between love and betrayal will now be unbridgeable except in terms of strictest narrative necessity. Consequently the poem must now be concerned with providing answers and consolations which may prove expedient in a situation otherwise unbearable and unacceptable. In Books IV and V, Chaucer ranges widely in search of philosophic and religious vantage-points from which to view his 'matere' with some composure: his imaginative range, however, is strictly narrowed by what he has to do. The great passages on Fate, Necessity, Free Will function seriously as the poem moves to its bitter conclusion, but they give, in many respects, 'a comfort serves in a whirlwind'; we should not mistake philosophic and religious reconciliation for imaginative committal. The sad bewilderment with which Chaucer watches his poem shrink to a tale of treachery cannot be wholly remedied: like Troilus, seeing Criseyde's love fade from him, he can only state, in all truth, what *was*:

> . . . I ne kan nor may,
> For al this world, withinne myn herte fynde
> To unloven yow a quarter of a day!
>
> (v, 1696–8)

But answers to the extreme dilemma of the narrative have to be attempted.

The crux of the matter lies in the last answer Chaucer chose to give— his closing stanzas. E. T. Donaldson has shown conclusively that the poetry from line 1750 onwards reveals 'the narrator's quandary'.[1] Anxiety and evasiveness are strongly apparent: the only conclusion left is one which is not congenial. And when at length Chaucer comes to draw that conclusion, it is with a surprising and terrible forcefulness:

> Swych fyn hath, lo, this Troilus for love . . .
>
> (v, 1828)

Now he makes obeisance to the medieval theme of *vanitas vanitatum*, and the severity of his expression can be seen as a measure of the reluctance he has shown, in the central part of his poem, to give any weight to that theme. It is, in fact, in this severity, rather than in conciliatory references to 'floures faire',[2] that we can discern Chaucer's recollection of what he achieved in Book III. Having enriched and deepened the implications of the Italian narrative, he is now forced to erase the memory of his actions. The pounding of his rhetoric is meant to still questioning, but we may inquire more thoughtfully than Chaucer's readers could about the relevance of that stanza

> Lo here, of payens corsed olde rites,
> Lo here, what alle hire goddes may availle . . .
>
> (v, 1849–50)

---

[1] 'The Ending of Chaucer's *Troilus*', p. 37.
[2] *ibid.*, p. 42.

PLC–H

It is a revealing and, at the same time, a problematic stanza: reveal-ing, because it shows quite clearly that Chaucer hopes we will not question this palpably unsatisfactory account of what we have just read or heard; problematic, because it is difficult to believe that any artist of integrity could turn his back on his work quite so decisively. 'Payens corsed olde rites', 'what alle hir goddes may availle', 'the fyn and guerdoun for travaille/Of Jove, Appollo, of Mars, of swiche rascaille', give poor coverage for the deliberate evocation of Christian belief and feeling in Books II and III. As an explanation of 'double sorwe' it is woefully inadequate, and we must not miss the fact that Chaucer offers it as an explanation:

> *Lo here*, what alle hir goddes may availle . . .
> *Lo here*, the fyn and guerdoun for travaille
> Of Jove, Appollo, of Mars . . .

The automatic listing of the gods (not all of them, as several critics have pointed out, properly operative in the poem) is in itself indicative of Chaucer's haste to be done with a troublesome matter. Automatic also is his dismissal of 'the high nobility of natural creatures'—

> Lo here, thise wrecched worldes appetites . . .

It was not this view which drew from him some of his finest poetry.

In short, Chaucer could never have intended his poem to be seen as a unified whole, except in the crudest narrative sense. It is a work of variable and fluctuating allegiances, of co-ordinate rather than complex construction, which relies on significant breaks and pauses between its separate parts. Beginning simply, it develops into a subtle and devout study of human 'worthynesse': ending simply, it fails to relate its findings meaningfully, and is even forced to revoke some of them—though not without some distress.

Like many of Chaucer's answers to complicated problems, the final answers given in *Troilus* do not match the intelligence and energy of the questions asked, the issues raised. For Chaucer, in the struggle between narrative authority and imaginative penetration, authority must win—'all/ Life death does end, and each day dies with sleep'. But we should not be afraid to recognize the struggle, nor to admit that while authority could literally conclude his poems for him, it could never conclude the business his imagination loved to engage in.

VI

Gower's 'Honeste Love'

Of all the revaluations forced upon us by the *Allegory of Love*, none was so unexpected as that suggested by the pages devoted to Gower. Here Lewis's descriptive criticism is at its genial best. Yet some of his warmest admirers have hinted that his judgement of the *Confessio* was partial, or even deliberately provocative. Those who feel that they are being provoked will doubtless class the half-chapter on Gower with the essays, printed elsewhere, on Morris, Kipling, and Rider Haggard. But there is good evidence that Lewis was captivated by the sheer craft and artistry of this little-read poet. How otherwise explain why he gave so much space to praise of the poem that he left himself almost no room for comment on the very features of its ethical scheme that should have earned it a special place in the history of Love-Allegory? Curiously enough, later critics of the work (almost all transatlantic) have continued to ignore its doctrine and, perhaps because of this, perhaps because of their surprising preoccupation with the massive French and Latin writers, have for the most part continued to damn or dismiss the *Confessio* as dull. J. H. Fisher's recent study even goes so far as to assert that 'the dullness cannot be palliated but must be recognised for what it is—success in its intended genre'. Dull the poem will doubtless seem if we take its genre to be social or political philosophy. But so to cabin it alongside the *Vox Clamantis* or *Speculum Meditantis* is to ignore the plain implications of its title. W. E. Dodd, writing on *Courtly Love in Chaucer and Gower*, did not ignore them. Unfortunately his method of proceeding produced its own kind of dullness. It was from the thraldom of such mechanical analysis that *The Allegory* rescued us. But to accept as definitive all the judgements of that masterpiece is to fall into another servitude.

I

The purely historical and verbal connexions between the *Confessio* and the *Roman de la Rose* Dodd and Lewis between them have adequately indicated. Each work may be described as an *Ars Amatoria*, so long as such a description is not taken to imply an identity of tone or an Ovidian flavour. So deep and pervasive was the influence of the *Roman* that Gower would not have had to read that rambling cyclopedia to learn of Malebouche (*C.A.* ii, 390), Danger (i, 2443; iii, 1538; viii, 2256; Balade x), Jalousie (v, 511–34). And long before the *Roman* was begun the roles of Venus and Cupid as King and Queen of Love had been firmly established; in presenting them Gower differs from his predecessors (and Chaucer) chiefly by eschewing any physical description of either—and he is almost equally reticent about Amans and his mistress. The blindness of the love they enkindle is the theme of a passionate lament that —without any warrant from Ovid—he puts into the mouth of Thisbe:

> O thou which cleped art Venus,
> Goddesse of love, and thou, Cupide,
> Which loves cause hast forto guide,
> I wot now wel that ye be blinde,
> Of thilke unhapp which I now finde
> Only betwen my love and me . . .
>   (iii, 1462)

It is concordant with this piteous complaint (in its language so similar to Crisseid's fatal outcry in Henryson's *Testament*) that Amans should describe suitors in the court of love as for ever climbing a wheel of fortune that lifts them only to hurl them down (iv, 2279). The Confessor himself, telling the tale of Canace and Machaire, represents Cupid not only as blind but as making his 'clients' blind (iii, 158–60); and he goes on to depict the ill-fated pair as further blinded by Nature:

> . . . sche which is Maistresse
> In kinde and techeth every lif
> Withoute law positif,
> Of which sche takth nomaner charge,
> Bot kepth hire lawes al at large,
> Nature, tok hem into lore
> And tawht hem so, that overmore
> Sche hath hem in such wise daunted,
> That thei were, as who seith, enchaunted.
>   (iii, 170)

Repeatedly the priest's *exempla* differ from their originals by such assertions of the power of 'Kinde', or natural law (it distinguishes his tale of

Constance, for example, from the Man of Law's).[1] It is as if Gower had combined the two characters of Genius and Nature in the *Roman*, where Genius is Nature's priest, spokesman, and confessor. And the constant awareness of the force of instinctive drives, of passion as a kind of enchantment that casts a spell on Reason, gives to Gower's priest a rare breath of sympathy and compassion that has its affinities with the specifically Christian *caritas* which is threaded through the whole system.

To the general tone of tenderness *courtoisie* has contributed as well as Christianity—if indeed it is possible in this respect to distinguish them. No one familiar with the literature of *courtoisie* will fall into the error of reading the Venus who controls the action of the poem as identical with the goddess of pagan worship. As Lewis noted, Gower faced some of the difficulties inherent in this personification when he came to consider heathen mythology in Book V; and really they are no greater than those arising from the ambiguities attaching to the word *love* itself (exemplified in the distinction Genius has to draw between the love he countenances and 'loves court nowaday', iv, 2279). Significantly, it is Amans himself who prompts Genius to the discourse on mythology. After hearing the story of Venus and Mars, he is moved to inquire (it is an attractive feature of the machinery that he is always depicted as having a mind of his own),

> Hou such thing to the heveneward
> Among the goddes myhte falle:
> For ther is bot *o* god of alle.
>
> (v, 730)

The Book shows the priest at his most orthodox, outlining the Christian faith and deploring the falling away of modern prelates whose avarice— he appeals to Colossians iii 5—was hardly different from the old idolatry. In this context *all* the heathen deities must be presented as 'fantasies'. But Amans rightly remarks that the god and goddess of love still 'stand in all men's speech' and wonders 'how thei ferst comen to that name'.

The question surely embarrasses Genius, not—as Lewis might seem to imply—because he can find no place for human love in his Christian apologetics, but because the Venus and Cupid of the pagan stories signify lust, lechery, promiscuity and even (v, 1426) prostitution. Genius is

---

[1] Genius also goes out of his way to maintain that Venus herself came forth 'by way of Kinde' (v, 800).

understandably ashamed that the deity he serves should figure in these stories; but he tells them

> for thei stoden nyh thi brest
> Upon the schrifte of thi matiere
>
> (v, 1384)

—in other words, so that Amans may avoid or clear himself of such sins, not so that he may abjure love. Admittedly there is a certain awkwardness here, but it hardly disturbs us as we read.

In making appropriate *exempla* out of other classical stories Genius does nothing more, and certain nothing more far-fetched, than had been done in the highly respectable *Ovide moralisé*, on which Gower doubtless drew; even the surprising interpretation of the tale of Mars and Venus has precedent in that popular work. And from the story of Pygmalion he extracts the unexceptionable moral (not to be found in Jean de Meun's version, where, as Gunn says, it represents 'the entelechy of feminine nature') that

> The god of love is favorable
> To hem that ben of love stable.
>
> (iv, 442)

If Genius's prime concern seems to be with a lover's faults and failings, we are never allowed to forget that these reflect vices common to all mankind. Though the discourse on Surquiderie (Presumpcio) is headed by elegiacs alluding to Cupid and the *laqueos Veneris*, in fact it touches on love only in so far as it portrays the self-love of Narcissus—presented, as always when reprehensible passion is involved, as a kind of madness or enchantment:[1]

> He sih the like of his visage,
> And wende ther were an ymage
> Of such a Nimphe as tho was *faie*,
> Whereof that love his herte assaie
> Began, as it was after sene,
> Of his sotie and made him wene
> It were a womman that he syh.
>
> (i, 2315)

[1] *cf.*, for example, Amphitryon's enchantment of Alcmena (ii, 2490). The spell that Estella throws over Pip, in *Great Expectations*, has something of the same sinister, magical power.

But the main drift of the preachment is against the presumptuous man who

> . . . seith nought ones 'grant mercy'
> To godd, which alle grace sendeth,
> So that his wittes he despendeth
> Upon himself . . .;
>
> (i, 1902)

whilst the description of the vainglorious lover (i, 2681–2717) who mistakes his own high spirits for lasting joys has moral and religious overtones that remove it far from the world of the *Roman*, and verbal anticipations of the fervent prayer with which the whole poem is to close. Judged by the standards Genius here sets up, Chaucer's Squire (and many another 'lovyere and lusty bacheler') would fall sadly short. When priest turns to penitent and bids him

> Now scrif thee, Sone, *in Godes pes*,
> And of thi love tell me plein
> If that thi gloire hath be so vein,

we are within a Christian confessional. And when later he cites scripture to his purpose it is not in parody:

> After the vertu moral eke
> To speke of love if I schal seke,
> Among the holi bokes wise
> I finde write in such a wise,
> Who loveth noght is hier as ded.
>
> (iv, 2321)

That this is a conscious attempt to relate the doctrine of courteous love to Christian teaching is indicated by the marginal direction, which runs: *Nota de amore caritatis*. The association reminds us that lack of *caritas*, in people and priest alike, is the main theme of the Prologue to the whole work; that at the beginning of Book I we turn from scenes of strife and discord to consider *naturatus amor*; and that at the end of Book VIII we come back to

> thilke love which that is
> Withinne a mannes herte affermed,
> And stant of charite confermed.
>
> (viii, 3162)

'The hyhe God'—so prays the poet—'such love ous sende'; of the same 'hyhe God' Genius had said that He

> Yaf to the men in Erthe hiere
> Upon the forme and the matiere
> Of that he wolde make hem wise.
>
> (iv, 2363)

The creed of Genius, then, is the poet's creed; and Amans accepts the ethics that Genius affirms. The one point on which the priest cannot move him is his refusal to win favour by fighting for his mistress abroad; it is the least logical and least defensible point of 'þe lel layk of luf', and Amans' appeal is to the Gospels:

> A Sarazin if I sle schal,
> I sle the Soule forth withal,
> And that was nevere Christes lore.
>
> (iv, 1679)

But he admits that his own desperate thoughts of self-slaughter were equally culpable as sins of intention (iii, 1513) and duly begs for and receives absolution from them; nothing brings out more sharply the difference between the *mores* Gower is depicting and those of Troilus (see *TC* iv, 1231–41). And when Amans calls his mistress 'vertuous' and 'devout' (iv, 1136) we should take these words at their face value. Nowhere is there any hint that she is married, still less is there any suggestion that Amans is: he is as 'innocent' as his antecedent in the *Roman*, and she, like the *amie* in the *Roman*, is a *damoisele* and a *pucele*. The adultery of an Iseult or a Guinevere has no place in Amans' thought.[1] Critics have argued that Gower substituted incest for *Luxuria* as a capital vice because 'Luxury naturally cannot be a sin against Venus'. It is at least as probable that Gower preferred to treat this perversion of love because it illustrates the strange workings of 'Kind' (by the same token, it is the mystery of transmutation as much as 'love-interest' that fascinated him in the *Metamorphoses*). *Luxuria* in its chief manifestation of adultery is, in fact, condemned wherever it appears, just as it had been in the *Vox Clamantis*. There (vii, 157 ff.) it figures as one of the *gallica peccata*, vices new come in from France: a false kind of love, 'Sic sub mendaci specie grossantur amoris'. Genius himself, on the other

---

[1] In the *Traitié* it is condemned as a *sotie*.

hand, sets forth at length the rationale of chaste marriage (employing a plain, earthy image which assures us that he speaks with Gower's voice):

> The Madle is made for the femele,
> Bot where as on desireth fele,
> That nedeth noght be weie of kinde:
> For whan a man mai redy finde
> His oghne wif, what scholde he seche
> In strange places to beseche
> To borwe an other mannes plouh,
> Whan he hath geere good ynouh
> Affaited at his oghne heste,
> And is to him wel more honeste
> Than other thing which is unknowe?
> Forthi scholde every good man knowe
> And thenke, hou that in mariage
> His trouthe plight lith in morgage,
> Which if he breke, it is falshode,
> And that descordeth to manhode . . .
>
> (vii, 4215)

'Corporis et mentis regem decet omnis honestas', says the Latin head-piece; and the margin directs us to his unimpeachable philosophical authority for this conception of 'honesty': Aristotle's 'de quinta principum regiminis Policia, que Castitatem concernit, cuius *honestas* impudicicie motus obtemperans tam corporis quam anime mundiciam specialius preseruat' [? = *Pol.* vii, 16]

II

To 'les amantz marietz' Gower had devoted the whole of his *Traitié*; its theme and argument are consistent with the attitude described above:

> Et puis dieus qui la loi ordina
> En un char ad deux personnes mis,
> Droitz est qe l'omme et femme pour cela
> Tout un soul coer eront par tiel devis,
> Loiale amie avoec loials amis:
> Cest en amour trop belle retenue
> Selonc la loi de seinte eglise due.
> Ovesque amour quant loialte s'aqueinte,
> Lors sont les noeces bones et joiouses.
>
> (iii, 3—iv, 1)

And on this the marginal gloss runs:

> Qualiter *honestas conjugii* non ex libidinis aut avaricie causa,
> set tantummodo quod sub lege generacio ad cultum dei fiat,
> primordia sua suscepit.

But it is the presence, indeed the pre-eminence, of Penelope, Lucrece,
Alceste, Alcyone in Venus's own court (in the *Confessio*) that underlines
most firmly his view of chaste marriage:

> Bot above alle that ther were
> Of wommen I sih foure there,
> Whos name I herd most comended:
> Be hem the Court stod al amended;
> For where thei comen in presence,
> Men deden hem the reverence,
> As thogh they hadden be goddesses,
> Of al this world or Emperesses.
>
> (viii, 2605)

This outdoes Chaucer, of whom the Man of Law—in the very act, it
seems, of censuring Gower—had said

> O Ypermystra, Penelopee, Alceste,
> Youre wifhod he comendeth with the beste!

And, in fact, Chaucer's commendation of Alcione (in the *Book of the
Duchess*) is far less moving than Gower's depiction of her as

> Sche fondeth in hire briddes forme,
> If that sche mihte hirself conforme
> To do the plesance of a wif,
> As sche dede in that other lif:
> For thogh sche hadde hir pouer lore,
> Hir will stod as it was tofore,
> And serveth him so as sche mai.
>
> (iv, 3109)

It is in key with this presentation that Genius should regard the love
that 'upgroweth with your age' as not only a sign of 'gentilesse' and,
if properly directed, a school of virtue, but also as finding its proper
consummation in marriage. Ironically enough, the sheer beauty of

the tale of Rosiphilee, in which this doctrine is most firmly embodied, has diverted attention from its sentence. The very fact that here for the first time Genius implies that 'mi ladi Venus' should not necessarily have the last word ought to alert us:[1]

> Mi ladi Venus, whom I serve,
> What womman wole hire thonk deserve,
> Sche mai noght thilke love eschuie
> Of paramours, bot sche mot suie
> Cupides lawe; and natheles
> Men sen such love sielde in pes,
> That it nys evere upon aspie
> Of janglinge and of fals Envie,
> Fulofte medlid with disese:
> Bot thilke love is wel at ese,
> Which set is upon mariage;
> For that dar schewen the visage
> In alle places openly.
> A great mervaile it is forthi,
> How that a Maiden wolde lette,
> That sche hir time ne besette
> To haste unto that ilke feste,
> Whereof the love is al honeste.
> Men mai recovere lost of good,
> Bot so wys man yit nevere stod,
> Which mai recovere time lore:
> So mai a Maiden wel thefore
> Ensample take, of that sche strangeth
> Hir love, and longe er that sche changeth
> Hir herte upon hir lustes greene
> To mariage, as it is seene.
> For thus a yer or tuo or thre
> Sche lest, er that sche wedded be,
> Whyl sche the charge myhte bere
> Of children, whiche the world forbere
> Ne mai, bot if it scholde faile.
>   (iv, 1467)

[1] *cf.* his later touch of independence (viii, 2079), preparing us for Amans's reservation in viii, 2392 ('sche which *seid* is the goddesse').

This same 'love honeste' is again commended later:

> for it doth aweie
> The vice, and as the bokes sein,
> It maketh curteis of the vilein:
> (iv, 2298)

lines which make clear the sense of Genius's dictum that

> Love is an occupacion,
> Which forto kepe hise lustes save
> Scholde every gentil herte have.
> (iv, 1455)

This is 'courtois' sentiment at its highest, and deserves to be set beside Malory's famous but confused chapter on 'trewe love' (Caxton xviii, 25). It might be read as a 'courtois' adaptation of the Pauline view that it is better to marry than to burn.[1] But Genius's praise of 'honeste love' reminds us of the nobler and more positive view that marriage is *honorabile connubium* (Heb. xiii 14).

Indeed, it comes close to what Chaucer's Parson saw as 'the cause finale of matrimoigne': 'engendrure of children to the service of God' (*C.T.* x, 935). Gower's broader view, that society must be continuated 'lest the world should fail', is consistent with that abiding concern for the commonweal which modern critics, from Dr. Wickert to A. B. Ferguson, have discovered in all of his works.[2] Equally characteristic is the equation of secret love *paramours* with 'disese' and of honourable love with peace. As an English comment on the subterfuges of a Jason, a Lancelot, or a Troilus it sorts well with the response that Chaucer anticipated as he told the story of how Troilus gained his Criseyde—'so nold I nat love purchace!' (*TC* ii, 33). But to Gower 'pes' meant more than the absence of difficulty or embarrassment. It is the keyword of all his poetry, the highest good that man may seek; and when he comes to describe heavenly felicity in his closing couplet it is to point us to that place 'wher resteth love and alle pes'.

---

[1] A marginal note in some MSS. runs: *Non quia sic se habet veritas sed opinio amantium*. But it is hard to believe that this is authorial comment, or even an expression of second thoughts. It probably represents a gloss by a literal-minded copyist who misunderstood part or all of the passage.

[2] *Studien zu John Gower*, by Maria Wickert (1953); *The Articulate Citizen and the English Renaissance*, by Arthur B. Ferguson (1965) (see ch. ii and iii).

III

Lewis, who so memorably described the closing scenes of the poem, thought this coda was a failure; 'Gower is not enough of a philosopher . . . even to attempt . . . any reconciliation between the claims of his two worlds'.[1] But is not the poet quietly adjusting these claims throughout the whole work? It is not only at the end that he goes 'a softe pas'; and the quiet unobtrusive manner may blind us to the nature of his achievement. But there is no mistaking the drift of the *moralitas* that crowns the end of his last and longest story:

> Lo, what it is to be wel grounded:
> For he hath ferst his love founded
> Honesteliche as forto wedde,
> Honesteliche his love he spedde
> And hadde children with his wif,
> And as him liste he ladde his lif;
> And in ensample his lif was write,
> That alle lovers myhten wite
> How ate laste it schal be sene
> Of love what thei wolden mene.
>
> (viii, 1993)

The doctrine illustrated by the tale of Rosiphilee at the centre of the poem and reaffirmed so emphatically near the end must surely remain valid, however irrelevant it may seem to Amans's plight as shortly revealed. And it surely forces us to give to the *Confessio* some of the historical importance that Lewis read into the *Kingis Quair*, a poem that perhaps does not praise Gower gratuitously. In King James's poem, says Lewis, 'the poetry of marriage at last emerges from the traditional poetry of adultery; and the literal narrative of a contemporary wooing emerges from romance and allegory'.[2] One can hardly assert that Amans's confessions give us a literal narrative of a contemporary wooing (or indeed be so sure that James gives us that), though in verisimilitude they surpass the later poem. One may, however, claim that the prose, if not the poetry, of fecund marriage is already emerging from the traditional poetry of *courtoisie*. And that Genius should link 'honest' marriage with child-bearing is not surprising if we recall his original

---

[1] *The Allegory of Love*, p. 218.
[2] *ibid.*, p. 237.

role, in the *Roman*, as sponsor of reproduction. Gower's 'toning down' of this aspect is all of a piece with his other modifications of the spirit and structure of the *Roman*; but he would hardly ignore the significance of Genius's name.

To recognize the meaning of that name, and to remember its history, is to see why the priest's attitude towards Amans's chances of personal success in his love-affair is throughout so non-committal. Being face to face with his penitent he knows from the outset what we as readers sense but slowly and do not clearly learn until the *dénouement*—that Amans is being shadowed by Elde. His persistence in unrequited love comes to have the quality of an obsession; and he himself admits that in this regard he is 'assoted': the word is used throughout the poem, as Malory was to use it throughout the *Morte*, of infatuation or ungovernable passion. This lovers' malady destroys Reason (which in Gower always connotes 'measure' and restraint). To persist in it, says Genius, is a sin (viii, 2098); and in so saying he first reminds us that his own priestly office makes it incumbent on him to instruct in virtue; then proceeds:

> Forthi to speken overmore
> Of love, which thee mai availe,
> Tak love where it mai noght faile.
>
> (viii, 2084)

As it stands, the advice is cryptic—the decorum of the poem forbids an explicit identification of this love with the Christian *caritas* that never faileth. But that we are moving out of the religion of love is clear a few lines later:

> For love, which that blind was evere,
> Makth alle his servantz blinde also.
> My Sone, and if thou have be so,
> Yit is it time to withdrawe,
> And set thin herte under that lawe,
> The which of reson is governed
> And noght of will
>
> (viii, 2130)

(though again the full implications are left to be drawn out by the poet himself, at viii, 3143 ff.) Amans, however, persists in presenting his

appeal to the deities of love, and in it, for the first time, and almost by
accident, he discloses his real plight. The ninth verse of his 'lettre' runs

> Ovide ek seith that love to parforne
> Stant in the hond of Venus the goddesse,
> Bot whan sche takth hir conseil with Satorne,
> Ther is no grace, and in that time, I gesse,
> Began mi love—
>
> (viii, 2273)

It began, that is, in the age assigned to malevolent Saturn, that last
stage of life in which, as Raleigh was to record, 'We find by dear and
lamentable experience, and by the loss which can never be repaired,
that of all our vain passions and affections past, the sorrow only
abideth.' And the plea in the next verse but one that Cupid if he cannot
give a 'salve' will withdraw his dart is another preparative for the final
farewell to love. Venus takes him at his word, and as she promises to
make him heart-whole again reveals that though he has feigned 'a
yong corage' his locks are grey:

> Mi medicine is noght to sieke
> For thee and for suche old sieke,
> Noght al per chance as ye it wolden,
> Bot so as ye be reson scholden,
> Acordant unto loves kinde.
>
> (viii, 2367)

Only Gower would make Venus, like a very schoolmistress, speak the
language of reason; and she is to resort to it again (2919). But it has
always been the language of her priest.

So the Senex comes to his senses, cured of love, conscious at last
that it may be just another name for desire. Gower's delicate art shines
through the little scene that follows:

> Venus behield me than and lowh,
> And axeth, as it were in game,
> What love was. And I for schame
> Ne wiste what I scholde ansuere . . .
>
> (viii, 2870)

'What is love?' is indeed the question that many of the *exempla* have
raised, though never so directly; and most of them, following the best

medieval pattern, have raised also the question of its relation to Reason.
As she dismisses Amans, Venus enjoins

> That thou nomore of love sieche.
> Bot my will is that thou besieche
> And preie hierafter for the pes.
>
> (viii, 2911)

This is doubly appropriate, for Venus herself espouses peace and tran-
quillity (*Venus otia amat*); and throughout his confessions Amans has
shown something of the fervour for peace that informs the Prologue
(in which war figures as destroying *charite*, 903–4). But, like the earlier
reference to unfailing love, 'the pes' is a phrase with spiritual overtones
(Amans himself has used 'werre, contek, strife' to signify inner discord,
iii, 1132); and the prayer that duly follows in the second recension
strengthens this impression. In it, returning to the theme of the Prologue,
where priests are censured for neglecting the duty of 'charite' (110), he
enjoins the clergy

> forto praie and to procure
> Oure pes toward the hevene above,
> And ek to sette reste and love
> Among ous on this erthe hiere.
> For if they wroughte in this manere
> Aftir the reule of charite,
> I hope that men schuldyn se
> This lond amende . . .
>
> (viii, 2998)

Thus there is no abrupt disjunction, but a gradually dawning sense that
in the last stage of life, when man no longer has dues to pay to 'Kinde'
(*cf.* viii, 2348), he must put by amorous concerns and both seek and
practise *caritas*. Macaulay labelled the closing passage of the whole work
a 'Farewell to Earthly Love'; but if these immediately preceding scenes
mean anything

> . . . thilke love which that is
> Withinne a mannes herte affermed
> And stant of charite confermed—

this love, though certainly contrasted with the worship of Venus, is not
wholly removed from secular concerns. Far from being asked, as

Chaucer asks us, to think 'al nys but a faire This world' (*TC* v, 1840),
we are to remember that God

> This large world forth with the hevene
> Of his eternal providence
> Hath mad,
>
>   (viii, 2972)

and to pray for peace, unity and good governance,

> With outen which, it is no les,
> To seche and loke into the laste,
> Ther may no worldes joye laste.
>   (viii, 2992)

The world will fail, Genius had argued, unless folk marry and bring
forth children. It will come to ruin, says the poet, here (as in the Prologue) *in propria persona*, unless men seek peace and practise charity and
kings seek 'Love and acord' (viii, 3018*). 'Honeste love' in wedlock,
caritas in the commonwealth, are wholly compatible ideals, and it is
Gower's distinctive achievement to have harmonized them in a single
poem, whilst still setting forth the graces and 'gentilesse' of *courtoisie*.

VII

On Romanticism in the 'Confessio Amantis'

In his stirring rehabilitation of the *Confessio Amantis*, Lewis finds 'Gower's point of maximum differentiation as a poet' in his being

'romantic' in the nineteenth-century meaning of the word. He excells in strange adventure, in the remote and the mysterious: like his own Jason, him

> sore alongeth
> To se the strange regiouns
> And knowe the condiciouns
> Of othre marches.[1]

The passages cited in illustration are the account of Medea's sorceries (v, 3957 ff.); the *beaute faye* upon the faces of the dead in *Rosiphilee* (iv, 1321); the heavenly light that descends in the story of Nectanabus (vi, 1981); and the 'strangely vivid, because strangely ambiguous, description of the dream' in *Ulysses and Telegonus* (vi, 1519–63).

The claim for 'romantic' quality raises, of course, questions of some depth and complexity. Lewis is the first to admit them: 'this quality in Gower', he continues, 'is worth noticing because it is rare in the Middle Ages. It is indeed what many expect to find in medieval literature, but we do not often find it.' Lewis notes its entire absence in some writers and its rarity in others ('it is, in places, even painfully lacking in Chaucer'); equates it with 'the fairy way of writing';[2] and although allowing that some may overrate it, finds for it a distinctive function (so that the 'shocking tale of *Tereus* acquires a bittersweet beauty not otherwise attainable'): 'Like all romantics Gower builds a bridge between the conscious and the unconscious mind.'

It is the purpose of this paper to ask whether the quality Lewis

---

[1] *The Allegory of Love* (Oxford, 1936), p. 210.
[2] The phrase is, of course, Dryden's: see pp. 127–8, below.

observes in Gower is truly to be termed 'romantic', with the function claimed for it.

I

The essential characteristic of the romantic would seem to lie in giving new significance to that which has ceased to command belief in terms of its actual or possible existence. For example, these lines from *The Rime of the Ancient Mariner*:

> Like one, that on a lonesome road
> Doth walk in fear and dread,
> And having once turned round walks on,
> And turns no more his head;
> Because he knows, a frightful fiend
> Doth close behind him tread.

This has its distinctive impact precisely because it is addressed to a reader who, like the writer, has no belief in the actual existence of fiends. It can therefore convey a dread otherwise unspeakable; through the merely imaginary shapes of bygone credulity the reader is admitted to true terror. The counter or symbol has to be cleansed from every tincture of belief—belief, that is, in possible existence—before it can become the perfect vehicle for nameless dread. In this sense, as Lewis had observed at an earlier point in *The Allegory of Love*, the old gods must die before they can 'wake again in the beauty of acknowledged myth'. Lucretius is one of the few in pagan antiquity who can contemplate the beauty of the gods; and he himself 'has laid his finger on the secret: it is *religio* that hides them'.[1] What is true of 'the gods' is true of all that moves between earth and heaven in man's apprehension of his universe. Grant the witches, fairies, ogres and demons a share in possible existence, and you have decisively modified the uses which they may serve in poetry. They can move terror, awe, or their counterpart in comic grotesquerie. But this they do in their own right; theirs is an unborrowed majesty, whether that majesty is reverenced or derided. What they cannot do is summon attention beyond themselves, to that which they merely represent or typify. One can imagine a child or an unduly credulous adult reading Coleridge's lines to the rising heartbeat of actual terror—the belief that a fiend may, at this as at any moment, stand behind him. The good ghost story is certainly of that kind, and

[1] *op. cit.*, pp. 82–83.

aims at that effect—to resurrect, in the realm of the possible, that which has never been wholly banished from it. For another instance we may turn to the 'spiritual shocker', as R. W. Chapman aptly christened the novels of Charles Williams.[1] Here the apparatus of the marvellous has the authority of the believed religion—unemphasized, certainly; but not less potent on that account. In *War in Heaven* (1930), for example, one character enacts a diabolical Sabbath which is no fantasy nor yet crude 'magic': 'By no broomstick flight over the lanes of England did Gregory Persimmons attend the Witches' Sabbath, nor did he dance with other sorcerers upon some blasted heath before a goat-headed manifestation of the Accursed'. It goes deeper than that; deeper even than the actual participation of 'abandoned spirits'—for

> That beyond them (which some have held to be but the pre-cipitation and tendency of their own natures, and others for the equal and perpetual co-inheritor of power and immortality with God)—That beyond them felt them and shook and replied, sustained and nourished and controlled.[2]

It does not, of course, matter whether or not the reader can accept Williams's theology—or the language in which it is expressed. What is relevant is the author's conviction, built into the fabric of his story, that the events he describes are possible manifestations of a believed system. I take the 'spiritual shocker' to be unlike the ghost story in one major respect. If the reader does *not*, in waking reality, accept its under-lying theology—a supernatural Good and Evil locked in conflict—then its terrors remain merely fantastic. It is theology that has called them into being—that, in Williams's story, invests a battered piece of antique silver with the wonder-working properties of the Holy Grail.[3]

[1] *Essays presented to Charles Williams* (London, 1947), p. viii.

[2] *op. cit.*, p. 81. (I have sometimes wondered whether a seed of *Screwtape*, forgotten by Lewis himself, lies in the description of Gregory's careful handling of his father's doubts 'whether there was anything in religion . . . He had—it had been his first real experiment—he had suggested very carefully and delicately, to that senile and uneasy mind, that there probably was a God, but a God of terrible jealousy . . .' (p. 79).)

[3] Williams is, of course, careful to mark the limits between this speculation and any necessary point of Christian belief. Archdeacon Davenant speaks: 'In one sense, of course, the Graal is unimportant—it is a symbol less near Reality now than any chalice of consecrated wine. But it is conceivable that the Graal absorbed, as material things will, something of the high intensity of the moment when it was used, and of its adventures through the centuries' (p. 40).

Take away that authority, and we are left with harmless diversion, at best a telling portrayal of merely human wickedness, at worst a flight of archaic whimsy. But the dead who rise in a good ghost story do not come at anyone's bidding; and the test of successful work in this kind is that while it can be made the material of light-hearted discussion and defensive parody, strong nerves are required to take it up when alone, at midnight, in an isolated house of some antiquity. In this sense, the ghost story, like certain kinds of rhetorical persuasion, and perhaps some *curiosa*, could be regarded as primarily stimulating the nervous system; and I suppose one main order of classification would distinguish the degree to which that stimulation had become preponderant in the finished work at the expense of other capacities. The author who actually frightens his reader, shocks him into action, or arouses his sexual impulses, may or may not do so out of conscious purpose. But the extent to which he remains unaware of the potential effect of his narrative must be one measure of his inadequacy as a writer—one unable, in Lawrence's phrase, to 'trust the tale', to co-operate in the organic development of the work instead of imposing, however involuntarily, his own solution. Of course, in any era readers may misuse the work of art, projecting upon it their own appetencies and deriving from it kinds of fulfilment which could scarcely have been foreseen. But the problem for the literary critic remains: to establish what is being offered in its own right as distinct from the accidental and marginal interests, however clamant, of the reader at any given time.

This approach leads immediately to the definitive characteristic of any literature truly to be called 'romantic'. It is this: the reader who brings, or comes to hold, a belief in its mythology as veridical is not gaining but is forfeiting insight. Anyone who takes up *The Rime of the Ancient Mariner* with some degree of belief in the objective existence of fiends is, in fact, missing something which is quite central to the poem, an *unmodified* experience of terror. Ghost, witch, fiend—these are all manifestations which, if true, would not heighten but would effectively lessen the terror. What Coleridge would express is, in Kierkegaard's phrase, 'the unconditional'. 'Man has a natural dread of walking in the gloom—what wonder then that he naturally has a dread of the unconditional?'[1] Coleridge's way forward in the poem is to work through the 'conditional', a mythology known to be untrue; what constitutes 'poetic faith' is the reader's initial step, 'a willing suspension of disbelief

[1] *Journals*, quoted in *The New Christian Year* (London, 1941), p. 125.

for the moment'. As the poem does its work, we may see the comfort of 'belief' (that which we agreed had no existence outside the world of the poem) as we are placed irrevocably beyond it. Indeed, in one aspect —not, certainly, the most important in any complete response—the poem can be said to create the conditions under which a real fiend could be preferred, as against a dread that can have no end because it has no objective source. At the turning-point, the Mariner finds himself —he knows not how—blessedly able to respond to the beauty of 'happy living things'. In that moment his burden is released; the journey homeward begins. It is for the reader to re-enact this experience; or fail to grasp the poem. The apparatus of past belief can become the vehicle of 'romantic' treatment only when it is freed from every touch of objective likelihood. That is the condition upon which we have the very possibility of an experience called 'romantic'; that, or not at all.

It may be worth while to point out, in passing, that the fact of disbelief does not in itself render the objects of former veneration 'romantic'. For example, Gower clearly disbelieves in the ancient pantheon, and says so in the long excursus on the four forms of religion 'Er Crist was bore among ous hiere' (v, 747–1970). The Greeks are put firmly in their place:

> Among the Greks, out of the weie
> As thei that reson putte aweie,
> Ther was, as the Cronique seith,
> Of misbelieve an other feith,
> That thei here goddes and goddesses,
> As who seith, token al to gesses
> Of suche as weren full of vice,
> To whom thei made here sacrifice.
>
> (v, 835–42)

The tone is jocular and derisory. 'Lo, which a god thei maden chief!' is the comment on Saturn; and as for the rest,

> sithen that such on was he
> Which stod most hihe in his degre
> Among the goddes, thou miht knowe
> These othre, that ben more lowe,
> Ben litel worth . . .
>
> (ibid., 864–9)

Pagan folly cannot be glossed over, even by Venus's priest:

> Ther was no cause under the Mone
> Of which thei hadden tho to done,
> Of wel or wo wher so it was,
> That thei ne token in that cas
> A god to helpe or a goddesse.
>
> (*ibid.*, 1447–51)

This is not so much to put the gods to death as to give them a Poor Law funeral. It is not upon these shrunken figures that men will project attributes of ideal strength, beauty, and the like. Certainly, the gods must first die. But a religion that totally supplants them allows no growing-place for new needs; and it is these needs which must be felt before the dead can be summoned into a new life. We return to Lucretius; *religio* hides the beauty of the gods. We may say of a truly romantic poetry that a primitively literal acceptance of its marvels would, in effect, be to substitute 'religion' for direct apprehension—to move the poem a decisive step away from its true nature into conformity with a pre-existing belief on the part of the reader; and so to commit in a specially irremediable way the great heresy of paraphrase.

II

The age in which medieval poetry is first systematically attended to is one strongly predisposed to find in its favour. Dryden's approbation of 'that Fairy kind of writing, which depends only upon the Force of Imagination'[1] was echoed by Addison. It is

> a kind of writing, wherein the Poet quite loses sight of nature, and entertains his Reader's imagination with the characters and actions of such persons as have many of them no existence, but what he bestows on them. Such are fairies, witches, magicians, demons, and departed spirits.[2]

Dryden, indeed, had thought to turn to good use some of the creatures to be found in the 'enthusiastic parts of poetry'. The Christian poet, it would seem, had an advantage over his pagan predecessors; were not good and evil spirits capable of employment as a specially effective order of 'machines'? 'Christian poets', Dryden declares roundly, 'have

[1] Epistle Dedicatory to *King Arthur*.
[2] *Spectator*, No. 419.

not hitherto been acquainted with their own strength'. There follows
the recipe for a truly heroic poem *de nos jours*:

> The perusing of one chapter in the prophecy of Daniel,
> and accommodating what there they find with the principles of
> Platonic philosophy, as it is now Christianised, would have
> made the ministry of angels as strong an engine, for the work-
> ing up of heroic poetry, in our religion, as that of the Ancients
> has been to raise theirs by all the fables of their gods, which were
> only received for truths by the most ignorant and weakest of
> the people.[1]

Whatever we may think of the application to the would-be heroic poet,
Dryden's spirited extension of the 'natural' beyond 'what is true or
exceeding probable' to 'visionary objects' had strong support in the
next century.[2] Addison, as we have seen, endorses Dryden's high estimate of the 'Fairy kind of writing'. It is 'indeed more difficult than any
other that depends on the Poet's fancy, because he has no patterns to
follow in it, and must work altogether out of his own invention'. The
poet needs 'a very odd turn of thought . . . an imagination naturally
fruitful and superstitious'. We see the drift of Addison's argument
when he speaks of descriptions that

> raise a pleasing kind of horrour in the mind of the Reader,
> and amuse his imagination with the strangeness and novelty of
> the persons who are represented in them. They bring up into
> our memory the stories we have heard in our childhood, and
> favour those secret terrors and apprehensions to which the
> mind of man is naturally subject.

The natural is not to be tied to the probable, as 'Men of cold fancies,
and philosophical dispositions' would require. For we know, Addison
says, that there are many sorts of intelligent being in this universe
besides ourselves; but we do not know their 'laws or œconomies'. We
may therefore yield to 'so agreeable an imposture' as witches, fairies,

---

[1] For the defence of the supernatural in the heroic poem see 'An Essay of
Heroic Plays'; and, on the 'machines', 'A Discourse concerning the Original
and Progress of Satire' (*Essays*, ed. W. P. Ker, I, 152–4; II, 34–37). Dryden's
own venture in this sphere, the astral spirits in *Tyrannic Love* (1670), had, of
course, been parodied in *The Rehearsal*.

[2] The general development has been attractively sketched in Arthur Johnston,
Enchanted Ground (London, 1964); on the argument descending from Dryden
and Addison, see pp. 72–74.

demons, and the like. They do not violate anything we *know* of other modes of being. This concession to amiable weakness is, of course, very far from a rapturous reception of the marvels from another age: but it is a serviceable point of entry. Later, when the 'Gothick' begins to find more ardent support, a balance of profit and loss, as between it and the poetry it bids to displace, can be seriously cast. In that reckoning, 'a great deal of good sense' is seen as outweighed by 'a world of fine fabling'.[1] The decisive factor making for an exalted estimate of medieval poetry is that primitivism which unhesitatingly equates 'early' with 'uncorrupted'. Even those who would not set Grecian and Gothic in mutual opposition, but seek rather to praise a 'mix'd Design', must elaborate a tradition of English minstrelsy which derives from 'consorted Druids' singing the triumphs of

> The Chiefs who fill our Albion's story.

To the latter-day poet, all constitutes a 'Fabric' of impressive antiquity:

> Ev'n now before his favor'd Eyes,
> In Gothic Pride it seems to rise!
> Yet Graecia's graceful Orders join,
> Majestic thro' the mix'd Design.[2]

It was not, perhaps, to be expected that so moderate a view would prevail. When Keats pictures the origins of poetry he, too, sees the altar shining 'E'en in this isle' and 'The fervid choir'

> that lifted up a noise
> Of harmony, to where it aye will poise
> Its mighty self of convoluting sound,
> Huge as a planet . . .

But in his vision there is not progress but sharp decline:

> a schism
> Nurtured by folly and barbarism,
> Made great Apollo blush for this his land.
> Men were thought wise who could not understand
> His glories: with a puling infant's force
> They sway'd about upon a rocking horse,
> And thought it Pegasus.[3]

[1] Hurd, *Letters on Chivalry and Romance*, Letter XII.
[2] Collins, *Ode to Liberty*, second epode.
[3] *Sleep and Poetry*, 172–60; 181–7.

It was not only the 'black-*letterati*', as Coleridge called them,[1] who in part created what they jealously guarded. Much more, it was those, poets and readers alike, who, unwittingly divesting medieval poetry of some kinds of appeal, whole-heartedly accorded it the highest authority. 'Should children be permitted to read romances and relations of giants and magicians and genii?' Coleridge's answer was decisive. 'I know no other way of giving the mind the love of the great and the whole.'[2]

III

Of Lewis's instances from the *Confessio Amantis*, I take first the general characteristic he attributes to Gower: 'like his own Jason, him

> sore alongeth,
> To se the strange regiouns
> And know the condiciouns
> Of othre marches.'

Since the instances cited in support of this contention are all of journeying in a metaphorical not a literal sense (Medea's sorceries, the 'fairy beauty' of the dead, etc.) a word must first be said on Jason and geographical 'adventure', the appeal of that which is remote in space; and one must observe at once that although Lewis freely equates this with magic, *faerie*, other-worldly manifestation and the region of compulsive dream, no such equation is inherent in the matter itself. Here, again, the world of belief and assumption which the reader brings to the text makes the vital difference. For the medieval voyager, there are marvels indeed to be discovered; but they lie in the real world. A man by journeying could hope to reach strange lands, of which there were reliable, if varying, reports—

> of antres vast, and deserts idle,
> Rough quarries, rocks and hills, whose heads
> touch heaven . . .
> And of the Cannibals, that each other eat;
> The Anthropophagi, and men whose heads
> Do grow beneath their shoulders.

[1] *Table Talk*, 15 March 1834.
[2] Letter of 16 October 1797. For the connexion between this and faith in an 'active universe', see H. W. Piper, *The Active Universe* (London, 1962).

Whatever degree of curiosity this stimulates, it is not, and by its nature cannot be, a thirst for that which lies beyond sense-experience. Of course, that which is imagined to be true readily colours what is in fact encountered. When the Elizabethan voyagers made their landfalls their accounts were shaped by what they had been led to expect. Raleigh reported that the people described by Mandeville were to be found in the hinterland of Guiana. More, the Terrestrial Paradise itself, in all essentials, was to be looked for across the Western Sea—along the thirty-fifth degree of north latitude was, he thought, the promising line.[1] As discovery went forward, so, too, did belief persist that 'oldest tales were true'. Dr. Wright soundly reminds us that 'Nothing was too strange, wonderful, outlandish, or tempting to be believed about the New World'.[2] Shakespeare turns this to good account when he puts Gonzalo the Golden Age idealist on the same island as the realists Sebastian and Antonio, and lets them not so much debate as run in counterpoint, Gonzalo's lofty generalizations being punctuated by the cynical comments of the *cui bono* men.[3] All, evidently, depends on the mind the traveller brings; and the same principle holds for those who inhabit the new lands. Miranda takes Ferdinand for 'a spirit', 'A thing divine'; and Caliban is certain that Stephano is 'a brave god', bearing 'celestial liquor'. But while each comes to learn better, there is still room for the wholly inexplicable. Prospero's may be a 'rough magic', which he finally abjures; but it is magic none the less, an unequivocal power over elemental Nature.

In other words, when knowledge has come in there is still room for wonder. Spenser, cautioning his readers not to dismiss 'Faery land' outright, conducts an ever-expanding argument. He begins, disarmingly, with his own limitations as poet of

> that happy land of Faery,
> Which I so much do vaunt, yet no where show,
> But vouch antiquities, which no body can know—

only to continue with an argument from contemporary exploration:

> But let that man with better sence aduize,
> That of the world least part to vs is red:

[1] Louis B. Wright, *The Elizabethans' America* (London, 1965), conveniently assembles narratives and descriptive reports of the period.

[2] *ibid.*, p. 1.

[3] *Temp.* II, 1, esp. 137–63 (Alexander). See Walter Raleigh, *The English Voyagers of the Sixteenth Century* (London, 1910), pp. 183–5.

> And dayly how through hardy enterprize,
> Many great Regions are discouered,
> Which to late age were neuer mentioned.
> Who euer heard of th' Indian *Peru*?
> Or who in venturous vessell measured
> The *Amazons* huge riuer now found trew?
> Or fruitfullest *Virginia* who did euer vew?

Discovery is not a bar to imagination, but a stimulus; for

> all these were, when no man did them know;
> Yet haue from wisest ages hidden beene.

The argument from past time has equal force for the future:

> And later times things more vnknowne shall show.

The conclusion is triumphant:

> Why then should witlesse man so much misweene
> That nothing is, but that which he hath seene?

Nor does the argument end there. If the entire globe lies parcelled out into exactly known areas, there is still scope for man's exploration, and so his continuing wonder:

> What if within the Moones faire shining spheare,
> What if in euery other starre vnseene
> Of other worldes he happily should heare?
> He wonder would much more: yet such to some
> appeare.[1]

We see, then, that there is no simple victory for 'truth' or 'reality'. Fanciful conjecture, the continued life of old beliefs driven into remote corners, characterizes a period of actual discovery. The unknown shifts its ground; the rainbow's foot is beyond the next ridge, never the one just attained: and Spenser's argument suggests that it always will be so, even in an age of space-exploration. But what, in all this, have we to do with romanticism proper? It is not the romantic who believes that the object of desire inheres in the real world. His concern is with 'The light that never was, on sea or land'; or, as Lewis himself once put it, with an 'object that is never fully given . . . in our present mode of subjective and spatio-temporal experience'.[2]

[1] *Faerie Queene*, II, Proem.
[2] *The Pilgrim's Regress* (London, new edn., 1943), p. 10.

If we scrutinize Lewis's specific passages from Gower, the same critique holds. Medea (the 'cunning one') in all forms of the story is an enchantress. Gower neither amplifies nor gives prominence to her sorceries. Certainly, his account is vivid:

> Thries sche torned hire aboute,
> And thries ek sche gan doun loute
> And in the flod sche wette hir her,
> And thries on the water ther
> Sche gaspeth with a drecchinge onde . . .

This is brisk, workmanlike, admirably pictorial: but nowhere does it go beyond a world in which magic is possible, conferring a power which ordinary mortals may well dread. Here, as with spatial travel, Gower and his readers inhabit a world in which some few could voyage farther than their fellow creatures. The marvels they experience, or may even command, are exciting matter, certainly. But the excitement resides in the things themselves and not in any order of awareness which they prefigure or symbolize.

With the tale of Rosiphilee we perhaps come to something more complex. The poet appears to have worked on the famous couplet; Macaulay records the variant:

> The beaute of hire face schon
> Wel bryhtere þan þe Cristall ston.

The difference is profound. This beauty, though transcendent, is immovably other than 'beaute faye', a quality which goes beyond the limits of mortal life:

> The beaute faye upon her face
> Non erthly thing it may desface.

In the presence of this marvel, ordinary experience is, like Rosiphilee herself, abashed and must stay silent:

> For as hire thoughte in hire avis,
> To hem that were of such a pris
> Sche was nought worthi axen there,
> Fro when they come or what thei were.

Rosiphilee does not know who they are: but we do. They are that class of the fairies (or *Longaevi*, as Lewis preferred to call them) who are drawn from the dead. In *Thomas the Rymer*, as Lewis himself reminds us, the road divides three ways, to Heaven, Hell, and 'fair Elfland'; and in *Sir Orfeo* we are left in doubt whether it is or is not the land of the dead to which Dame Heurodis has gone.[1] That which is *faye* in the sense which concerns us is thought of as a possible mode of being, not to be exactly located, for some among the dead. So the stories which tell of encounters with them convey awe, a reverence for that which is not mortal but once was. The stories are not mysterious, to speak properly: they have no reference beyond themselves. Here, as with the ballad of the supernatural, the dead come and go with their own dignity and self-possession. It is a later generation which fastens obsessively upon such stories as expressing the very quintessence of a Gothick middle age and breeds from them at best high poetic mysteries, at worst ruin-and-terror tales to gratify a 'degrading thirst after outrageous stimulation'.[2] Whatever the end-product, we are not to confuse it with the material upon which romantic taste can work. In itself, that material is not romantic at all.

In citing the story of Nectanabus, Lewis might well have included the magic which, like that in Medea's tale, is faithfully recounted:

> thurgh the craft of Artemage
> Of wex he forgeth an ymage.
> He loketh his equacions
> And ek the constellacions,
> He loketh the conjunccions,
> He loketh the recepcions,
> His signe, his houre, his ascendent,
> And drawth fortune of his assent . . .

The heavenly light that comes upon the Queen in her dream is, of course, the product of 'enchantement'. 'For', Gower has been careful to warn his reader,

> it was guile and Sorcerie,
> Al that sche tok for Prophecie—

and the tale of Nectanabus's misdeeds is emphatically reckoned:

> With guile he hath his love sped,
> With guile he cam into the bed,
> With guile he goth him out ayein.

---

[1] *The Discarded Image* (Cambridge, 1964), p. 137.
[2] Wordsworth, *Preface to Lyrical Ballads* (1800).

The conclusion is sturdily moralized—

> He was a schrewed chamberlein,
> So to beguile a worthi queene—

as is the ending of the tale itself:

> And thus Nectanabus aboghte
> The Sorcerie which he wroughte.
> Thogh he upon the creatures
> Thurgh his carectes and figures
> The maistrie and the pouer hadde,
> His creatour to noght him ladde,
> Ayein whos lawe his craft he useth,
> Whan he for lust his god refuseth,
> And tok him to the dieules craft
> Lo, what profit him is belaft . . .

This story, least of any, is susceptible of romantic feeling, if we read it in its entirety and do not simply isolate the first enchantment which Nectanabus effects. To do so would be as if a reader of Chaucer's *Franklin's Tale* were to dwell upon the enchantments of the magician—

> His tables Tolletanes forth he brought—

and disregard not only the Franklin's moralizing upon 'supersticious cursednesse' and the ways of 'hethen folk' in far-off days, but the whole tender and realistic setting in which enchantment is placed. Here, least of all, can Gower be allowed any tincture of romanticism.

Lewis's final instance is the 'strangely vivid, because strangely ambiguous' dream in *Ulysses and Telegonus* (vi, 1519–63). The dream, it must be allowed, presents an ambiguous personage:

> A man it semeth was it non,
> Bot yit it was as in figure
> Most lich to mannyssh creature,
> Bot as of beaute hevenelich
> It was most to an Angel lich:
> And thus betwen angel and man
> Beholden it this king began.

Similarly, the 'pensel' which the apparition bears is mysteriously embroidered:

> Thre fisshes al of o colour
> In manere as it were a tour—

being, as 'the wyht' has to tell Ulysses, 'A signe . . . Of an Empire'.
If we read the dream out of its context, we may think we are dealing
with mysterious symbols. Indeed, to take the dream by itself would be
to construct our own 'medieval' romantic poem—the unearthly visitant,
the brightness in which he is bathed, and the pattern of the three
fishes: what could be more promising? Alas! we must read the tale,
and nothing less than the whole tale, if we are not to beat the air. The
figure, I am afraid, remains as he is: a remarkable creature, more than
mortal, one proper to all august tradition of dream-announcement, or
Oraculum—but nothing other than that. He is costumed for his
traditional role; and there's an end. As to the 'pensel' with its 'strange
device', Gower tells us plainly, even prosaically, that there is nothing
mysterious in that:

> It was that time such usance,
> That every man the conoiscance
> Of his contre bar in his hond,
> Whan he wente into strange lond;
> And thus was every man therfore
> Wel knowe, wher that he was bore:
> For espiaile and mistrowinges
> They dede thanne suche thinges,
> That every man mai other knowe.

It is the heraldic device of Telegonus; and Telegonus, born of Ulysses
and Circe, will later slay his father. In this, Fortune's wheel comes full
circle for Ulysses:

> Thurgh Sorcerie his lust he wan,
> Thurgh Sorcerie his wo began,
> Thurgh Sorcerie his love he ches,
> Thurgh Sorcerie his life he les.

If we wish to construct a romantic poem, we can. But it is not the poem
Gower gives us. Everything that seems to us promising leads nowhere.
The apparition speaks no more than is set down for him; the light is
functional, not ethereal; the 'pensel' signalizes downfall not by any
inherent symbolism but by being the badge of Telegonus. Whatever
overtones of wonder there could be in a story of unlooked-for doom

they are simply irrelevant to Gower's tale. His purpose is plain, his meaning neither strange nor ambiguous.

IV

From this we can construct a general principle and, I think, make some serviceable distinctions. The principle is clear. Where the object of interest or desire lies within the region of possible attainment, we cannot have anything properly to be called romantic. If the 'strange regiouns' that excite Jason's longing are practicable landfalls, reported by those who have travelled so far; if Medea's sorceries are a possible accomplishment; if the light that surrounds a figure of 'enchantement' is the common attribute of efficient 'guile and Sorcerie'; and if figures 'betwen angel and man' are to be looked for in the dream of oracular warning—then it matters not how rare such manifestations are in the reader's own experience. If some few choice or malign spirits can go uniquely far, whether literally, in physical space, or metaphorically, in spiritual voyaging, then the reader's awareness, with whatever over-tones of scepticism or plain disbelief, remains within the region of the possible-fantastic. The marvels exist in and of themselves. They may, as in a good deal of medieval Romance writing, exist for themselves; or, as in most homiletic and moralizing work, including this of Gower's, they will serve the author's didactic and illustrative ends. In the *Confessio Amantis* the marvels, along with the matter of love, constitute that element of 'lust' which, paired with 'lore', yields the sum of Gower's undertaking. There is no question of Gower doing better than he knew—at least, not in the sense of being a romantic before the dawn. Certainly, the material which he, like many another medieval writer, provides can be read romantically by a later reader. But for that to happen, the map of knowledge must have undergone decisive change. So long as some part of the world remains undiscovered, all remains possible. When, in a later age, everything has been explored, desire shifts its ground; and it is then that the apparatus of the old world, the monsters, the demons, all the exciting glimpses at the margin of the map, come into new life. Free from every limitation of the possible, they offer themselves as the perfect vehicle for that joy or terror, exalta-tion or despair, which otherwise can have no distinctive utterance. It is then, and only then, that bridges can be built between 'the conscious and the unconscious mind': and in that age the medieval poets are the first to be assiduously quarried by the bridge-builders.

We may ask, what difference does it all make? Is there not a 'liberty of interpreting'[1] which is naturally prior to these overexact considerations? I suppose one answer might run as follows. To misread Gower as a romantic is in principle the same error as to misread Wordsworth as an exalted moralist. They are equal, not opposite, errors: in each instance the work is moved away from its distinctive quality into a preconceived area of meaning. To do this is, of course, as was said earlier, to substitute a poem of the reader's own invention for the poem that lies before him. The final answer to the question why not, is that the reader has taken one more step in insulating himself from contact with that which, being other than he expects, has most chance of challenging him into awareness—of poetry, of external reality, and of the assumptions he has brought to his reading and which, it may be for the first time, he now sees laid bare.

It follows that to go to Gower for what is in him in his own right is, so far from diminishing a poetry truly to be called romantic, to heighten it; and this leads to a serviceable distinction. If we see what in medieval poetry tempted eighteenth-century enthusiasts we are better able to discriminate between the sub-romantic—the poetry in which fancy plays around the apparatus of an imagined past—and romanticism full-grown. When romanticism has come of age, the poet knows nothing of 'romances and relations of giants and magicians and genii' save as reading for children, implanting 'the love of the great and the whole'. The apparatus of past belief serves, as nothing else can, to body forth mysteries.

Was it not much the same with Lewis himself? His first enthusiastic reading of medieval literature—and few men ever read so widely for a first book as he did for *The Allegory of Love*—led him to ascribe to Gower the qualities he most admired in human nature: 'The heart is insular and romantic, the head cool and continental: it is a good combination'.[2] Lewis later found a scope for his own narrative writing in the space-fiction ('scientifiction', as he liked to call it) which, in the 'thirties and 'forties, was dealing still with possibilities so remote from

[1] *cf.* Lascelles Abercrombie, 'A Plea for the Liberty of Interpreting', Annual Shakespeare Lecture of the British Academy, 1930 (*Proceedings*, XVI). Abercrombie's position has recently been cogently defended by L. C. Knights ('On Historical Scholarship and the Interpretation of Shakespeare', *Sewanee Review*, LXIII (1955)); for some comments on this by the present writer, see the same journal, LXIV (1956), 186–206.

[2] *Allegory of Love*, p. 222.

actuality that there was an ample field for sustained imagination.[1] In this, Spenser's confidence seemed to be vindicated:

> What if within the Moones faire shining spheare
> What if in euery other starre vnseene
> Of other worldes he happily should heare?
> He wonder would much more . . .

The last of the 'space' trilogy, *That Hideous Strength*, pits medieval wizardry against modern technological barbarism. Ransom, returned to Earth, is joined by Merlin, raised from his age-long sleep, and the planet Venus herself descends to take part in the final conflict. Is it fanciful to suppose that Lewis was prescient of the changes to come in the possibilities for science-fiction, once space flight became not only a serious possibility but an established fact? At all events, he turned from space-romance to children's stories, in which 'giants and magicians', if not 'genii', play their exhilarating parts and the whole sequence moves towards a profound climax. Perhaps it is more significant that his highest achievement in narrative is neither science-fiction nor fairy-tale, but the myth of *Till We Have Faces*. There, for once, we have an instance of the quality of 'myth' which Lewis himself defined better than anyone. Myth offers a pleasure which 'depends hardly at all on such usual narrative attractions as suspense or surprise. Even at a first hearing it is felt to be inevitable.' Lewis goes on to link anthropological investigation into myth with the 'impulse which makes men allegorise the myths. It is one more effort to seize, to conceptualise, the important something which the myth seems to suggest'.[2]

Perhaps we have in this the explanation of his own misreading of Gower as a romantic. What the voyagings, the sorceries and the dreams suggested to Lewis's exalted imagination bore good fruit in his own narrative writing—not so much in particular felicities of science-fiction or fairy-story as in his constant awareness of that myth which he

---

[1] 'What set me about writing the book [*Out of the Silent Planet*] was the discovery that a pupil of mine took all that dream of interplanetary colonization quite seriously . . . You will be both grieved and amused to hear that out of about 60 reviews only two showed any knowledge that my idea of the fall of the Bent One was anything but an invention of my own . . . any amount of theology can now be smuggled into people's minds under cover of romance without their knowing it' (from a letter written on 9 July 1939, which I quote with W. H. Lewis's permission).

[2] *An Experiment in Criticism*, Cambridge, 1961, pp. 43, 45.

understood as prompting all curiosity and desire. It is the myth which he in part retells in *Perelandra*, when a new Fall of the divine creation appears imminent; and which achieves near-perfect expression in *Till We Have Faces*, where unassuming mortality puts on immortality. It is not strange that Lewis should have developed in this way. The myth he reverenced was to him expressive of ultimate truth, underlying, and constituting the only final justification for, the romantic impulse itself.[1]

[1] On Lewis's conception of romanticism, see my '*Rasselas*, Romanticism, and the Nature of Happiness' in *Friendship's Garland: Essays presented to Mario Praz* (Rome, 1966).

VIII

Love and 'Foul Delight': Some Contrasted Attitudes

His habitual generosity of mind is nowhere more evident in the writings of C. S. Lewis that in his account, in the opening chapter of *The Allegory of Love*, of the *De Arte Honeste Amandi* of Andreas Capellanus. Lewis does Andreas the honour of supposing him as serious a writer as he is himself, and worthy to be mentioned in the same breath with Chaucer, as one concerned about the same high things. He sees him as the celebrant of an earthly spirituality, propounding a clearly reasoned code of behaviour, based in the belief that *amour courtois* is a source of noble virtue:

> . . . When Andreas talks of the *bonum in saeculo* he means what he says. He means the really good things, in a human sense, as contrasted with the really bad things: courage and courtesy and generosity against baseness.

And when, at the end, Andreas turns his neat professional somersault, repudiating the system he has so lovingly propounded, Lewis credits him with the same sincerity, faith and vision that he finds in Chaucer's palinode at the end of *Troilus and Criseyde*:

> . . . The Chaplain's palinode does not stand alone. In the last stanzas of the book of Troilus . . . it is the same. We hear the bell clang; and the children, suddenly hushed and grave, and a little frightened, troop back to their master.

What are we to make, asks Lewis, of the volte-face? Is the love-lore of Andreas pure joking, or is his religion rank hypocrisy?

I

I doubt if Andreas's state of mind when he wrote his book could fully have been described in such a clear antithesis. Dr. D. W. Robertson[1] has come recently to the Chaplain's aid by pronouncing his dialogues to be satirical, and his recantation orthodox; he believes him a man of probity, another generous judgement. For me the voice of Andreas is too often the voice of Screwtape, and nowhere more loudly than in the recantation of his Third Book, where the core of his creed is discovered as an unhealthy hatred of sexuality, especially in women, which at the same time renders them objects of fascination to him. From the start he has the inner knowledge (withheld from his readers) that this hatred will in the end bring him out on the side of a safe orthodoxy, but meanwhile he can indulge his flippant pen in a pleasantly detailed manual of sexual instruction, posing as an adept; and there will be many pleasures for his imagination to indulge on the way to the supreme pleasure of battering down its bower of bliss. There is, for instance, the pleasure of being 'in the know', even of posing as the instructor of those already 'in the know', a highly fashionable in-group of lascivious and apparently aristocratic laity; and he himself a celibate priest. There is the pleasure of showing one's paces in casuistry, a dazzling exhibition of brinkmanship; and there is the more general pleasure, known to us all, of inventing day-dream conversations, rallies in the duel of sex, that inch their way towards the forfended place, and reach it at last by the pretence of preferring to forgo it. Chaucer invests Troilus at the moment of ecstasy with a sense of its holiness, albeit a pagan holiness. Andreas is incapable of conceiving of holiness of any kind, to judge by this work. Holiness does not go with hatred of what God has made, but he is haunted by a hatred in which he puts his trust. A true courtesy is beyond him.

Andreas is a master, if not of courtesy, at least of urbanity: he is naturally nearer to Ovid than to Plato in his account of love. His affinity to the former arises from his aggressive heterosexuality, which imports the whole panoply of the sex-war into the argument. In Plato jealousy stands aloof; there is no thought of conflict, still less of contest, between lover and beloved; there is a clear ascent into the spirit, the flesh not being so much denied as transcended. But in Andreas, as Lewis observes, jealousy is central. Socrates received no practical tips from Diotima, because, for Plato, love was not an 'art', but something nearer to 'the holy bond of things' which Chaucer's Troilus so seriously

[1] *A Preface to Chaucer*, by D. W. Robertson, jun. (Princeton, 1963); see especially p. 448.

and so beautifully calls it. Shakespeare's Troilus, so close to Chaucer's, thinks of it in terms of 'sanctimony': but to think of love in terms of casuistry and protocol instead is to enter a country of trappers and encroachers and strategists. Andreas-country, in fact. Shakespeare's Troilus—and he might have been speaking for his Chaucerian ancestor —says:

> I am as true as truth's simplicity
> And simpler than the infancy of truth.

None of the puppets of Andreas could say that, any more than he could have said it of himself. There are artifices practised in *Troilus and Criseyde*, but they are all Pandar's, as when he tells his friend how to write a love-letter:

> Ne scryvenyssh or craftily thow it write;
> Biblotte it with thy teris ek a lite.

If Troilus obeyed him in this, it was because he could not hold back his tears, just as, when Pandar told him to feign sick before the dinner-party at the house of Deiphebus, Troilus could honestly answer that he had no need to feign:

> For I am sik in ernest, douteles,
> So that wel neigh I sterve for the peyne.

That Andreas is only offering his friend Walter (if he existed) springes to catch woodcocks is clear from a hundred indications; that the woodcock turns out, in the recantation, to be the Enemy is to be expected of his *amo-odi* character. God is much in his mouth and in the mouths of his puppets, and what is said of Him in the first two Books undercuts what is said of Him in the last; the reader may take his choice which to trust. The palinode tells us how God hates and punishes the servants of Venus, according to both Testaments, but says nothing about the mercy shown to the woman taken in adultery, an incident so familiar to the Middle Ages as to have been a scene in three out of our four surviving English miracle cycles; and this casts doubt on the value, if not on the sincerity, of what Andreas and his Pauline thunders have to say. The reader cannot but match it against his earlier pronouncement that 'God cannot be offended by love, for what is done under the compulsion of nature can be made clean by an easy expiation'. And there are greater and more cynical effronteries than these; as when we are told that the

initiation of a novice into the mysteries of love is a better action in a
woman than to set her choice on an already experienced lover, just as
the conversion of one sinner to repentance is more pleasing to the King
of Heaven than the virtue of the ninety and nine just persons. On two
occasions one of Andreas's puppet-lovers adjures the woman he is
attempting to seduce in the following impudent terms:

> And I beseech God in Heaven that of His grace He may grant
> me to do those things that are wholly pleasing to your
> desire . . .[1]

that is, to *her* desire, not to *His*. But the pagan Troilus treats his gods
with no such flippancy, even though we are reminded by Chaucer, at
the end of the poem, that his gods were rascals.

Although Andreas makes great play with the importance of truth
in love, and has for his fifth commandment the complete avoidance of
all falsehood, his structures of seduction are rooted in pretence. The
chief pretence is that good character alone makes a man worthy of love,
and that therefore, on moral grounds, the lady ought to yield herself to
the lover with the best character; consequently these 'lovers' are loud
in their own excellences. But we never hear Troilus boasting his virtues.
So far from thinking well of himself, he repeatedly tells us he is a
'wrecche', and means it. But Andreas has a second barrel to the gun of
this pretence. If the lady will not yield because the lover's character is
worthy of this reward, she can be told that only she can make him
worthy; as if the object of the lover was the improvement of his
character and not the seduction of the lady.

Yet with all this talk of the power of love to improve character
Andreas affirms that love and jealousy are the same thing, and in this
opinion declares he has the backing of the Countess of Champagne,
with her dictum that a man incapable of jealousy is incapable of love.

Now, jealousy can by no pretence be thought to improve character,
or to belong to the *bona in saeculo*; it belongs, on the contrary, to what
Lewis calls 'baseness'. And this is also clearly Chaucer's opinion, though
he puts it in the mouth of Criseyde:

> Ek al my wo is this, that folk now usen
> To seyn right thus, 'Ye, jalousie is love!'
> And wolde a busshel venym al excusen

[1] All quotations from Andreas are taken from *The Art of Courtly Love*, by
John Jay Parry (New York, 1941).

> For that o greyn of love is on it shove.
> But that woot heighe God that sit above,
> If it be likkere love, or hate or grame,
> And after that, it oghte bere his name.

All that Andreas tells us of the 'art' of love leads, deviously or directly, to the sexual act. Yet, when at last he gets there, he pretends to shy away from it, asserting that final consummation is love mixed with impurity. There is a 'pure' and there is a 'mixed' love, he tells us, and though both are good (he says) the 'pure' is better than the 'mixed'. This 'pure' love (he would have us believe) consists in the contemplation of the mind and affection of the heart:

> it goes as far as the kiss and the embrace and the modest contact with the nude lover, omitting the final solace . . . This is the kind that anyone who is intent upon love ought to embrace with all his might . . . and we know no one that ever regretted practising it, and the more one has of it the more one wants. This love is distinguished by being of such virtue that from it arises all excellence of character, and no injury comes of it, and God sees very little offence in it.

This is the kind of love propounded by Iago in extenuation of the conduct he ascribes to Desdemona with Cassio:

> Or to be naked with a friend in bed
> An hour or more, not meaning any harm . . .

Othello's judgement follows:

> It is hypocrisy against the devil.

It is, indeed, such hypocrisy as almost to make one accept Dr. Robertson's explanation that Andreas intended this part of his work to be taken satirically. Yet we must pause before so easy an interpretation. It appears to have been not impossible in the Middle Ages to regard this at-the-last-moment inhibited way of love as an ideal. It is lyrically recommended by Christine de Pisan in her *Duc des vrays Amans*, and the fact that she was a ninny does not alter the case. It is true that she does not precisely state that her lovers were naked, but they lay all night in each others' arms, kissing. Farther, we are told, they did not go:

> Then my lady, in whom dwells every grace, very tenderly embraced me, and kissed me more than a hundred times. And

I remained thus happy all the night, and be assured, you lovers
who hear this, that I was very contented. . . . Thus I asked
her for naught beside, for I had all that I desired . . .[1]

Chaucer had no taste for these refinements in prurience. He describes
the union of Troilus and Criseyde, at its consummation, with grave
simplicity and, if the tone of poetry means anything, with no dis-
approval:

> Therwith he gan hire faste in armes take,
> And wel an hondred tymes gan he syke,
> Naught swiche sorwful sikes as men make
> For wo, or elles when that folk ben sike,
> But esy sykes, swiche as ben to like,
> That shewed his affeccioun withinne;
> Of swiche sikes koude he nought bilynne.

This is the first expression of an idea later found in Donne:

> Love's mysteries in souls do grow,
> But yet the body is the book.

Andreas's puppet-woman, confronted with the suggestion of such a
naked feast, is not deceived. It is another encroacher's trick; 'I wonder'
she says,

> if anyone was ever found with such continence that he could
> resist the promptings of passion and control the actions of his
> body.

When we come to Andreas's retraction, sex-war is openly declared.
Bodily pleasure is a snare of Hell, adultery may lead to murder,
passion of love is enslavement to jealousy and terror, one is in danger
of earning a scandalous reputation, love *par amour* is an idolatory that
leads to obsession and incapacitates one for the business of life. The
Devil himself is the author both of love and of lechery, and these are
harmful biologically as well as spiritually and intellectually: to yield to
them is to make yourself the enemy of God. And finally there comes a
tirade, in the tradition of patristic misogyny, in which *his hatred of
women*, which is the other side of the coin of their fascination for him,

---

[1] *The Book of the Duke of True Lovers: now first translated from the Middle
French of Christine de Pisan: with an Introduction: by Alice Kemp-Welch* (London,
1908), p. 91.

is at last released. We learn that no woman ever loved a man; that she is a natural miser, slanderous and full of envy; a liar, a drunkard, a babbler, vainglorious and given to lechery as much as to pride; her god is her belly, she is consumed by jealousy and hatred; so great is her avarice that she contemns all law, whether human or divine; and *there are no exceptions to the rule*. Fickle, as she is also double-tongued, there is no honesty in her, and her arrogance is past endurance: often drunk, she is abusive and overbearing in her cups, as she is insatiable in her bed. No woman, however, can give a man what he seeks, since no woman is capable of love; prone to every sort of evil, women are never to be trusted. Divine authority declares that there is no more serious sin than fornication.

All this, of course, is common form in certain monkish ways of thinking, and had been so for centuries. Four hundred years before, King Cormac was instructing Carbery to the same tunes,[1] and four hundred years before that St. Jerome held similar opinions.[2] The palinode of Andreas would fit in more convincingly with these if his first two Books, whether deemed satirical or not, had not shown a certain bent of mind. Prurience thrusts through the satire and his hatred of the flesh is not holiness; for Langland tells us that chastity without charity will be chained in Hell, and Browning suggests that there's a text in the Galatians that may easily be tripped upon. He does not tell us which, but perhaps it is the text in which those born after the flesh and those born after the spirit are so mightily opposed.[3] The hatred in Andreas does not seem a hatred of sin, but a hatred of the flesh itself, and it is this that trips him up and sends him flying off to Hell, a Manichee.

For Chaucer voices no hatred of Criseyde, except through Pandarus. Pandarus, speechless at the falsity of his niece, with all his stratagems come to nothing, is reduced to stammering

What sholde I seyen? I hate, ywis, Cryseyde!

But Chaucer has no hatred for her; he would excuse her, for pity; and Troilus could not find it in his heart to unlove her a quarter of a day.

The Chaucerian vision of mortal love, as it is shown us in *Troilus and Criseyde*, imperfect and brittle as it may be, is the beginning of

[1] *Selections from Ancient Irish Poetry*, translated by Kuno Meyer (London, 1911), pp. 106–7.
[2] As in the *Epistola adversus Jovinianum*.
[3] Gal. iv 29.

English romanticism, a romanticism which by no means excludes the mockery of its heroes. Troilus is frequently foolish, and sometimes funny, but that does not make him an unsympathetic, still less an unromantic figure. Indeed, it greatly endears him to us, and at the end of the story we are allowed to escort him to a felicity which appears not to have been denied him by his creator. It is only in comparison with this felicity that he condemns the blind desires[1] of mortality as ephemeral. And why should he have attained felicity, if he had not shown himself worthy of it by an innocent and steadfast love, maintained against the falsity and transience of a mortal world?

The tradition of innocent sincerity in sexual love is carried farther in Shakespeare, Chaucer's natural successor in romance; the tradition of Andreas reappears, with many diminutions and some developments, in a certain attitude that seems mainly Gallic, though it is found here and there in the English tradition, for instance in the comedies of the Restoration; and it is akin to the libertinism of Robert Lovelace in *Clarissa*, and of the Vicomte de Valmont in *Les Liaisons Dangereuses*. Jealousy reappears as the central passion in love in *A La Recherche du Temps Perdu*. Indeed, wherever love is thought of in terms of possession rather than of gift, of adroitness rather than of innocence, or encroaching, predatory males, at heartless war and skirmish with a sex they desire and despise, there we will find the ghost of Andreas Capellanus, sitting crowned upon the grave thereof.

We are told that his work was very popular: a dozen manuscripts and many early reprintings testify to this, no less than an episcopal condemnation in Paris, in March 1277. This popularity, taken with the condemnation, suggest that if Dr. Robertson is right in supposing the first two Books to have been written with satirical intention, this was

> [1] And in hymself he lough right at the wo
> Of hem that wepten for his deth so faste;
> And dampned al oure werk that folweth so
> The blynde lust, the which that may not laste,
> And sholden al oure herte on heven caste.
>
> v, 1821–5

Some critics, including Dr. Robertson, have taken the laughter of Troilus to be 'ironical'; if by this hackneyed adjective they mean, or wish to imply, that it was a sneering laugh, there is no justification for it in the poem. It is the laugh of a man newly entered (so we are told) into felicity. In time those who are lamenting his death may enter it themselves and cease to mourn, and can laugh for joy with him.

not suspected at the time. It was taken to be a useful manual of the works of Venus.

II

Let us now turn from the Courtier-Poet and the Courtier-Casuist-Teaser-Puritan-Priest, to the educated gentlefolk for whom they may be thought partly to have written, and to their less articulate mixtures of instinct, prejudice and opinion on the theory and practice of love. I suppose one could hardly find a more illustrative sample of the average country aristocrat of the fourteenth century than the Knight of the Tower of Landry. His family had had its home there, tucked away between the Angevin villages of Cholet and Vezins, since 1200; that is, from about the time when Andreas was composing his little three-decker treatise. But although more than a hundred and fifty years had passed since then, I cannot think the *De Arte Honeste Amandi* had ever come into the hands of the Knight of the Tower, for the noise of the explosion would surely have reached us.

In the book which the Knight was inspired to compile and put forth, to guide his daughters in the conduct of life (and particularly through the dangers of love *peramours*), only the faintest awareness of the premises and sophistications elaborated by the Chaplain is perceptible. That some sort of plausible apology could be offered in the pursuit of free love, the Knight knew well enough; but he could have known this from general tides of gossip. Andreas may (at many removes) have been an influence on his awareness, however much diluted, but an influence is not necessarily a source.

The Knight had, however, been touched by love-vision poetry, and he actually began his book in verse, with a conventional, yet charming, spring-time flourish in the manner of the *Roman de la Rose*; the translator has almost caught a Chaucerian mood.[1]

> In the yere of the incarnacion of oure lord Miij^{c}lxxj, as y was in a gardin, al heui and full of thought, in the shadow, about the ende of the monthe of Aprill, but a litell y reioysed me of the melodie and song of the wilde briddes; thei sang there in her langages, as the Thrustill, the thrusshe, the nytingale, and other briddes, the whiche were full of mirthe and ioye; and thaire

[1] All quotations from this work are taken from *The Book of the Knight of La Tour-Landry*, ed. by Thomas Wright, for the Early English Text Society (O.S. 33) (London, 1906).

suete songe made my herte to lighten, and made me to thinke
of the tyme that is passed of my youthe, and loue in gret dis-
tresse had holde me, and how y was in her seruice many tyme3
full of sorugh and gladnesse, as mani louers ben. . . . (p. 1).

This note, personal and poetic, is one that recurs—rarely, alas!—in the
Knight's book, when he recalls the past. The book has two other
intermingled moods, one of a secular, the other of a theological com-
plexion, when he abandons reminiscence and gets down to business.
Occasionally one can distinguish the clerical voices of his four ghost-
collaborators (the priest, and clerks of his household), but more often
his own anecdotal gusto seems to be in charge of this work of edification, dedicated to his daughters.

In many ways it is not remarkable; it gives all the expected advice,
and many of the expected illustrations. What is conventional can be
quickly epitomized. Begin the day with prayer, hear three masses a
day, make regular confession, honour the Blessed Virgin, observe the
proper fasts, avoid the deadly sins. Do not gormandize or affect new
fashions in dress; do not fard your faces or pluck your eyebrows. Be
humble, courteous, and charitable to the poor; to your husband be
loving and obedient; keep his secrets and maintain his honour. Talk
little; never answer back; avoid all possibility of scandal. Outface all
attempts at your seduction; send your children to school and teach them
to fear God. If you have stepchildren, be kind to them; if you should
be widowed, remarry (if you must) by the advice of your friends and
family, and not for the pleasures of the flesh.

This is the gist of his teaching and were it not for the wild medieval
fantasy of some of his anecdotes (as of the husband who sought to test
his wife's capacity to keep a secret by informing her, with strict
injunctions to tell no one, that he had laid two eggs; within a week
word came back to him that he had laid a clutch of them), and some
incidental and surprising value-judgements (as when he lets slip that
the purgatorial tariff for the sin of fornication, if properly confessed
before death, is seven years for each act), there would be little to draw
a modern reader except the momentary sense, from time to time, that
we are in homely conversation with an authentic old buffer from the
fourteenth century, who comes out with unexpected turns of phrase,
notwithstanding that we only hear him in translation.

He agrees emphatically with Andreas on one major premiss: lechery

is, of all the sins, the sin that God most abominates—the Knight, however, couples it with pride (p. 67). But the Knight is no hater of women;
on the contrary, he shows every sign of a decent normality, capable of
warm admiration for their virtues and of pleasure in their company; he
loved his first wife and respected his second, and was fond of his
daughters. Although theological considerations are allowed pride of
place in his book, one cannot help feeling that secular ones were
inwardly more important to him, whether he knew it or not. His
overriding anxiety is lest his daughters should '*lose their marriage*' by
some imprudence. To lose her marriage, he seems to consider the
greatest misfortune that can befall a girl in this world; and this is ever
accompanied or caused by some diminution of respect in the world's
eye, the supreme reason for which is the suspicion, or certainty, that
she has given herself to a lover in 'foul delight'. This also brings in its
train the loss of God's favour and the most ferocious punishments of
Hell, or, if repented and confessed, of Purgatory.

It is tempting to see in his perpetual insistence on the necessity of
avoiding the slightest act or even mannerism that could 'lose a marriage'
the lasting effect of his own first amatory experience (or at least the
first he records). Although he makes no such admission, he was partly
to blame in an episode which had a tragic consequence; the incident
haunted him and he recurs to it later in his book. It is fully related in
his thirteenth chapter, and is by far the most interesting thing he has
to tell us. It includes a conversation that carries the stamp of authenticity
in every line; for once we are reading life, not literature. We see clearly
the way in which a match between two young people was actually set
on foot, the way in which they actually spoke to each other, and the
way in which it was broken off, with sad consequences for the unwanted
girl.

He tells us how his friends 'spake to me to be maried into a noble
place', and how his father brought him to see the girl, 'and sette me in
language with her, that y shulde haue knoulech of her speche and
langage' (p. 18). On this point, the custom of the times is in as full
harmony with Andreas as it is with Chaucer. Andreas listed 'readiness
of speech' as the third of the graces that beget love (p. 33), and Chaucer's
happiest praise is given to the Duchess Blanche for her conversation:

> Of eloquence was never founde
> So swete a sownynge facounde.
>
> (*BD*, 925–6)

The young Knight of the Tower and his designated bride began to exchange words. He opened, very naturally, by talking about the war, and how the English treated their prisoners; and from this gambit he adroitly took off, and was soon airborne in allegory with

> Damesell, it were better to fall to be youre prisoner thanne to mani other, for y trow youre prison shuld not be so harde to me as it shulde be and y were take with Englisshe men.

To this sally she returned the charming answer 'Y haue saie sum not long sethe that y wolde were my prisoner.' If she had a prisoner to keep, she said, she would keep him as she would her own body; and he replied that it would be a happy man indeed who came into so noble a prison (p. 18).

But now he was lying to her. She had already made a fatal blunder, and he had swiftly decided against her. *She was too pert.*

> What shall y saie? she loued me wel ynough, and hadd a quicke yee, and a light, and ther was mani wordes. And so atte the laste she waxe right familier with me, for she praied me ij or iij tymes that y shulde not abide longe, but that y shulde come and see her how euer it were; of the whiche y had meruaile, seing that y was neuer aqueinted with her, nor hadd spoken, nor see her afore that tyme.

The young Knight, alas, shows himself to have been something of a prig, on the way to becoming something of a puritan. The willing friendliness of her conversation, that now reads so charmingly and freshly, gave him deep offence. When, as they rode home, his father asked him how he liked her, he replied that

> she was bothe good and faire, but she shulde be to me no nere than she was . . . for she was so pert and so light of maners that caused me to be discoraged from her . . .

It may, of course, have been the tone of her voice, rather than what she said. Yet he seems to have had a double standard of judgement. Alle-gorical innuendo was permitted to him, but not to her. And this double standard, one for men and one for women, permeates his thinking. Men may fornicate, and wives ought to tolerate it if they do. An aunt of his, he tells us, had a husband that was 'merueilously lecherous'

(p. 23); but, by ignoring his infidelities, she retained his affection and saved her marriage, saying to him:

> Y were a fole to slee my selff for youre sportes.

But there was to be no such tolerance for adulterous wives, and he commends the ferocities of God and Moses, and of the countries less civilized than France and England. In the days of Israel they made short work of an adultress:

> . . . she shulde be brent or stoned vnto the dethe, so noble and trwe was the lawe of God and of Moyses . . . (p. 162).

And he laments that 'there is no iustice do thereon in this Reaume, as ther is do in other'—he means in Provence, in Spain and in Aragon, where, he says, their throats are cut or they are burnt alive.

The story of the sprightly girl his friends had chosen to be his bride has a sad ending. Somehow she soon had got herself talked about (perhaps for the very virtue of obligingness):

> For in sothe it was not half a yeere after that she was blamed; but y note whedir it was fals or true. And after she deied (p. 18).

He could not shake the experience out of his mind and he returns to it in the dialogue between himself and his second wife (for so she seems to be), the Lady of the Tower, near the end of his book (p. 177). Into her mouth he puts words that amount almost to a rebuke to him, or as nearly a rebuke as he felt able to allow her: 'Ye prayd her of loue', she reminds him,

> but by cause that she whiche was not wyse ynough to ansuere yow curtoysly and wel, ye demaunded her not; and yf she had hold her self more secrete and couered, and more symply, ye had take her to your wyf. Of whome I haue syn herde saye that she hath be blamed, but I wote not for certayne yf it was so . . . many wymmen haue lost theyr maryage by cause of theyr amerous loke and fayr semblant . . .

Fair-Semblant was the name of the least grievous of the arrows of Cupid in the *Roman de la Rose*; and though the Lady may not consciously have been alluding to the poem in what she said, there is a line in it, telling us about this arrow, which she might have quoted:

> Yit can it make a ful gret wounde.
>
> (965)

She was blamed. It did not matter whether truly or not. To be blamed was enough. And she died.

No wonder the old Knight set such store on the avoidance of immodesty, let alone of inchastity, in his daughters. It is the pole upon which his world of women turns.

The only love he allows a woman is the love of her husband; he makes it clear that this love includes their sexual life together as well as all other aspects of their union. Obedience, affection, care for him in sickness and affliction, and tolerance for his faults, are also written into his concept of the marriage contract, and he has the seeming *naïveté* to approve the question, asked by a father of a daughter, in one of his illustrative anecdotes:

> Whi loue ye or haue more plesing to ani man than to youre husbonde? (p. 48).

As he poses it, it sounds to him an unanswerable question, as if the two kinds of love—married love and love *peramours*—were of the same kind. And if we accept his double standard, it is unanswerable. It assumes that women are not moved to love in the same ways, or for the same considerations, in all respects, as men. And this is still an observable fact.

That love *peramours* could exist between husband and wife, or at least that a chosen woman can keep such a love alive in her husband, was also the experience of the Knight of the Tower. It had happened to him, a sudden and lasting miracle, twenty years before he set himself to write his book: it had been the source of all joy and poetry for him. Love, he tells us,

> gaue me a fayr wyff . . . that was bothe faire and good, and of all good she was the bell and the floure: and y delited me so moche in her that y made for her loue songges, balades, rondelles, virallës, and diuerse nwe thinges in the best wise that y couthe. But deth, that on all makithe werre, toke her from me . . . And so it is more than xx yeere that I haue ben for her ful of gret sorugh. For a true loueris hert forgetith neuer the woman that enis he hathe truli loued (pp. 1–2).

And as he was meditating this love, walking (as he tells us) in the shadows of his garden and its vernal birdsong, his three daughters came out to join him. In that moment he conceived the notion of writing a book for their instruction; and he gave it such a shape as to make his lyrical meditation on his dead 'wyff' its Prologue. The word 'wife' is, of course, ambiguous. Are we to understand it here as *woman* (in the sense given to it by Iago when he tells us that Cassio is almost damned in a fair wife) or are we to understand it as *wedded wife*? I think the latter.

It is hardly possible to suppose he would begin a book for the edification of his daughters, particularly a book that so vehemently and repeatedly warns them against the foul delight of sexual union outside matrimony, with a personal rhapsody of such a kind unless it could claim the innocence of marriage. Moreover, the Knight later deplores the promiscuity of the companions of his youth and denies that he had any share in it (pp. 2–3). This we may believe or not, as we please; but if the image of himself that he wished to establish for the benefit of his daughters was one of chaste behaviour, how could he be thought to have begun with one which they could have taken as guilty? Like most people, the old Knight seems to have made the best of both worlds, the world of poetry and the world of ethic. A man could find them both in marriage, if he knew how to choose; but more was permitted to a man than to a woman in the way of romance. He had no need of a palinode; he had nothing to retract.

And yet, towards the end of his book, without warning, he changes sides and enters into an argument with his wife, as *Advocatus Diaboli*. There can be no evil thought in love, he says, for if it is evil it is not love. Why should not ladies and damsels love *peramours*? (p. 171).

> I tell you that grete almesse it is, whanne a lady or damoysell maketh a good knyght eyther a good squyer (p. 172).

It is the old, agreed basis of justification, argued in Andreas and enacted in Troilus: requited love elicits all the virtues a man and a soldier should have.

The Lady of the Tower has a short answer to this argument:

> Ye say, *and so done all other men*, that a lady or damoysell is the better worth whan she loueth peramours, And that she shall be the more gay, & of fayr maner and countenaunce, And how she shalle do grete almesse to make a good knyght. *These wordes are but sport and esbatement of lordes and of felawes, in a langage moche comyn* . . . but these wordes *coste to them but lytill to say* . . . but how be hit that they saye that 'for them and

for theyr loue they done hit'. *In good feyth they done it only for to enhaunce them self, and to drawe vnto them the grace and vayne glory of the world* . . . (p. 172).

I have supplied italics to suggest her tone of voice. If what she says is true, there is no honest art of love, and the casuist is undermined; but not the poet. For Chaucer does not tell us of any such argument advanced by Troilus, or even by Pandar, to overcome the resistance of Criseyde. On the other hand, he takes the right, as an omniscient author, to tell us, not a cause but an effect:

> But Troilus lay tho no lenger down,
> But up anon upon his stede bay,
> And in the feld he pleyde the leoun;
> Wo was the Grek that with hym mette a-day!
> And in the town his manere tho forth ay
> Soo goodly was, and gat hym so in grace,
> That ecch hym loved that loked on his face.
>
> For he bicom the friendlieste wight,
> The gentilest, and ek the mooste fre,
> The thriftiest and oon the beste knyght
> That in his tyme was or myghte be.
> Dede were his japes and his cruelte,
> His heighe port and his manere estraunge,
> And ecch of tho gan for a vertu chaunge.

If the Lady of the Tower had lived to read this, she might have wavered in her opinion.

IX

The Worshipful Way in Malory

I

Although I do not agree with everything they say, my own conviction is confirmed by the contributors to *Essays on Malory* (Oxford, 1963) and *Malory's Originality* (Baltimore, 1964): in general, Malory's romance is one. Though imperfect in unity, according to our modern expectations of a work of art, it is a true *corpus* of tales, more or less loosely articulated, and correctly described as 'the hoole book of Kyng Arthur and of his noble knyghtes of the Rounde Table' (p. 1260).[1] It now becomes clear that, in this respect, the distinction of Professor Vinaver's great edition was not in definitively dismembering the *Morte Darthur* and displaying its separated limbs as the *Works*, but in stimulating us by his bold scholarship to reconsider what exactly Malory achieved and with what kind and degree of unity: in what way and how much does his romance cohere, and with what significance?

To this revaluation Mr. P. E. Tucker has made a major contribution by his article, 'Chivalry in the *Morte*', in *Essays on Malory*. With a great deal of what he has to say in an essay obviously closely related to mine I agree and I shall refrain from repeating, when that would only be for the sake of completeness, what he has often said so well. I find it difficult, however, in the light of the inconclusive evidence, to accept the contention that any one interpretation of Malory can give 'a satisfying view of the whole work' (p. 64), and, in particular, am not

---

[1] All unqualified page and line references, unless obviously to a work cited in their context, are to *The Works of Sir Thomas Malory*, ed. E. Vinaver (Oxford, 1947). I am very grateful to the editors of *Review of English Studies* and *Studies in Philology* for their kind permission to use in this essay material that first appeared in their periodicals, *viz.* 'Malory's Launcelot and the noble way of the world', *R.E.S.* NS VI (1955) and 'Malory's "vertuouse love"', *S.P.* LIII (1956).

entirely able to accept the interpretation of Mr. Tucker. I understand a passage or two of Malory differently, sense some differences of emphasis, see less obvious consistency, am less content to explain difficulty away by acknowledging Malory to be 'a wayward and even a careless writer' (p. 64), true though this is, and, in the outcome, am not quite so clear as he. I have some sympathies, rather, with Lewis, who, after a consideration of Malory and his work that included something of my theme, admitted that he ended 'in uncertainty' (*Essays on Malory*, p. 19). It seems to me that different interpretations of Malory are possible and my uncertainty is which to choose.

Mr. Tucker says that Malory's 'interpretation of his material developed as he progressed' (p. 72) and that what appears as he progressed is 'that he believes strongly in natural—that is, unsophisticated—love and fidelity' (p. 73). In general, I agree, and it is important for the view I wish to explore to emphasize this, but with the reservation that something of such love is to be found as early as Caxton's first three books: 'the Kynge caste grete love unto hir and desired to ly by her. And so they were agreed' (p. 41 and *cf.* p. 7, ll. 10–18, and p. 77, ll. 17–19), and ' "Hit ys well done," seyde Merlyon, "that ye take a wyff. . . . Now is there ony . . . that ye love more than another? . . . thereas mannes herte is sette he woll be loth to returne" ' (p. 97).

In the tale of Sir Gareth or Bewmaynes, for which no source is known and which it is not impossible to believe Malory created himself, a fairly typical medieval literary love-affair between gentlefolk ends naturally in marriage after appropriate tribulations. But romantic adultery is predominant in Malory's presentation of love, a fact which makes him exceptional among the English writers of romances[1] but points his close relationship to his French sources. That unrewarded, abjectly obedient lover's service, however, that is characteristic of the French romances is not so of Malory. It is true that Palomides says of Isode, 'by her, and bycause of her, I have wonne the worshyp that I have. . . . And yet I had never rewarde nother bounte of her, dayes of my lyff, and yet I have bene her knyght longe gwardonles' (p. 781). But the relationship of Launcelot and Gwenyver is, in this respect, more typical: Launcelot declares that he has been always her 'poure knyght and trew', but, then, she has 'ben ever my speciall good lady' and, time and again, she has rewarded him with her company and her

---

[1] *cf.* G. Mathew, 'Ideals of Knighthood in late-fourteenth century England', in *Studies in Medieval History presented to F. M. Powicke* (Oxford, 1948), pp. 354–62.

bed (p. 1166 and *cf*. p. 253, ll. 15–19). Sir Dinadan would certainly have agreed with Sir Bewmaynes, 'thou to love that lovyth not the is but grete foly' (p. 322, *cf*. pp. 689, 692–3), and his lady, Lyonesse, assures Bewmaynes later, when she shows him 'straungenesse', that neither his 'grete travayle nother your good love shall not be loste, for I consyder your grete laboure and your hardynesse . . . as me ought to do' (p. 327, and *cf*. p. 129, ll. 18–19). It is no sophisticated love, excited, frustrated and refined beyond all reason and reality, which causes Lamerok to say to Launcelot, who has bridled on behalf of Gwenyver (in a passage for which no source can be found) 'every man thynkith hys owne lady fayryste, and thoughe I prayse the lady that I love moste, ye sholde not be wrothe' (p. 487). The sensibility of Malory's lovers—unlike that of many others in the literature of the Middle Ages, who are hypersensitive and passionately extravagant—is, in the main, immediately convincing.

In general—though some of the difficulty of interpretation arises because it is not invariably so—Malory writes about love with candour and an unaffected reverence. If it is predominantly his honest-to-goodness plainness that convinces the modern reader, so also does his spontaneous delicacy, simple and occasional though it may be. It is these facts that must be given their full weight, as they ought to be in an evaluation of any literary work, when we are trying to assess what Malory's romance is saying to us about love and duty; for, whatever may be the eventual fate of his great lovers or whatever overt criticism may be made of them, these facts declare the worth that Malory, the writer, knows there to be in 'love'. There is no reason to believe that he set out from the beginning to embody in his imagined world a well-developed philosophy or code of love, and certainly nothing like what he found in the French romances. But, whatever was his initial purpose in writing, at all, or his reason for treating the great love-stories, in particular, there is now general agreement that his artist's skill grew with practice and his literary achievement became more authoritative—and so, in Caxton's last three books especially, did Malory's implicit affirmation of 'love'.

This claim should not be made, however, without saying also that his ability to make character, dialogue and action convince the reader extends to several very diverse kinds. Malory is able to enter, apparently indifferently, into a Dinadan, who mocks the senselessness of chivalry and love, into the mysterious appearances of the Holy Grail, and into the bloody battles of countless knights—though never into the craven disposition of a King Mark. There is something in him of Keatsian 'negative capability', a capacity doubtless closely related to the suggestion made by Professor Lewis (exaggerating just a little), that 'he has no style of his own, no characteristic manner' (p. 24), but several styles, and these often reflections of his different sources.

By two paragraphs, for which no source is known, Malory makes it clear that, in Caxton's last books, 'the grete angur and unhappy that stynted nat tylle the floure of chyvalry of the worlde was destroyed and slayne . . . was longe uppon two unhappy knyghtis. . . . For thys Sir Aggravayne and Sir Mordred had ever a prevy hate unto the Quene, Dame Gwenyver, and to Sir Launcelot' (p. 1161); and the complaint of Arthur himself is not against the two sinners, though he is at first prepared to prosecute their punishment to the death, but rather against Sir Aggravayne, who forced the whole affair into the open. Had Gawayn permitted it, Arthur would readily have ended the war and been reconciled to Launcelot and Gwenyver (pp. 1184, 1190, 1192, 1194, 1213). So that, although Launcelot and Gwenyver eventually declare that it was their pride and their love that destroyed King Arthur and the Round Table, and although what Launcelot does and why he does it are a chief constituent of the tragic denouement, Malory has diverted blame from the lovers; and he presents them so sympathetically that he would be insensitive and narrow who, brought up in our Western culture, did not feel himself somewhere with Sir Bors on the side of Launcelot:

> 'My lorde, Sir Launcelot,' seyde Sir Bors, 'be myne advyce ye shall take the woo wyth the weall . . . And also I woll counceyle you, my lorde, that my lady, Quene Gwenyver, and she be in ony distres, insomuch as she ys in payne for youre sake, that ye knyghtly rescow here; for, and ye ded ony other wyse, all the worlde wolde speke you shame to the worldis ende. Insomuch as ye were takyn with her, whether ye ded ryght othir wronge, hit ys now youre parte to holde wyth the Quene' (p. 1171).

As we shall see later, those words, 'whether ye ded ryght othir wronge' pick up another and eventually dominant thread in the total meaning of Malory's romance; and we should note that Malory feels it exceptionally necessary to screen the conduct of the two lovers in a passage which significantly alters his sources: 'And whether they were abed other at other maner of disportis, me lyste nat thereof make no mencion, for love that tyme was nat as love ys nowadayes' (p. 1165). But the point that I want to make here is that Launcelot's sinful conduct and its motivation is so presented by Malory that, even when he prays 'Jesu Cryste, be thou my shylde and myne armoure' (p. 1167) in his chivalrous defence of the adulterous Queen, his lady, against her just but treasonous accusers, our sympathy is with him, much as the sympathy of Honoré Bonet and Christine de Pisan, in their works on chivalry,[1] was with knights who defended themselves or accused women by force of arms against charges of adultery, although they disallowed trial by combat in general. Taking Gwenyver in his arms, Launcelot addresses her as 'moste nobelest Crysten quene' (p. 1166), and begs her to pray for him should he die in her defence. Perhaps more provocative is his assuring King Arthur that Gwenyver's accusers must have been liars, for, 'had nat the myght of God bene with me, I myght never have endured with fourtene knyghtes' (p. 1197 and cf. p. 1133): the ultimate implication of this is that God is on the side of the truly chivalrous though they are sinful. It is this kind of thinking that may have led Malory in the most provocative passage of all, for which no source is known, to the conclusion that because Gwenyver 'was a trew lover . . . therefor she had a good ende' (p. 1120). It may be that Malory implies that fidelity in love conduced to Gwenyver's final fidelity to God: loyalty in the one sphere perhaps educated her for loyalty in the other. But whatever he means, this conclusion and the other points we have just been considering make me certain that I cannot go all the way with Mr. Tucker when he maintains that Malory found Launcelot's relationship with Gwenyver an embarrassment and resolved his difficulty by distinguishing between a secular chivalry eschewing extra-marital love of women, which he approved, and one which, involving it, he showed must lead to a tragic end.

Nor need those occasions on which Launcelot rejects love outside marriage be taken as significant instances of Malory's own attitude. When he refuses the offer of the Fair Maid of Astolat to be his paramour, saying, 'Jesu deffende me! . . . for than I rewarded youre fadir and youre brothir full evyll for their grete goodnesse' (p. 1089), he

[1] Bonet, The Tree of Battles, tr. G. W. Coopland (Liverpool, 1949), p. 197. Christine, The Book of Fayttes of Armes and of Chyualrye, tr. W. Caxton, ed. A. T. P. Byles, E.E.T.S., O.S., 189 (1937), p. 265.

appears to condemn, also, his own disloyalty to King Arthur in his affair with his wife. But the two situations are different because, feeling no passion for Elayne, Launcelot has a will clear-sighted and free: but its focus is so altered by his passion for Gwenyver that he is gloriously but blindly led. The contradictory attitudes are consistent in entirely human terms.

The second instance of Launcelot's apparent rejection of love outside marriage is one on which he rejects marriage, too, because then 'I must couche with' my wife 'and leve armys and turnamentis, batellys and adventures' (p. 270). Then he goes on to reject, also, taking his 'pleasaunce with peramours . . . in prencipall for drede of God, for . . . who that usyth peramours shall be unhappy [= shall suffer misfortune], and all thynge unhappy that is aboute them'. If it could be shown that the word *peramours* is never used of Gwenyver in the *Morte Darthur* it might be argued that Launcelot's opinion here is quite consistent with his conduct elsewhere in that he is excluding from his rejection such a lover as the Queen to whom he is as faithful as if he were committed to her in marriage. But what is more likely is that Launcelot is here speaking 'in character' and defending the good name of Gwenyver, mentioned just before as his lady, by denying that he has any appetite for love at all, let alone for any particular person. Stronger arguments are needed against this possibility than Mr. Tucker's undefended assertion that this 'motive attributed to Lancelot is too subtle for this stage of Malory's work' (p. 71). After all, Launcelot has already been shown able to lie in Gwenyver's defence by denying that she is untrue to Arthur under pressure from Morgan le Fay (p. 258); and, as for the idea that marriage weakens a knight, this is scarcely to be regarded simply as Malory's view in that King Arthur, for example, is himself presented as married but far from uxoriously inactive.

II

In the passage in which, according to Caxton, 'trewe love is lykened to sommer', Malory undoubtedly expresses his own view and makes his own distinctions. He distinguishes between love in 'Kynge Arthur's dayes' and 'love nowadayes' (pp. 1119–20). The old-fashioned love he calls 'vertuouse'. Here, in his own unsystematic way, impulsive and not reasoning, often ambiguous and opaque, he elaborates his very simple reconciliation between romantic love and Christianity. For him two facts are given: for him it is from these that one must start. First, that

'there was never worshypfull man nor worshypfull woman but they
loved one bettir than another', and, secondly, that a knight will always
be wanting to gain honour by his fighting: 'worshyp in armys may
never be foyled' [= defiled]. (Thus Sir Percival explains that since he
and his brother are 'comyn of kynges bloode of bothe partis . . .
therefore . . . hit ys oure kynde to haunte armys and noble dedys'
(p. 810).)

From these positions Malory goes on to say that the knight should
first honour God (and I presume he means, specifically, in fighting), and
'secundely thy quarell muste com of thy lady. And such love I calle
vertuouse love.' The knight must serve God first and the lady second:
such love is the proper development of an inevitable relationship
between worshipful men and women 'in the world'. What Malory has
at the back of his mind here is probably something of the traditional
Christian doctrine of the proper love of creatures (cf. the second
quotation from Gavin Douglas on p. 168). What he says is illuminated
by King Arthur's charge to his Knights of the Round Table to 'take
no batayles in a wrongefull quarell for no love ne for no worldis
goodis' (p. 120). How differently it may be thought that Launcelot acts!

And yet, though Malory seems to regard love between the sexes as
acceptable when it is not contrary to the service of God, there is no
mention whatsoever of the sacrament of marriage. Instead, what seems
to be significant to Malory is that such 'vertuouse love' is essentially
stable. It is essentially loyal. It is essentially not promiscuous and not
impetuous. This true love is likened not, as Caxton's edition wrongly
suggests by giving the chapter such a title, to summer, the hot season
opposed to the cold winter, but to May, in which month new life
returns to the world, the same old world, 'and in lyke wyse lovers
callyth to their mynde olde jantylnes and olde servyse, and many
kynde dedes that was forgotyn by neclygence'. And so 'trew love . . .
that coste muche thynge' is restored. The old love, after whatever
winter, is revived. That it should be otherwise would be 'no wysedome
nother no stabylite, but hit ys fyebleness of nature and grete disworshyp,
whosomever usyth thys'. The important word is *stabylite*. Malory
presents the lack of it as an essential in Launcelot's own situation, and
the presence of it as a mark of the superiority of the way of renunciation
over the ways of this unstable world below the moon, about both of
which more later.

Malory is obviously not alone in putting faithfulness above fulfilment of passion. One of the first courtly love writers, Andreas Capellanus, called slavery to passion the behaviour of beasts not men (tr. J. J. Parry, p. 33). Cresseid, in Robert Henryson's 'Testament of Cresseid', laments her incontinence and unfaithfulness to Troilus after her affair with Diomeid has ended in misfortune and the anger of the gods against her blasphemy. She acknowledges her 'instability', saying that,

> Sa elevait I was in wantones,
> And clam upon the fickill quheill sa hie,

that she counted Troilus's loyalty 'small in my prosperitie', whereas of Troilus, whose conduct was the opposite of hers, she says,

> For lufe, of me thou kept gude continence,
> Honest and chaist in conversatioun.
> Of all wemen protectour and defence
> Thou was, in helpit thair opinioun.
> My mynd in fleschelie foull affectioun
> Was Inclynit to Lustis Lecherous:
> Fy fals Cresseid, O trew Knicht Troylus.
>
> (ll. 554 ff.)

And in our own country today, if there is to be love outside marriage, steady faithfulness to one person puts it in an entirely different category from that of gay promiscuity. Though in both cases it may be sinful, the first is, at least in one of mature years, the more respectable.

The contemporary attitude is paralleled by fifteenth-century connivance at the faithful, but, of course, illicit, relationship of a priest to one concubine, whereas common opinion had no respect for priestly promiscuity. Such intemperance met with as little favour in medieval society as, for the most part, in the *Morte Darthur*. There Gwenyver calls it the conduct of a 'comon lechourere' (p. 1047).

That she has been faithful to Launcelot and not a 'comon lechourere' is Elayne's defence when her confessor bids her put aside thoughts of love. She explains her confidence in her innocence by saying, 'I loved never none but hym, nor never shall, of erthely creature', as well as by going on to say, 'and a clene maydyn I am for hym and for all othir' (p. 1093).

In passing, it is to be noted that she then makes her own reconciliation between romantic love and the Christian way by begging God to let her mortifications as an innocent lover in this world relieve the suffering for her sins that would otherwise be hers in purgatory. Since, she says, God now suffers me to die, may he count the pains I suffer—and I presume she means, in love—as part relief for my sins: '. . . have mercy uppon me and my soule, and uppon myne unnumerable paynys that I suffir may be alygeaunce of parte of my synnes'. Similarly, but with aggressive confidence, Gawayn in Caxton's Book XIII, ch. 16, refuses to do penance as his confessor bids, because the ordinary life of a knight adventurer is already painful penance enough.

The point is that, as Malory presents it, Elayne suffered love. Love happened to her, and she could resist it no more than a disease: 'of myselff, Good Lorde, I had no myght to withstonde the fervent love, wherefore I have my deth'. And the final implications of the whole episode are that Launcelot and King Arthur regard her death as one of life's unavoidable tragedies (p. 1097). One is reminded of Chaucer's Troilus and Criseyde, for the complex vision of the human lot, in the poem named after them, which is brought into focus through their destiny, is strongly characterized by unavoidable tragedy, in particular that of romantic love.

Elayne's apologia, itself, in some respects resembles other medieval defences of love rather than Malory's own, which stresses the righteousness of a lover's faithfulness and temperance. It is argued, for example, by one lover in Andreas Capellanus's De Amore Libri Tres that since love is natural it extenuates any sin there is in it: 'God cannot be seriously offended by love, for what is done under the compulsion of nature can be made clean by an easy expiation' (tr. J. J. Parry, p. 111). This lover allows that love can offend God, but only venially. And earlier he argues, with a sophisticated casuistry which distinguishes Andreas the subtle clerk from that plain Malory who was in life probably a country gentleman and soldier, that since a man cannot serve two masters, if it is God you would serve, then you should renounce the world wholly. But if you keep one foot in the world then you should enjoy love thoroughly without any pretence.

Thus Elayne's defence, when her confessor bids her reject her amorous thoughts, takes this course:

Why sholde I leve such thoughtes? Am I nat an erthely woman? And all the whyle the brethe ys in my body I may complayne me, for my belyve ys that I do none offence, thou[gh] I love an erthely man, unto God, for He fourmed me thereto (p. 1093).

Elayne is arguing that if you do not renounce the world as a religious person but remain, like her, an *erthely* person, then to resist love is unnatural and unreasonable. Her attitude is made clearer by a similar remark of Chaucer's Criseyde. Debating with herself whether she should allow love to grow between her and Troilus, she asks,

> Shal I nat love, in cas if that me leste?
> What, pardieux! I am nat religious.
>
> (ii, 758)

I am not, says Criseyde, one who has renounced the world: why should I not love? Another aspect of Elayne's position, to which she now goes on, is further developed by Chaucer elsewhere in the poem when he argues casuistically, 'God loveth, and to love wol nought werne' (iii, 12), for Elayne, whose argument began by saying that love was natural to human beings and therefore pleasing to God, continues: '. . . and all maner of good love comyth of God. And othir than good love loved I never sir Launcelot du Lake.' By this change of course, made without comment, Elayne has shirked the deep waters, for she has not tried to show where lies the distinction between the good love to which she is finally referring, and that love in general with which she began.

But later she confesses one reason why, in the light of other observations in the *Morte Darthur*, we might consider hers was not, in fact, good love. 'I take God to recorde I was never to The grete offenser nother ayenste Thy lawis, but that I loved thys noble knyght, sir Launcelot, oute of mesure.' She admits, I think, that the extravagance of her love does offend God. Moreover, because her death came of love that was incontinent, Launcelot himself feels his conscience clean. He is supported also by the thought that he did not find his heart returning her love, and 'I love nat', says he, 'to be constrayned to love' (p. 1097).

Love 'oute of mesure', or inordinate love, is not Elayne's offence alone. In the chapter we have already considered, called in Caxton's edition, 'How trewe love is lykened to sommer', where Malory praises that love which is not impetuous but has *stabylite* and is utterly *trew* to one person, he deplores the fact that love nowadays is otherwise. Nowadays, he says, 'men can nat love sevennyght but they muste have all their desyres', and

> where they bethe sone accorded and hasty, heete sone keelyth
> . . . Thys is no stabylyte. But the olde love was nat so. For

men and women coude love togydirs seven yerys, and no
lycoures lustis was betwyxte them, and than was love, trouthe
and faythefulnes. And so in lyke wyse was used such love in
kynge Arthurs dayes.

The older order, says Malory, has changed. He is by no means alone
among medieval writers on love in looking back to an ideal past.[1]

Launcelot himself confesses that he has loved Gwenyver 'un-
mesurabely and oute of mesure long'. He is brought to make this
confession by his failure to succeed in quest of the Grail which causes
him to 'se and undirstonde that myne olde synne hyndryth me'. In
taking upon him 'the adventures to seke of holy thynges', he recognizes his sin of intemperance in love, a sin which had not inhibited his
success in secular adventures at all: 'whan I sought worldly adventures
for worldely desyres I ever encheved them'. But his confessor assures
him that he 'shall have the more worship than ever ye had'—and the
implication, though uncertain, is that he will have it in quest of the
Grail—so long as Launcelot will assure him that he will 'no more com
in that quenys felyship *as much as ye may forbere*' (pp. 896–7). This very
liberal condition would appear to be some guide to what is meant by
love that is *oute of mesure*.

Launcelot tries to practise what he had been taught when he returns
to Camelot, for, his confessor having bidden him 'to sew knyghthode
and to do fetys of armys', 'in all such maters of ryght sir Launcelot
applyed hym dayly to do for the plesure of oure Lorde Jesu Cryst', and
to Gwenyver's grief he fights as often for other ladies as for her: 'And
ever *as much as he myght* he withdrew hym fro the company of quene
Gwenyvere for to eschew the sclawndir and noyse.' He points out to
the Queen, when she takes him to task, that he has only recently been
in quest of the Grail, 'and wyte you well, madam, hit may nat be yet
lyghtly forgotyn, the hyghe servyse in whom I dud my dyligente
laboure' (pp. 1045–6). This reminder of a holy intention does something to correct the impression that Launcelot avoided the Queen's
company for the worldly reason that he wanted to avoid scandal, but
it seems unlikely, though difficult to believe, that Malory intended any
sharp distinction to be felt. Here worldly and holy values appear to be
confused.

[1] *cf.* Chrétien de Troyes' *Yvain*, ll. 17 and 5394; Chaucer's *Canterbury Tales*,
F95 and F287.

The idea of *mesure* as the mark of virtuous love is illuminated by parallel observations in Gavin Douglas's Prologue to Book IV of his translation of the *Aeneid*.[1] After saying plainly that there are 'twa luffys, perfyte and imperfyte' of which only one is *leful*, he continues in praise of virtuous love,

> . . . quhar that lufe is rewlyt by messure,
> It may be lyknyt to ane hail mannis estait,
> In temperat warmnes, nowthir to cald nor hait.

Rebuking 'fresch gallandis, in hait desyre byrnyng' and bidding them 'Found ʒow on resson', he defines inordinate love very much in the way Malory does when he says, in Caxton's 'How trewe love is lykened to sommer', 'firste reserve the honoure to God, and secundely thy quarell muste com of thy lady':

> Than is thi lufe inordinat, say I,
> Quhen ony creatur mair than God thou luffis.

It may be the ideal of this stable love, all faithfulness and continence, that inhibits Malory, as we have seen above, when he hesitates to say how Launcelot and Gwenyver were enjoying themselves at the time Sir Aggravayne and his knights discovered them together in the Queen's room (p. 1165). Somewhat like Chaucer, when the tale requires him to say unpleasant things about Criseyde, Malory shelves the responsibility:

> as the Freynshhe booke seyth, the quene and sir Launcelot were togydirs. And whether they were abed other at other maner of disportis, me lyste nat thereof make no mencion, for love that tyme was nat as love ys nowadayes.

This refusal to commit himself is not, of course, altogether honest. It is true that, when describing 'vertuouse love' (p. 1120), he says that, in King Arthur's days, 'men and women coude love togydirs seven yerys, and no lycoures lustis was betwyxte them'. But there are several instances of Malory's lovers *abed* and they can leave little doubt of his conception of the normal relationships of great Arthurian lovers (pp. 394, 434–5, 612, 1131). They are not 'platonic'.

[1] I am much indebted to Professor J. A. W. Bennett, who pointed this out to me and the benefit of whose learning and judgement I had in earlier versions of this essay. I am also very grateful to Mr. B. Nellist, who criticized my final draft.

III

Malory's values, both stated and enacted, evince again and again what Lewis has called 'the civilization of the heart' (*Essays on Malory*, p. 9). But the subject perhaps most dear to Malory's heart is knights in combat. Through battle after tedious battle we dodge the cloven heads and guts of horses while once again he compares two angry soldiers to two wild boars. The virtues of his ideal knights seem scarcely more subtle or elaborate: they are those of a country gentleman and soldier. 'Bretherne, ye ought to be ashamed to falle so of your horsis! What is a knyght but whan he is on horsebacke?' (p. 667 and *cf.* p. 29). This is to go to the very root meaning of *chivalry*. It is to make exactly the same appeal as Caxton in his epilogue to his *Book of the Ordre of Chyvalry* [*E.E.T.S.* O.S. 168 (1926), p. 123]: 'How many knyghtes ben ther now in Englond that haue th' use and th' exercyse of a knyghte?—that is to wete, that he knoweth his hors and his hors hym?' Thus, in the end, when the remaining knights become clerks in emulation of Launcelot, the first detail of their changed way of life occurring to Malory is that, then, 'their horses wente where they wolde, for they toke no regarde of no worldly rychesses' (p. 1255). And as Sir Ector praises the dead Launcelot in a passage of unaffected dignity and winning simplicity, he refers to the typical occasions of his nobility: '. . . And . . . the truest frende to thy lovar that ever bestrade hors' (p. 1259). In much the same way, when 'vertuouse love' is under consideration it is with specific reference to 'quarrels' that arise out of it and to *worshyp in armes* (p. 1119).

Throughout his romance, however, as well as praising his knights' physical strength, skill and courage—their *prouesse*—Malory most often calls them *curtayse, kynde, jantyll* and *trew*. An analysis of his various uses of these words shows, on the whole, that for him there are two prime pairs of virtues and vices, which occur in relations with both ladies and fellow knights: they are, first, loyalty or keeping faith, and its opposite, falseness or betrayal, and, second, courteous service and mercy, and their opposite, treason or murder. Murder is, principally, of course, physical, but it can be spiritual. In a 'gentle man' is to be expected, above all, mercy, for it is not only in Chaucer, Boccaccio and Dante that 'pite renneth sone in gentil herte'. The 'gentle' character is not, then, revealed, despite the emphasis of frequent mention, only by its appetite for horse and armour, battles, hunting and noble deeds, and by its recoil from mere servile labour. It has a moral quality: 'a knyght withoute mercy ys withoute worshyp' (pp. 100, 106–7, 294, 375, 795, 810). Murder and betrayal are to be expected in those who are not Christians or who are of low birth. Although 'nobleness of the hands' and *prouesse* are praised for themselves, they must be virtuously employed, for attention is always drawn to the fact when they are used 'falsely' or 'treasonously' (p. 717). Malory's values are the traditional ideals of the English literature of knighthood, as Fr. Mathew makes clear.[1]

The two relationships that, perhaps most of all, engage Malory are prime examples of the practice of these virtues. They are the relationship of Launcelot and Gwenyver and that of Launcelot and Arthur. The essential element in both cases is loyal service, mercifully performed. Of all Malory's knights, Launcelot is the one who most draws the attention by the frequency of his appearance, the rarely rivalled praises showered upon him, and the attractiveness of his disposition. It is he who, more than all the other knights, follows a way of life which, practising the virtues just discussed, and, therefore, not ignoble like that of King Mark (*cf.*, e.g., p. 680) is none the less not holy like that of Sir Galahad, but is the highest way for any gentleman who did not give himself to perfection as a religious. It was the way of a secular chivalry, which tried to make of this sinful and mutable world as fine and noble a place as could be. Launcelot lived as nobly as can a man who frankly accepts and does not renounce his disposition to sin. Thus Malory repeatedly refers to him as 'the trewest lover *of a synful man* that ever loved woman', or 'the best knyght . . . *of ony synfull man of the worlde*' (pp. 1259, 863, 930, 941, 948). Far on one side of him is Mark, a sinful man of the world, but not a *trew lover* and not a good knight. Far on the other is Galahad, who is not a sinful man at all, but utterly chaste, a pure knight of the Grail.

Launcelot is, as a consequence, unable to achieve Galahad's spiritual success; but, what is more important, his getting as near to it as he does is a kind of vindication, even by these highest standards, of the noble way of worshipful men and women in the world. The first appearance of the Grail in Malory is to Launcelot. It is said that he *sees* it and its bearer. In the second episode (which is more typically indefinite, and only partly filled in) Launcelot, half asleep, half awake, is unable 'to ryse agayne the holy vessell'. But even so he appears to see it, and also the sick knight who is healed by actually kissing it (pp. 793 and 894–5).

[1] *op. cit.*

On the other hand, it is said several times that the prime necessity for the knight in quest of the Grail is *stabilite*, or 'perseverance', in a state of grace, and the sin most likely to impede him, if one can judge by the frequency of reference to it, is concupiscence (pp. 895–9, 946–7, 955–6). That Launcelot should have been given the privilege of seeing the Grail in these two episodes is, then, typically and provocatively inconsistent with what one might have expected in the light of Malory's other comments on the spiritual prerequisites for any stage in the revelation of the Grail mysteries. And it is, of course, Launcelot's lack of perseverance in the way of holiness, his thought inwardly of Gwenyver while he seems outwardly for God (p. 1045), that prevents him from seeing on other occasions than these more than an outer fringe. Even so, he thanks God that he has been allowed to see 'as much as ever saw ony synfull man lyvynge'. Malory makes Launcelot's failure when seen from the highest plane appear, when seen from the lower, a triumph (pp. 801, 1046). A hermit says in praise of Launcelot,

> nere were that he ys nat stable, but by hys thoughte he ys lyckly to turne agayne, he sholde be nexte to enchev[e] hit sauff sir Galahad, hys sonne; but God knowith hys thought and hys unstablenesse. And yett shall he dye ryght an holy man, and no doute he hath no felow of none erthly synfull man lyvyng (p. 948).

Further 'spiritual' vindication of Launcelot and the way he follows is afforded by his healing of Sir Urre (p. 1152). Launcelot's weeping after he has performed the miracle shows how well Malory knows exactly what is proper in a spiritual as well as an amatory crisis, and he presents as one of Launcelot's glories the spiritual virtue that accompanies the 'symple worshyp and honeste' of this best of all secular knights.

A hermit says of Launcelot, 'sith that he wente into the queste of the Sankgreal he slew never man nother nought shall, tylle that he com to Camelot agayne, for he hath takyn [upon] hym to forsake synn' (p. 948). Of course, when he returned to Camelot what he found it impossible to do, even though he tried hard, was to persevere in purity and to avoid the company of Gwenyver; and the sin that Launcelot has forsaken, as he confesses, is that of having loved Gwenyver 'unmesurably and oute of mesure long' (pp. 896–7). That a concupiscent knight will be a 'murderer' is an idea which Launcelot elsewhere expresses, as we have seen, when he says that knights who are *lecherous* will probably 'sle . . .

bettir men than they be hemself. And so who that usyth peramours shall be unhappy, and all thynge unhappy that is aboute them' (pp. 270–1). Malory has, as so often, failed to say things clearly, and it would be foolish to try to read too much into this passage. Mr. B. Nellist has suggested to me that the explanation may be that a knight involved in love-affairs is inevitably involved in battles on his mistresses' behalf and is thus forced into more (and less righteous) slaying than he would be if unattached. But may it not be, rather, that, on this occasion, Launcelot rejects love outside marriage because a knight, alienated from God by sin, especially that of concupiscence, can never properly fulfil his role? Cursed in one thing, he is cursed in all.

That this is what Launcelot means is at least partly supported by the hermit's explanation of his rebuke of Sir Gawayne for having 'used the moste untrewyst lyff that ever I herd knyght lyve'. Referring to the death of seven knights at the hands of Gawayne and his fellows, the hermit, in a context suggesting that the wickedness referred to is that of concupiscence, says

> had ye nat bene so wycked as ye ar, never had the seven brethirne be slayne by you and youre two felowys: for sir Galahad hymself [earlier described as a *mayde* who has *synned never*] alone bete hem all seven the day toforne, but hys lyvyng ys such that he shall sle no man lyghtly.

Although it is not clear whether a Sir Galahad deliberately eschews murder, or whether it happens in the nature of things that such a man never kills, it is implied that a sinful, a concupiscent, knight can be expected to act unbefittingly.[1]

Another of the values of the noble way of the world appears in King Arthur when he is represented as nobly unsuspicious of the relationship between his wife and Launcelot. Arthur shows that freedom from fear of peril which elsewhere (p. 1134) Malory says characterizes men of worship, 'for they wene that every man be as they bene'. Thus, though Malory wastes an artistic opportunity and does not incise it, irony is latent in such a scene as that where Gwenyver gives a banquet to suggest her disregard for Launcelot's absence. He has left the court because of

---

[1] pp. 891–2. The propriety of 'unbefittingly' here is supported slightly by a possible sense of *unhappy*, the word used by Launcelot above. It may perhaps have meaning 5 in O.E.D. '(not) successful in performing what the circumstances require, (not) apt or dexterous'; or meaning 6, '(not) appropriate, (un)befitting'.

her displeasure, but she finds that she now has a desperate need of his presence to defend her honour, so that Arthur in apparent innocence, seeing this need, asks, 'What aylith you that ye can nat kepe sir Launcelot uppon youre syde?' (p. 1051).

Ultimately, however, Arthur's attitude is more than unsuspicious-ness. When he knows of his betrayal, it becomes, rather, tolerance for the sake of peace. It is also tolerance for the sake of his love for Launcelot and Gwenyver (p. 1163). Then, when all is public, it is forgiveness. In contrast, King Mark, of course, always suspects Trystram and Isode and does his utmost to impede their love; and our immediate sympathy is rather with the more noble attitudes of Arthur. But, after all, he was in part deceived, and Malory implies that he was a finer man for not having suspected what was true. One can hardly maintain, simply, as Professor Vinaver does, that Malory's is a 'realist' attitude: whether or not the differences between Malory and his probable French sources point preponderantly to 'realism', his 'unrealistic' presentation of the nobility of the way of secular chivalry as opposed to the shrewd but unlovable way of King Mark must not be forgotten. In this, to be as wise as serpents is not a virtue he expects of his ideal 'man of worship'.

Not that King Arthur himself does not show shrewdness on occasion. Exceptional though it may be, it prompts him to reply to Gawayne's confident comment on Launcelot's ability to prove by his military skill that Gwenyver is no traitor to her husband,

> That I beleve well, but I woll nat that way worke with sir Launcelot, for he trustyth so much uppon hys hondis and hys myght that he doutyth no man. And therefore for my quene he shall nevermore fyght, for she shall have the law (p. 1175).

The King appreciates that the cogency of Launcelot's denial of the Queen's unchastity is entirely the power of his arm. The truth depends on his martial skill—'that woll I make good with my hondis' (pp. 1188 and 1171). Now that the likely truth about the affair of Launcelot and Gwenyver has been forced into the open by the malice of Sir Aggravayne, King Arthur is no longer, it would seem, governed by this value of the chivalric way. A quite different code now applies, that of the law, and Arthur shrewdly insists on what is truthful rather than what is honourable.

IV

That there may be a distinction between truth and honour, worship and goodness, is forced into recognition by the events of the last books, and the consequence is that Launcelot and Gwenyver enter a way which, like that of the Grail, is one of 'perfection', 'penance' and prayer (pp. 1253 and 1255). After Arthur's death, his widow and her lover might otherwise have married—but there is no suggestion of this, unless it is implied by Launcelot's 'yf I had founden you now so dysposed, I had caste me to have had you into myn owne royame'. But she is not so disposed, and though Gwenyver bids him '[go] thou to thy realme, [an]d there take ye a wyff', Launcelot replies, 'I shall never be so false unto you of that I have promysed. But the selff desteny that ye have takyn you to, I woll take me to, for the pleasure of Jesu.' That destiny is the way of 'perfeccion'.

So far as Gwenyver is concerned she follows this changed way of life because it is their love that has caused the death of so many knights, including her own lord. She is therefore in the convent 'to gete my soule hele'. She does not doubt her eventual salvation, 'for as synfull as ever I was, now ar seyntes in hevyn' (p. 1252). Eventually Launcelot, too, has so mortified his corrupt desires that when Gwenyver dies and he looks on her face, 'he wepte not gretelye, but syghed'; and though at her interment he swooned, he replied to the hermit who reproved him for such sorrow-making that his conscience was clear, 'for my sorow was not, nor is not, for ony rejoysyng of synne' (p. 1256).

It was not simply his old love that wrung his heart. What it was we must pick out from a passage of typical difficulty. As we have seen before, Malory's style tends to become opaque whenever any revealing comment promises. 'No', says Launcelot,

> when I remember of hir beaulte and of hir noblesse, that was bothe wyth hyr kyng and wyth hyr, so whan I sawe his corps and hir corps so lye togyders, truly myn herte wold not serve to susteyne my careful body.

Launcelot, I think, is wrung by a concrete example of transience. It is made more poignant because of the lying together in death of those he had offended so: the poignancy is partly from his guilt, partly from a resurgence of his old loyalty to them both, and especially to them as a pair, his lord and lady; but predominantly it is the poignancy of the tears in things. Thus, too, in the palinode to his *Troilus and Criseyde*, Chaucer refers succinctly to the 'false worldes brotelnesse' which has caused Troilus so much pain, and which he can now correctly recognize for what it is from the stability of the heavens. Thus, too, when Launcelot has left Gwenyver in the nunnery and heard from Bedyvere an account of how Arthur and the last knights of the Round Table had passed away, he 'threwe hys armes abrode and sayd, "Alas! Who may truste thys world?"' (p. 1254), and renounced it and became a religious. Galahad had earlier warned Launcelot to 'remembir of this worlde unstable', and Launcelot, banished from England, had already complained that 'fortune ys so varyaunte, and the wheele so mutable, that there ys no constaunte abydynge' (pp. 1035 and 1201).

Launcelot's renunciation is not only of a transient and sinful world, but also of a way of life that tried to make it fine and noble. In the same way, at the end of *Troilus and Criseyde*, Chaucer laments not only the *brotelnesse* of a *false world* but also the final insignificance of its refinements, *worthynesse*, *noblesse*, and all the other glorious virtues of the noble lover. Eventually Launcelot is ordained priest, and then, in this spectacle of 'the nobleste knyght of the world' taking 'such abstynaunce that he waxed ful lene' (p. 1255), the ideal of the knight suffers a dramatic death before that of the clerk. It is not only concupiscence that Launcelot renounces, but the whole orientation of a knight whose life is devoted to 'worldly works'. So that, when his old comrades join him, Malory says that 'there was none of these other knyghtes but they redde in bookes and holpe for to synge masse, and range bellys, and dyd lowly al maner of servyce. And soo their horses wente where they wolde.'

Launcelot has attempted this renunciation before. It was in quest of the Grail, when concupiscence was condemned in its holy light, and when, in his first confession for fourteen years, he saw that

> all my grete dedis of armys that I have done for the moste
> party was for the quenys sake, and for hir sake wolde I do
> batayle *were hit ryght other wronge*. And never dud I batayle
> all only for Goddis sake, but for to wynne worship and to cause
> me the bettir to be beloved, and litill or nought I thanked never
> God of hit (p. 897: *cf*. pp. 1058 and 1166).

He now looks God-ward, to truth and goodness, and away from himself, away from the earthly goddess, Gwenyver, and away from the pursuit of honour.

Launcelot's confession of pride is repeated in his final expression of grief for Gwenyver and Arthur. That grief is also contrition for his fault and pride. These, he says (p. 1256), laid his lord and lady low. His lord and lady were 'kynde', but he was 'unkynd'. This is at least an expression of humility, and a recognition of his own responsibility. It is an expression of his freedom from all blame of others. Presumably his exact meaning is that both Arthur and Gwenyver in their several ways as his superiors, his lord and lady, were generous to him, and so were true to their noble natures, while all that he, their subject, did in return was to act unnaturally and by his noble liaison with the Queen to bring enmity between them, and between them and their people. There, presumably, were his pride and fault.

Gawayne, as he dies (p. 1230), repents that Arthur is suffering because of his refusal to allow the King to accord with Launcelot on account of his blood-feud for his dead brothers. If Gawayne's fault were simply a failure in mercy, it might be possible to interpret his repentance strictly in terms of the chivalrous way, for without mercy a knight was without worship, and the romances have as a common subject a conflict of loyalties. But Gawayne calls his single-minded, heroic, epic loyalty to his brothers, pride. Thus, though Malory by no means develops the point, so that its significance may be doubted, Gawayne, too, it would appear, finally doubts the 'nobility' of the earthly code.

Whereas Launcelot was unsuccessful as a knight of the Grail, and his defeat was due to his instability in a state of grace (for while she was alive and accessible, Gwenyver could not be kept out of his mind), Malory implies at the end that in his final renunciation of the world Launcelot has remained stable and made satisfaction for all his offences: for in a dream at the time of Launcelot's death the Archbishop sees him carried to heaven. And however and to what extent Malory may have seen the long love of Gwenyver and Launcelot as 'vertuouse love', Gwenyver in the end renounces it, and is afraid that to see Launcelot again would destroy that state of grace in which she is determined to die. ' "I beseche Almyghty God that I may never have power to see Syr Launcelot wyth my worldly eyen!" "And thus," said al the ladyes, "was ever hir prayer these two dayes tyl she was dede" ' (pp. 1255–6).

V

Such a renunciation of the world, however, may not be taken to mean that Malory himself now felt valueless all that he had earlier felt and shown to be valuable about the noble way of worshipful men and women in the world. Such a renunciation and such a turning of the eyes to Heaven in one's last days is what any parish priest would have taught as the last stage in the worldly pilgrimage of any layman. But Malory was not (and is not) alone in finding that, whoever it is, whether it is a theologian expounding doctrine or the creator of a romance, the themes and motives with which he has been dealing inevitably issue in paradox and ambiguity. In Malory's case, however, our difficulty in eliciting one clear and satisfactory interpretation is particularly acute; and, again paradoxically, it is just as likely that this was because of his potentiality as a creative artist (only partially developed though this may well have been) as because of his carelessness, or foolishness, or mere country crudity.

X

Order, Grace and Courtesy in Spenser's World

C. S. Lewis taught us to see the close relationship between Books III and IV of *The Faerie Queene*, and indeed to treat them as a single book on the subject of love. It was only one of the illuminations given us in that transcendent piece of interpretation and enrichment, Chapter VII of *The Allegory of Love*. Yet his writing on Book V does not illuminate but darkens, and I have long wondered that he did not draw Books V and VI together. It is the purpose of this essay to explore the connexions between them; between Book V and *A Viewe of the Present State of Ireland*; and between Books V and VI, taken together, and the Cantos of Mutability; and also to explore some other connexions and links—the Blatant Beast, the Hercules image, and the relationship between the Graces, the 'Charites' and Charity.

After Artegall had freed Irena

> His studie was true Justice how to deale,
> And day and night employ'd his busy paine
> How to reforme that ragged commonweale.
>
> (V.12.26)

But he was recalled to Faerie Court before he could reform it thoroughly and on his journey home he was assailed by the Blatant Beast. For the first time in *The Faerie Queene* the Knight's achievement is incomplete. The Red Cross Knight killed the dragon; Sir Guyon overthrew the Bower of Bliss and bound Acrasia; Britomart chained Busirane and saw the destruction of his house; and in Book IV, although there is no central knight or adventure and no culminating contest, Paridell and Blandamour were discomfited, Braggadocchio and False Florimell exposed, Amoret rescued from Lust, Corflambo slain, happiness was achieved by Marinell and Florimell, and a culminating symbol of Concord was shown in the marriage of Thames and Medway. These books seem complete; they all close in the finality of virtue's triumph.

But now in Book V Artegall is 'forst to stay' his course of justice before he can thoroughly reform Irena's disordered land.

It would seem reasonable to associate this ending, with its clear statement that much remains to be done in Irena's land, with the Proem to Book V, in which Spenser writes of the sad contrast between 'the state of present time' and 'the image of the antique world . . .'

> When as mans age was in his freshest prime,
> And the first blossome of faire vertue bare.

He goes on:

> Such oddes I finde twixt those, and these which are,
> As that, through long continuance of his course,
> Me seemes the world is runne quite out of square,
> From the first point of his appointed sourse,
> And being once amisse growes daily wourse and wourse.
>
> (V, Proem 1)

He makes further reference in the Proem to 'present dayes, which are corrupted sore' and to the fact that all things 'are chaunged quight': the spheres have 'wandred much' from their courses, the sun is declined

> Nigh thirtie minutes to the Southerne lake:
> That makes me feare in time he will us quite forsake
>
> (Proem 7)

and the planets have run amiss. The deterioration of the world is further complained of in the account of Astraea in Canto 1, stanzas 5–12. Astraea, Goddess of Justice, while she lived on earth in the days of its perfection, brought up the child Artegall and taught him 'all the discipline of justice', how to

> weigh both right and wrong
> In equall ballance,

and 'all the skill of deeming wrong and right'. But when sin came into the world she returned to heaven. Spenser is clearly thinking, in his characteristic way, of several ideas at once: of Hesiod's view of the degeneration of mankind since the Golden Age; of Plato's idea of cyclical retrogression in the cosmos; of the Elizabethan theory of the degeneration of the world; and of the violence of the last days and the darkening of the sun, when the stars shall fall from heaven before the destruction of the world and the establishment of a new heaven and a new earth.

But principally he is thinking of the world since the Fall, and Irena's land provides the image of this corrupted world. Naturally he drew it from his own experiences in Ireland. To the Protestant Englishman of Elizabeth's day Ireland provided a palpable image of Disorder, indeed of Chaos, because it was a land of Antichrist; because of its troubled and warlike condition and the series of insurrections during Elizabeth's lifetime; and because there was no government and no order beyond the Pale, where the Irish, steadfast only in resisting all attempts to impose English standards of order and government, were as strongly resistant to any attempts to order themselves. The violence and cruelty of Sanglier; the extortions of Pollente and Munera; the discord shown in the quarrelling brothers Amidas and Brasidas; the treachery of Dolon; the guile of Malengin; the wicked oppressions of the Souldan, Geryoneo, and Grantorto—these are the fictional counterparts of Irish reality. In *A Viewe of the Present State of Ireland* Spenser wrote of that

> unrulye people . . . [whom] no lawes no penalties Cane restraine but that they doe in the violence of that furye treade down and trample underfoote all bothe divine and humaine thinges and the lawes themselves they do speciallye rage at and rend in peces as moste repugnaunte to theire libertye and naturall fredome which in theire madnes they affecte;[1]

and of the Irish soldiery that they

> oppress all men they spoile as well the subjecte as the enemye they steale they are Cruell and bloddye full of revenge and delightinge in deadlye execucion licentious swearers and blasphemours Comon ravishers of weomen and murderers of Children.[2]

Although Book V is subtitled 'The Legend of Justice', and although it contains many examples of injustice and of justice being executed, its emphasis is on the horror of disorder, and what it desiderates is not so much justice as that greater condition without which justice is impossible, the existence of God's Order.

It is true that what Artegall does, usually by means of his iron man

[1] *A Viewe.* Variorum ed., *Spenser's Prose works* (Baltimore, 1949), p. 55.
[2] *ibid.*, p. 123.

Talus, is to execute a certain amount of rough justice and to deliver some judgements of Solomon. But the great adversaries encountered by Artegall or by Arthur stand not so much for injustice as for disorder. Injustice is only one of the forms disorder takes. The communistic giant of Canto 2; the unnatural order of the women's realm presided over by Radegund in Cantos 4, 5, and 6; the oppressions of the Souldan and his wife Adicia in Canto 8 and of Grantorto in Cantos 11 and 12, provide the most conspicuous examples. Artegall has to be rescued from Radegund by Britomart, it is true; but he learns his lesson. Spenser immediately goes on to say, at the beginning of Canto 8, that although nothing can so strongly allure man's

> . . . sense, and all his minde possesse
> As beauties lovely baite

(examples are Samson's subjection to Delilah and Antony's to Cleopatra), yet Artegall is not detained from his mission by the beauty of his beloved and staunchly pursues his quest.

Samson and Antony were two potent examples to the Renaissance mind of the penalty of one form of defiance of the natural order, when a man puts himself in the power of a woman. The Souldan seeks 'by traytrous traines' to kill Mercilla, a maiden queen of high renown. Godless, faithless, a tyrant, he is 'provokt and stird up day and night' by his wife Adicia, who counsels him 'to breake all bonds of law, and rules of right'. Arthur fights

> for honour and for right
> Gainst tortious powre and lawlesse regiment.

The 'unnaturalness' of the Souldan is further shown in such details as the chariot drawn by 'cruel steedes' who have been fed

> With flesh of men, whom through fell tyranny
> He slaughtred had, and ere they were half ded,
> Their bodies to his beasts for provender did spred.
>
> (8.28)

After defeating the Souldan, Arthur takes on another enterprise, to free Belge from the murderous oppression of Geryoneo, a tyrant who has killed and eaten twelve of her seventeen sons and sacrificed their blood to his Idol. As if to emphasize still further his unnaturalness, Spenser draws him as having three bodies growing from one waist, and the arms and legs of three to succour him in fight.[1] Geryoneo slain, there yet remains the hideous monster that lurks under the altar: a huge Sphinx-like beast with maiden's head, the body of a dog, lion's claws, dragon's tail and eagle's wings, a further 'unnatural' enemy to be overcome. The final adventure, Artegall's own, is to free Irena from Grantorto, who is of that company whom not

> lawes of men, that common weales containe,
> Nor bonds of nature, that wild beastes restraine,
> Can keep from outrage, and from doing wrong.
>   (12.1)

These great examples of Disorder are overcome, and the way perhaps is open for Artegall to 'reforme that ragged commonweale'. But he is called away before he can 'reforme it thoroughly', and he takes his leave of Irena, 'There left in heavinesse'.

The Irishman in C. S. Lewis came uppermost as he wrote about Book V of *The Faerie Queene*: 'Spenser,' he declares, 'was the instrument of a detestable policy in Ireland, and in his fifth book the wickedness he had shared begins to corrupt his imagination.'[2] His illustration of this is cursory. He mentions Artegall's cruelty, without examples, writes of Talus as 'the rack as well as the axe', and of the 'rough' justice of Artegall—and that is all. Eighteen years later,[3] he wrote of Spenser's prose *Viewe of the present state of Ireland*: 'The morality of his own plan for the reduction of Ireland has been shown to be not so indefensible as quotations might make it appear, but any stronger apologia would be a burden beyond my shoulders.' Rarely have shoulders been so pointedly shrugged in print. In neither place does he connect Book V with *A Viewe*, and few critics have done so at all firmly. Yet Irena's land is Ireland, and in a dozen places the poem reminds one of the prose work, not only in its instances of violence and cruelty, but in the writer's sad acceptance of the truth: that the world is disordered, and therefore true

---

[1] Here, as elsewhere, some of the details—perhaps it is their primary function—also further the historical allegory. Belge's seventeen sons are also the seventeen provinces of the Netherlands of which the five survivors are the five provinces which combined for self-defence in the Union of Utrecht in 1579; and the three bodies probably refer also to Charles V's three areas of dominance—Spain, the Netherlands and the Spanish Empire.

[2] *The Allegory of Love*, p. 349.

[3] *English Literature in the 16th Century* (Oxford, 1954), p. 378.

justice does not reign, evil is at large, and virtue is precarious, always in danger.

It is true that Spenser in *A Viewe* advocated a 'thorough' policy in Ireland, and believed it was necessary. As Irenius, who stands for Spenser himself, says:

> all those evills must firste be Cutt awaie by a stronge hande before anie good Cane be planted, like as the Corrupt braunches and unholsome boughes are firste to be pruned and the foule mosse clensed or scraped awaye before the tree cane bringe forthe anye good fruite . . .[1]

But the end of the policy he advocates, which Lewis ignored, Spenser set down immediately after the passage quoted:

> by the sworde I meante the Royall power of the Prince which oughte to stretche it selfe forthe in her Chiefe strengthe to the redressinge and Cuttinge of all those evills which I before blamed, and not of the people which are evill: for evill people by good ordinaunces and government maye be made good . . .

A Viewe begins with Eudoxus addressing Irenius:

> But if that Countrie of Irelande, whence you latelye come be so goodlie and Comodious a soyle as yee reporte I wonder that no course is taken for the turninge thearof to good uses, and reducinge that salvage nacion to better government and Cyvilitye.[2]

In the discussion on laws that follows, Irenius declares that the laws 'at firste intended for the reformation of Abuses and peaceable Continuance of the Subjecte' are now 'either disannulled or quite prevaricated throughe Change and Alteracion of tymes'.[3] The Common Law of England is not suitable to the Irish, a people altogether stubborn and untamed, and indeed they have ignored it and have always preserved their own law, the Brehon Law. The abuses of Brehon Law, together with Irish customs such as Tanistry, not only make it difficult for order to be maintained in Ireland by the English but encourage the Irish in their natural stubbornness, barbarousness, indiscipline, and

---

[1] Variorum ed., p. 148.
[2] *ibid.*, p. 43.
[3] *ibid.*, p. 46.

quarrelsomeness. Yet Irenius, outspoken though he is in describing the native deficiencies of the Irish nation, looks forward to the 'Temperinge and menaginge of this stubborne nacion of the Irishe to bringe them from theire delight of licentious barbarisme unto the love of goodness and Civilitye'.[1]

Behind the advocacy, in *A Viewe*, of a stern and thorough policy of subjugation lies a hopeful vision of an evil people being made good by good ordinances and government, and so brought to the love of goodness and civility. From the very condemnation of the violent strife and enmities of Irena's land may be deduced Spenser's vision of a world disposed according to God's order, in which true justice—God's not man's—will hold sway. Artegall's charge against the giant in Canto II is that, presuming

> to weigh the world anew,
> And all things to an equall to restore,
> Instead of right me seemes great wrong dost shew,
>
> . . .   .
>
> For at the first they all created were
> In goodly measure, by their Makers might . . .
>
> (34, 35)

and there follows in stanzas 39–43 an eloquent exposition of the theory of degree, which symbolizes the Order God intended for the world. The first stanza of Canto 7 also defines the inseparability of the concepts of Order and true Justice:

> Nought is on earth more sacred or divine,
> That Gods and men doe equally adore,
> Then this same vertue, that doth right define:
> For th' hevens themselves, whence mortal men implore
> Right in their wrongs, are rul'd by righteous lore
> Of highest Jove, who doth true justice deale
> To his inferiour Gods, and evermore
> Therewith containes his heavenly Common-weale.

In the prose work, of course, this Order and this state of virtue cannot be shown to have been achieved. The facts of history defeat the fancies

[1] *op. cit.*, p. 54.

of myth, and Spenser, writing so unmistakably of Ireland, cannot show them achieved in Book V, either. The further implication, which from this point onwards dominates the poem, is that they cannot be wholly achieved in a fallen world. The dream which Britomart has in the Temple of Isis—the episode which forms, in Lewis's valuable definition, the 'allegorical core' of the book—carries this implication. When the priest interprets her dream of the goddess Isis and the crocodile Osyris to mean

> that clemence oft in things amis
> Restraines those sterne behests, and cruel doomes of his,
>
> (V.7.22)

he means that Britomart's clemency will temper Artegall's judgements after their marriage, that justice will be tempered with love. We do not see the foretold marriage of Britomart and Artegall. The time is not yet when God's love will inform the world and God's Order in the world will again be the expression of his loving justice.

Spenser brings in the Blatant Beast in the twelfth canto of Book V, initially no doubt because of the historical reference to Lord Grey (Artegall) to whom he also pays great tribute in *A Viewe*, defending him from the calumnies ('how ever envye liste to batter againste him') which had beset him at the conclusion of his period as Lord Governor in Ireland: 'most untrewlye and malitiouslye do these evill tonges backebite and slaunder the sacred ashes[1] of that most juste and honorable personage';[2] 'and now that he is dead his imortall fame survivethe and florisheth in the mouthes of all the people that even those which did backebite him are Choked with their owne fenim and breake theire galls to heare his soe honorable reporte'.[3] Most of the surviving manuscripts read 'blatter' for the 'batter' of the Ellesmere manuscript used by the editors of the Variorum edition; the Blatant or Blattant Beast does 'backebite and slaunder' and break its gall to hear honourable report. If we think Spenser invented only a childish monster and an insignificant adversary in the Blatant Beast, we should remember that the spirit of envy and detraction is a creature of Evil's and Evil will often do its work by such foul agents. We should acknowledge, too,

---

[1] *A Viewe* was almost certainly written in 1596, although not published until 1633. Lord Grey had died in October 1593.

[2] *ed. cit.,* p. 162.

[3] *ibid.,* p. 64.

that in times of arbitrary rule a poisoned word can be enough to kill a man. Nevertheless, the Beast's role in Book V is small. It has nothing to do with the subject of justice, though it is an active agent of Disorder. However, it is the chief enemy of the hero of Book VI, Sir Calidore, whose mission is to subdue it; and the fact that it links the two books of Sir Artegall and Sir Calidore is significant.

The Blatant Beast is a monster bred of hellish race, begotten, Spenser says, of Cerberus and Chimera (VI.1.8), and of Typhon and Echidna (VI.6.9–10). Any Elizabethan at all well read in the classical authors would recognize him as a monster, monstrously born of monsters, a fiend of hell. Milton had it and its ancestry in mind when he created his appalling picture of Sin and Death in *Paradise Lost*, Book II. Possibly here Milton understood Spenser better than others have done. Commentators, strangely, have not made much of the fact that the Blatant Beast is the son of the watchdog of Hell, Cerberus, and of Chimera, the monstrous daughter of Typhon and Echidna. Nor have they paid much heed to Typhon himself, the son of Tartarus, and Echidna, daughter of the Gorgon Medusa. One hundred tongued (V.12.41) or one thousand tongued (VI.1.9), grandchild or greatgrandchild of the Gorgon, nephew of Geryon and so related to Spenser's monster Geryoneo, defeated by Arthur in Book V, Canto 10—one can hardly be satisfied that this creature merely represents Slander or Backbiting, or the spirit of Unfriendliness, glossed to include Malice, Malevolence, Envy and Contentiousness,[1] or even Shame.[2] I think Spenser is dealing in bigger concepts here, and the Spirit of Slander accompanying Envy and Detraction in Book V, Canto 12, becomes increasingly in Book VI the Spirit of Evil. Perhaps the hermit most helps us to see that the Blatant Beast represents not only evil calumny which can do infinite harm to individuals (in Canto 6 his bite has festered and begun to putrefy the flesh of Timias and Serena), but general Evil in the world of men. The Hermit sees that Timias and Serena need to be disciplined

> With holesome reede of sad sobriety,
> To rule the stubborne rage of passion blinde:
> Give salves to every sore, but counsell to the minde.
>
> (VI.5)

[1] W. F. DeMoss, 'Spenser's Twelve Moral Virtues "according to Aristotle"', *Modern Philology* XVI (1918), 23–38.
[2] W. Nelson, *The Poetry of Edmund Spenser* (Columbia, 1963), p. 289.

He tells them plainly:

> . . . in your selfe your onely helpe doth lie,
> To heale your selves, and must proceed alone
> From your owne will, to cure your maladie.
>
>   . . .   .
>
> First learne your outward sences to refraine
> From things, that stirre up fraile affection;
> Your eies, your eares, your tongue, your talk restraine
> From that they most affect, and in due termes containe.
>
> ---
>
> For from those outward sences ill affected,
> The seade of all this evill first doth spring,
> Which at the first before it had infected,
> Mote easie be supprest with little thing:
> But being growen strong, it forth doth bring
> Sorrow, and anguish, and impatient paine
> In th' inner parts, and lastly scattering
> Contagious poyson close through every vaine,
> It never rests, till it have wrought his finall bane.
>
> (VI.7–8)

The Blatant Beast is not, then, some grotesque externalization, a yelling monster to be briskly overcome by the sword of a virtuous knight. It is much more persistent, insidious, and elusive than that. Spenser invented it at the end of Book V because he wanted to conclude the historical allegory accurately, and slander and detraction had greeted Lord Grey on his return from Ireland; because, too, he wanted to show that Order had not yet been restored to the earth, despite Arthur's and Artegall's victories. In Book VI it certainly still damages reputations and fosters lying and detraction, but it is not something which directs its attention only where it has seen fruitful soil: it exists, and can grow, in anyone, whether the gentle Timias or the virtuous Serena, through the senses. Evil can be overcome if swift action is taken at the beginning of the infection, but if the initial attack is ignored or neglected it will quickly overcome the whole body. It can be something external which attacks virtuous and unvirtuous alike; but it is also something which can mine within the soul of the virtuous as the unvirtuous. In Book VI the Beast retains its superficial function of back-biting and slander, but it comes increasingly to represent Evil-at-large.

As Spenser shows at the end of the poem, it is still at large in the world. It is true that Spenser's final words in Book VI revert to the superficial aspect of Evil expressed in calumny and detraction, and specifically refer to some example, not positively identified, in his own career. But that in Book VI Evil is the antagonist, whatever form or forms it takes—whether as slander, contempt, detraction, the cankering evil which can destroy a man or the restless destructive spirit of disorder—is indisputable. We should remember the ancestry of the Blatant Beast, a monster bred of hellish race.

If Book V, as I have suggested, presents the world as a place of Disorder, one in which true justice, if it existed, would epitomize and comprise God's Order, Book VI presents the world as a place in which, because God's Order has been broken and not yet restored, true Virtue cannot reign. If at the end of Book V the Blatant Beast appeared, a final symbol of evil in the world, at once the cause and the result of disorder, its reappearance in Book VI, its role as chief quarry of the hero Sir Calidore, and the fact that it breaks out into the world again at the end of that book, all assert the continuing existence of evil and disorder in the world, and so its continuing imperfection.

The linking of Books V and VI by the Blatant Beast and by the obvious connexion between Order and Virtue (or, as we have it in these two books, between Disorder and Evil) goes deeper. The Blatant Beast is a sort of Cerberus, Hell-born. In classical mythology Cerberus was captured and bound by Hercules and then returned by him to Hell. Neither Artegall nor Calidore finally overcomes the Blatant Beast, but the figure of Hercules looms behind the heroes of Books V and VI and forms another link between the two books. Hercules was a ready symbol of Right and Justice to the Renaissance imagination. Spenser recalled that he

> . . . all the West with equall conquest wonne,
> And monstrous tyrants with his club subdewed;
> The Club of Justice dread, with kingly powre endewed.
> (V.1.2)

He declares that Artegall is the peer of Bacchus and Hercules, the civilizers and law-givers of the East and West (V.1.2). His enslavement by Radegund (Cantos 4–7) resembles that of Hercules by Omphale, cited by Spenser, but mistakenly with reference to Iole (V.5.24). The conquest of the Souldan by Arthur resembles Hercules's slaying of the tyrant Diomedes, who, like his Spenserian descendant, feeds his horses on human flesh. Arthur's victory over Geryoneo is like that of Hercules over Geryon, said by Spenser to be the father of Geryoneo (V.10.9). The rapid changes of shape of Malengin, ultimately killed by Artegall's lieutenant Talus, recall those of Achelous, slain by Hercules. Indeed, Spenser's picture of the cruel disordered world through which Artegall and Arthur have to force their way is often reminiscent of the nightmare world through which Hercules struggled to perform his great Labours. The Elizabethan reader would also know Hercules as a symbol of virtue, shown in the story of the Choice of Hercules, or Hercules at the fork in the Road, where, pondering which road to take, he is confronted by two goddesses representing Pleasure and Virtue, a subject extremely popular both in literature and in pictorial art.[1]

Hercules figures much less prominently in the background of Book VI, indeed only in the last canto in which Calidore muzzles the Cerberus-like Blatant Beast. But he is assuredly there, and Calidore-Hercules is a kind of protraction of Artegall-Hercules. His quest is Hercules's Labour to overcome Cerberus. Hercules striving with and vanquishing Cerberus represents the overcoming of death; Hercules, as it were, performs a pagan harrowing of hell. If Calidore had for ever vanquished the offspring of Cerberus, the Blatant Beast, he would have conquered evil in the world. But Calidore failed to overcome it finally. In mythology a hero can overcome death; in Spenser's mythology, which by this stage in the poem's development is not a free mythology but one tied to the facts of the world he knows, failure must attend the hero's efforts, however virtuous and valiant, in a fallen world. This failure is not the only one. Calidore 'fails' when he steps forward from the covert of the wood, to get a closer glimpse of the Graces dancing on Mount Acidale. A third instance of setback to virtue in Book VI is the destruction of Meliboe's pastoral paradise by lawless invaders. Taken together, and adding the incompleteness of Artegall's success in Book V, they strongly counterpoise the earlier books of *The Faerie Queene*, which end in complete and final victory for virtue.

The pastoral world, of course, has always had for poets special attributes of virtue and innocence. In *The Shepheardes Calender* and *Colin Clout's Come Home Again* it stands for virtuous simplicity, simple piety, devotion to duty, innocence as opposed to sophistication,

[1] See Hallet Smith, *Elizabethan Poetry* (Harvard, 1952), pp. 292–301, 337–8; and W. Nelson, *op. cit.*, p. 257.

honesty as opposed to deceit, Virtue as opposed to Evil. In many places in *The Faerie Queene* the simplicity of natural life is contrasted with the corruption of courts and palaces, and with dens, bowers and castles where evil or corruption of various kinds is practised. Simple persons, like Sir Satyrane or Timias, noble wild beasts like the lion in Book I, and the savage men who yet protect Una, are contrasted with sophisticates like Paridell, or with unnatural creatures like the monsters representing Lust in Books III and IV and the giants of Book V. Always the simple, virtuous and natural are celebrated; but always their vulnerability is shown. Spenser carries the idea farthest in Book VI, presenting a whole pastoral world in Canto 9 and showing it invaded and despoiled in Canto 10. There can be no mistaking the delight with which Spenser always describes virtuous people and virtuous places. In Canto 9, as elsewhere in his work, the poetry moves with jubilant poise and certainty as he describes the happy state of the pastoral world. It is a place of ordered, peaceful, fruitful, creative activity. It is not often in romantic epics, or indeed in fiction of any kind, that we see people working. Here we are clearly shown the pleasant pattern of constructive work, and we hear Meliboe extolling its virtue and its charm—which he is well qualified to do, for he knows from long experience in his youth the idle hopes, the 'wrackfull yre', the disillusionment that attend the courtier's life, and the serene contentment of the 'lowly quiet life' he now leads. Because it is a place of virtuous employment, Calidore's sojourn in the shepherd world is not mere truancy. It would be convenient if I could claim that the Hercules motif in Books V and VI is also employed here—as, that Calidore is faced with a 'Hercules's choice' when he comes 'yet sweating' from his arduous and so far unsuccessful pursuit of the Blatant Beast to the shepherd world in Canto 9; that the shepherd world is the world of pleasure; and that Calidore is un-Hercules-like in even temporarily abandoning the quest of duty. A temporary errancy from his physical quest it undeniably is; but that period of his journeying which leads him to an ideal world and which gives him a glimpse of order and perfection can hardly be called a truancy. It is not entirely unequivalent to the Red Cross Knight's sojourn and instruction at the House of Holinesse, or Sir Guyon's visit to the House of Temperance.

But contrasted with the shepherds and their ideal society are the Brigants who invade and destroy the happy pastoral world. This 'lawlesse people'

> . . . never usde to live by plough nor spade,
> But fed on spoile and booty, which they made
> Vpon their neighbours. . . .

They broke in upon the pastoral dream

> And spoyld their houses, and them selves did murder;
> And drove away their flocks, with other much disorder.
>
> (VI.10.39)

The Brigants might well have appeared in Book V, so palpably do they stand for evil and disorder. Their dwelling is a kind of hell, deep underground (VI.10.42), and they are like damned fiends (VI.10.43), or like fiendish dogs that fight each other fiercely over their prey (VI.11.17) down in the filthy darkness of their Cerberean den.

It is Spenser's most powerful picture of the vulnerability of virtue in the fallen world, of which there are countless examples throughout *The Faerie Queene* and in the minor poems, too, especially in *The Ruines of Time, The Teares of the Muses, Muiopotmos, Daphnaida*, and the Vision poems. It is arguable that this is his favourite theme, and that his early frequentation of the world of the emblem-books and of the poetic of complaint and vision developed his taste for melancholy and nostalgic moralizing, and deepened his sense of the transitoriness of the world and the vulnerability of virtue and of its outward manifestation, beauty. *The Faerie Queene* becomes, whatever it was originally intended to be, a poem concerned with the imperfection, indeed the imperfectability, of the world. It is not, ultimately, an escapist celebration of the universal triumph of virtue.

If the pastoral world in Book VI provides an example of virtuous ordered life, the scene of the Graces dancing on the hill within the confines of that world concentrates and clarifies the symbol. There is no enormity in the fact that the Graces dance, surrounded by the hundred naked maidens and encircling a fourth Grace, on whom they lavish flowers and 'fragrant odours', to the piping of Colin Clout; for he is, here as always, the poet Edmund Spenser himself. This, indeed, has led critics to an interpretation of the meaning of Book VI based on Colin Clout's relation to the Graces, not Sir Calidore's.

It is strange that very few commentators have asked why the vision on Mount Acidale vanished when Sir Calidore stepped forward from the covert of the wood in order to see it more closely. Lewis says,

obscurely enough, that the important thing about the Graces is that
they vanish if disturbed; their meaning, he continues, 'in their relation
to Colin Clout, is perfectly clear: they are "inspiration", the fugitive
thing that enables a man to write one day and leaves him dry as a stone
the next, the mysterious source of beauty'.[1] This may be true in relation
to Colin Clout; but why should the Graces vanish from Calidore?
While Colin played his pipes alone they conducted their gracious
ordered dance,

> An hundred naked maidens lilly white,
> All raunged in a ring, and dauncing in delight,
>
> (VI.10.11)

in their midst the three Graces dancing round 'Another Damzell' and
casting sweet flowers and fragrant odours upon her. They vanished
only when Calidore rose out of the wood 'and toward them did go',
when

> soone as he appeared to their vew,
> They vanisht all away out of his sight,
> And cleane were gone, which way he never knew;
> All save the shepheard, who for fell despight
> Of that displeasure, broke his bag-pipe quight,
> And made great mone for that unhappy turne.
>
> (VI.10.18)

The idea that in Book VI Spenser is really paying a great tribute to
poetry itself—that, as Kathleen Williams claimed, 'the ordering power
of the book of Courtesie . . . is really the ordering power of the poet,
creator of the small universe of the poem'[2]—is an extension of Lewis's
interpretation of the Graces as standing, in relation to Colin Clout, for
poetic inspiration. It is true that poetry itself has a role in Book VI
which it does not have elsewhere in *The Faerie Queene*. It is true that
Spenser begins Book VI by calling on the Muses, the 'sacred imps, that
on Parnasso dwell', to guide his footing and conduct him well

> In these strange waies, where never foote did use,
> Ne none can find, but who was taught them by the Muse;

---

[1] *The Allegory of Love*, p. 351.
[2] 'Courtesy and Pastoral in *The Faerie Queene*, Book VI', *Review of English
Studies*, NS XIII (1962), 343.

and that, apart from the apostrophe to the Muses with which the whole poem opens, there is no other invoking of them anywhere. It is true that Colin Clout appears in Book VI and nowhere else, and that he represents the poet himself. It is true that the whole pastoral episode can reasonably be interpreted, as pastoral always could be interpreted, as standing for the ordered world of poetry in a world otherwise disordered and often hostile and dangerous. And it is true that to the Elizabethans poetry was a great civilizing influence upon men. William Webbe in his *Discourse of English Poetrie* said that 'the best wryters agree that it was *Orpheus* who by the sweete gyft of his heavenly poetry withdrew men from raungyng uncertainly and wandring brutishly about, and made them gather together and keepe company, make houses and keep fellowshippe together.'[1] Puttenham, in *The Arte of English Poesie*, told how Orpheus 'by his discreete and wholsome lesons vttered in harmonie and with melodious instruments . . . brought the rude and savage people to a more civill and orderly life'.[2] More significant for our study of Book VI is the preface of T. Wilson's *Arte of Rhetorique*, entitled 'Eloquence first given by God, after loste by man and last repayred by God agayne', in which he describes the Fall, as a result of which 'mans reason and entendement were both overwhelmed', and continues:

> Long it was ere that man knewe himself, beinge destitute of Gods grace, so that all thinges waxed savage, the earth untilled, societye neglected, Goddes wille not knownen, man agaynste manne, one agaynst another and all agaynste order. Some lived by spoyle, some like brute beastes grased upon the ground, some wente naked, some romed like woodoses, none did anye thing by reason . . . For vertue, vyce bare place, for right and equitie might used authoritie . . . when man was thus paste all hope of amendemente, God still tendering his owne workemanship, stirred up his faythfull and elect to persuade with reason, all men to societye . . . after a certaine space thei became through nurture and good advisement, of wilde sober: of cruel, gentle: of foles, wise: and of beastes man. Suche force hath the tongue and such is the power of eloquence and reason that most men are forced even to yelde in that which

[1] *Elizabethan Critical Essays*, ed. G. G. Smith (Oxford, 1937), I. 234.
[2] *ibid.*, II.6.

most standeth againste their will. And therefore the poetes do
feyne that Hercules being a man of great wisdome had all men
lincked together by the eares in a chaine to drawe them and
leade them even as he lusted. For his witte was so great, his
tongue so eloquente and his experience suche that no one
man was able to withstand his reason.[1]

I quote this at length because it repeatedly reminds us of the world
of *The Faerie Queene*, and especially of Books V and VI. Spenser must
surely have known *The Arte of Rhetorique*, and it is difficult not to
believe that this passage from its preface particularly appealed to him
and influenced him.

But just as in Book V the poet's concern is ultimately with something
much larger than Justice (the ostensible subject of the book) namely
God's Order, so in Book VI it is with something much more than the
civilizing power of poetry, or the nature of poetic inspiration, or
indeed courtesy in the ordinary sense. The episode of the Graces
dancing on the Acidalian hill is the symbolic core of the book, providing
the key to the poet's central preoccupation. It also provides another link,
a thematic one, with Book V; for the dance of the Graces is an example
of ordered activity and so a symbol of virtuous order. That it is
transitory and vanishes from sight is all-important, and makes the
connexion between the themes of Book V and Book VI clear. What
the Graces symbolize is not actually attainable in the fallen world, any
more than the pastoral ideal is practically valid in the fallen world of
disorder. If Calidore's sojourn in the pastoral world has affinities with
the Red Cross Knight's at the House of Holiness and Sir Guyon's at the
House of Temperance, it has also an affinity with Britomart's brief
stay at the Temple of Isis, and the vanishing of the Graces with Britomart's evaporating dream. For whatever bliss or contentment is
glimpsed is shown also to be not yet within the knight's grasp. Britomart's marriage with Artegall will happen, but not yet, not, in fact,
within the bounds of *The Faerie Queene*. Order will not yet be re-
established, nor Justice and Love yet embrace for ever in an ordered
world. The ideal virtue of the pastoral world does not, in fact, exist: if
it did, it would be swept away as it was in Book VI. And the Graces
are not at any time, much less all the time, to be seen dancing on the

---

[1] T. Wilson, *The Arte of Rhetorique* (1553), sig. A3–A3v. I am indebted for
this reference to Mr. J. A. Kissell.

Acidalian mount; nor are they to be seen by everyone; nor, once seen, can they be counted on not to disappear. The time is not yet, in Book VI as in Book V, for the settled achievement of perfection and the universal triumph of virtue.

If this is so, then either Book VI is not chiefly about 'courtesy' at all, or it is about Courtesy in a much deeper sense than has been assumed. Of course, many of the characters and incidents epitomize or display courtesy and courteous behaviour, and to that extent the book is a Book of Courtesy as Book V is a Book of Justice. Spenser shows many of the other virtues that he has displayed in the knights and ladies of earlier books as contained in his ideal of courtesy. Sir Calidore loathes 'leasing, and base flattery' and loves 'simple truth and stedfast honesty' (VI.1.3). He is temperate and self-controlled; he can 'his wrath full wisely guyde' and does 'him selfe from fraile impatience refraine' (VI.1.30). When he spares Crudor's life, the poet, commending him, writes

> For nothing is more blamefull to a knight,
> That court'sie doth as well as armes professe,
> How ever strong and fortunate in fight,
> Then the reproch of pride and cruelnesse.
> In vaine he seeketh others to suppresse,
> Who hath not learnd him selfe first to subdew.
>
> . . .   .
>
> Who will not mercie vnto others shew,
> How can he mercy euer hope to have?
>
> (VI.1.41 and 42)

So Calidore is brave, self-controlled, just, merciful, not blemished with pride or cruelty. He is also kind (3.15), compassionate (2.41), considerate (3.21), and delights in 'doing gentle deedes' (7.1). Through him Spenser shows that courteous conduct can influence the behaviour of others and bring them great happiness, in the conversion of sad Briana in 1.45 and 46. Spenser shows that he shares with his master Chaucer the view that 'pitee renneth soone in gentil herte', in Calidore's sympathy with the wounded Aladine (2.41). In short, Calidore is a paragon, almost the apotheosis, of the virtues Spenser has displayed in earlier books. It is not surprising that Prince Arthur's function in Book VI is less significant than in any of the other books of *The Faerie Queene*, for his virtues and his nature repose already in Calidore. Arthur's role in this book is not to rescue the knight-hero from some appalling peril, but to rescue his own squire from Defetto, Decetto, and Despetto in Canto 5; to destroy Turpine, the oppressor of Sir Calepine and many another, in Cantos 6 and 7; and again to rescue Timias, from the giant Disdaine, in Canto 8. Indeed, Prince Arthur and Sir Calidore do not meet. Is it because, in fact, Calidore is his equivalent, 'The image of a brave knight, perfected in the twelve private morall vertues'? Does not Calidore seem to be 'the perfection of all the rest' as, Spenser wrote in the Prefatory Letter, Arthur was intended to be? In Book VI, the knight who, although reasonably virtuous, is a prey to many a temptation and many a peril is not Sir Calidore but Sir Calepine. (Spenser confuses the two in 6.17, when he shows Prince Arthur pursuing Turpine, who 'wrought to Sir *Calidore* so foule despight'.) That Sir Calepine bears the brunt of infamy, evil, slander, oppression—an unparalleled deviation from the normal pattern of the books of *The Faerie Queene*—leaves Calidore free to appear as a paragon of virtue.

For he is more than a paragon of merely human courtesy. Perhaps Spenser had read *The Young Children's Book*. If so, he might well have felt disposed to include himself among the clerks that know the seven sciences and say

> þat curtasy came fro heven
> When gabryell owre lady grette,
> And elyzabeth with here mette.
> All vertus be closyde in curtasy,
> And alle vyces in vilony.[1]

The Courtesy of Book VI, reflected in courteous and gentle behaviour, is a gift of God's from Heaven. Sir Calidore is given a glimpse of perfection in the dance of the Graces, as the Red Cross Knight is given his view of the new Jerusalem, Sir Guyon his meeting with Alma and his sojourn in her comely court, Sir Scudamour his visit to the Temple of Venus, and Britomart her apparently disquieting but actually auspicious dream in the Temple of Isis. It is through no fault or inadequacy in him that the vision vanishes when he steps forward to get a nearer view of the dance; it is the imperfection of the world that frustrates. That the Graces represent an ideal of civil and courteous behaviour, of generosity and loving kindness, goes without saying; but they represent much more. Spenser has taken the classical Graces,

[1] *E.E.T.S.*, 32 (1868), p. 17, ll. 6–10.

with all their beauty and their generosity to men, and has invested them with something of Christian Grace. Indeed, the maid in their midst who 'Seem'd all the rest in beauty to excell', on whom they bestow special gifts and favours, who, says Spenser, is a sort of fourth Grace, having

> Divine resemblaunce, beauty soveraine rare,
> Firme Chastity, that spight ne blemish dare;
> All which she with such courtesie doth grace,
> That all her peres cannot with her compare
>
> (VI.10.27)

—she may be thought of as symbolizing Grace itself. Of course, the issue is not simple. Spenser has complicated it, seemingly, by making the central figure 'but a countrey lasse' and the beloved of Colin Clout. But one of the messages of Book VI, indeed of *The Faerie Queene* at large, is that virtue does not only live in courts; it may grow on lowly stalk, and may, in fact, most readily be found among simple people and wild animals, and in the pastoral world. We know that Spenser will always multiply significances and is always extending the area and the application of his symbols. It is perfectly in keeping with his practice that the maiden in the middle of the Graces should be at once a country lass; his own beloved; a fourth Grace; the poet's inspiration (as Lewis claimed); and Virtue itself. She it is 'to whom that shepheard pypt alone' (VI.10.15). In the romantic narrative it is she alone to whom the shepherd (poet) Colin Clout piped. To transliterate: she it is who was Spenser's only inspiration and the only subject of his poetry—Virtue itself, his constant theme and poetic vocation. It is again perfectly consistent and credible that Spenser should present virtue as something which may be glimpsed but not attained in this world, and should show its vulnerability in the scenes of the destruction of the pastoral world.

It will be objected that the obvious concern of Book VI is with courtesy and courteous behaviour, and that it is a long step from courtesy to Grace. Lewis claimed that courtesy is 'the poetry of conduct, an "unbought grace of life" which makes its possessor immediately lovable to all who meet him, and which is the bloom . . . on the virtues of charity and humility'; and he wrote of the spiritual aspect of courtesy, 'its affinity with the sterner or more awful forms of the good'.[1] To be sure, Spenser recognizes courteous behaviour as the poetry of conduct,

[1] *The Allegory of Love*, p. 352.

and analyses courteous conduct in great detail. In his work, virtue is always seen as active and the actions of the virtuous man will naturally exemplify courtesy as well as virtue. But by the time Spenser wrote, the word 'courtesy' had long carried a profound spiritual sense as well. The *Pearl* poet called our lady 'Quene of cortasye' (456–7), and the writer of *The Young Children's Book* found that courtesy came from heaven when God's messenger Gabriel greeted the Virgin Mary. Chaucer quite naturally calls the son of God 'the curteis Lord Jhesu Crist' (*Parson's Tale*, 245); and the courtesy of God or of Christ is a commonplace in medieval literature—to be found in the *Ayenbite* (97/36); Langland (*Piers Plowman*, B. xii, 79); the Sermons of Wyclif (1.378: Crist, of his curtasie interpretiþ þer wordis to goode); Mirk's *Festiall* (80/8: Saynt Brandon . . . saw þys Judas syttyng on a stone yn þe see . . . 'I am Iudas, Godis traytour, þat have þis place of Godys curtesy for refreschyng of þe gret hete þat I suffred wythyn'); and the *Castel of Love* (3.125: God all-myȝht dyde hym þat grete curtasy, Of paradys gave hym þe mastery.) In all these examples, it is the special loving generosity of God or our Lord which is meant, and it is the generous love of God's grace to man which Spenser celebrates as the central Virtue of Book VI. In classical literature the Graces are the generous and giving ones, who 'to men all gifts of grace do graunt' (VI.10.15). In Spenser we see them giving their gifts especially to the maiden they dance around. She is something more than they are, their apotheosis. She symbolizes the Courtesie celebrated in this final book.

There is in the fourth grace more than a suggestion of the Christian *agape*. Christ's ethical claims upon men present demands ever beyond their reach, to be met only through the grace of God. But Christ was more than a teacher. He was also a pattern of love and generosity; and God gives love to man, requiring it of man again in an endless cycle of giving and receiving. This is what the Graces signify,[1] and their Greek name is Charites. The New Testament translates *agape*, 'charity'. As the Collect for Quinquagesima reads, charity is 'the bond of all virtues', that by which every virtue is made valid, the root and the soil out of which all spiritual fruits grow. *Agape*, charity, is a social concept. Virtue can have little meaning in isolation, but only in association or relationship between man and man. The most important of social virtues is the loving, selfless generosity that, as it came first from

[1] See Edgar Wind, *Pagan Mysteries in the Renaissance* (London, 1958), Ch. II and III.

God, binds man to man and man to God. St. Paul knew it for the greatest of virtues. Charity, love, generosity, grace, the medieval *courtesie*, virtue itself: the scene of the Graces implies all of these. Although the play of words, Graces, Grace, Charites, Charity, was not certainly in Spenser's mind, it is legitimate and I hope illuminating to indulge in it here.

The connexions would be obvious to an Elizabethan reader, and so, I think, would the connexions between Books V and VI. Order, the Order of God, was shown not to have been successfully restored in Book V, and so Justice cannot properly exist in the world. This same Order in Book VI, shown in the ways of the pastoral world and in the ordered dance of the Graces, is still not assured, and so true Courtesie, the grace and love of God, Virtue itself, does not reign on earth. This is not to say that it does not or cannot exist in individuals. Calidore is a living refutation of this, and there are many others elsewhere in *The Faerie Queene*. Book VI asserts the need, in a fallen world, for the utmost exercise and extension of it.

Any schematizing of the poem is bound to falsify. I do not suppose that Spenser would recognize what I have written as an accurate account of his deliberate intentions. Any poet or creative writer will acknowledge interpretations which he did not mean, much less fully comprehend, as he wrote his narrative or made his rhymes. Besides, in a poem written over a period of at least sixteen years, written piecemeal in the intervals Spenser could wrest from an active life as a public servant in occupied territory, and while he grew from the age of about 28 to about 44, changes, developments, subtleties, variations were certain to suggest themselves that he had not time fully or efficiently to incorporate into the continually growing fabric of his work. Constancy can hardly be demanded in a work constantly under the influence of mutability. I call the wise sanity of C. S. Lewis to my aid:

> Spenser expected his readers to find in it not his philosophy but their own experience—everyone's experience—loosened from its particular contexts by the universalizing power of allegory. It is, no doubt, true that Spenser was far from being an exact thinker or a precise scholar in any department of human knowledge. Whatever he had tried to write would have had a certain vagueness about it. But most poetry is vague about something. In Milton the theology is clear, the images vague . . . What is clear in Spenser is the image . . .[1]

[1] *English Literature in the 16th Century*, p. 387.

To me the clearest images in Books V and VI are the gigantic image of Disorder drawn in Book V, and in Book VI the fleeting images of virtue and happiness in the pastoral world and the vision on Mount Acidale. The victories of Arthur, Artegall and Calidore are not so clear. But almost as clear again is the image with which both books conclude—that of the Blatant Beast, hell-born, monstrous, the restless tormenting figure of Evil-at-large, still abroad in the world.

I add a postscript, because Spenser added one to the six books of his poem. I cannot agree with Lewis that in the Mutability Cantos we have 'the core of a book without the fringe', the core of an unwritten book of Constancy. There is something at once too cosmic, too complete and too final about the cantos. And what knights or ladies and what adversaries and encounters could fringe them in? What they present is too protracted for a vision, too varied for a masque, too detailed and substantial for a dream—a happening more immense than any in the poem. With the other 'cores', the reader feels that he, like the knights or ladies concerned, has seen something which might well continue indefinitely, or could start up again, or which goes on even when there is no character from the 'fringe' to see it. With the Mutability Cantos the reader feels that something has been brought to a climax and then to a conclusion; after that conclusion nothing more will happen, or needs to happen as it used to. For what the Cantos foreshadow is really the final victory of God and the second coming of Christ, when all shall be changed and made anew.

In the Mutability Cantos, Spenser gives the answer to those who might complain that he has shown in Books V and VI not the perfecting of a knight in a virtue, not the establishment of a virtue, but the partial defeat of virtue in the fallen world. There was nothing sad about Books V and VI, but at their endings there was no place for jubilation. Irena's land was not completely reformed; the Beast escaped; the pastoral world was invaded and destroyed; the Graces vanished from Calidore's sight; the Beast is loose still and ranges about the world. The world was shown to be constant indeed, but only in defeat and change. Justice and Order do not reign on earth; and, although there are virtuous knights and ladies, the Graces and the fourth Grace do not move for ever in their grave and lovely dance. They are only to be glimpsed, and then by few; for in a world deprived of God's Order there cannot begin again the great reign of God's Love.

The judgement given in the Mutability Cantos is that the time will come when Mutability will bow to God's unchangingness. It is not suggested that that time is come; but it is certain that that time will come. Nature, God's vicar, acknowledges the love of change that all things and creatures feel, but declares that

> . . . time shall come that all shall changed bee,
> And from thenceforth, none no more change shall see.
>
> (VII.7.49)

Britomart's dream at the Temple of Isis prophesies a fulfilment that will come; Calidore's glimpse of the Graces is a glimpse of something that will assuredly come, when the prediction in the Mutability Cantos is fulfilled.

I find it impossible to escape the feeling that Books V, VI, and the fragment called 'Two Cantos of Mutabilitie' with its 'VIII Canto, vnperfite', are closely interconnected. Spenser may not originally have planned this, but the connexion between them appears too strong to overlook. Sir Calidore in Book VI seems to bring together in himself the knightly and human virtues of the heroes of the earlier books, almost displacing Arthur from the commanding, if aloof, dominance he had everywhere else exerted. The virtue celebrated in Book VI, as I claim, is the ultimate virtue, Grace itself, 'Courtesie' like God's or Christ's. Where could Spenser have gone from here? Far from *The Faerie Queene* remaining a half-finished work, I believe that Spenser deliberately worked it to a conclusion, and that what we have is a completed poem, not a fragment only of the projected poem of 1580, or of that outlined in the Prefatory Letter of 1590. We have also the postscript of the Mutability Cantos, which resolve all, silently declaring that the adventures of Faerie Land are concluded and all that now has to be done is to await with confidence and hope and desire the second coming, when the world will return to the virtuous perfection God always intended for it.

Spenser left an even more personal postscript in the two final stanzas in which he comes at last on to his own stage—not now as Colin Clout, but as Edmund Spenser, oldish, tired, loathing 'this state of life so tickle' in our fallen, disordered world,

> whose flowring pride, so fading and so fickle,
> Short *Time* shall soon cut down with his consuming sickle.

Then, comforting himself, he comforts us with his assurance that the time will come

> . . . when no more *Change* shall be,
> But stedfast rest of all things firmely stayd
> Vpon the pillours of Eternity,

and that

> . . . thence-forth all shall rest eternally
> With Him that is the God of Sabbaoth hight.

In December 1598, as the latest Irish uprising spread into Munster, Spenser was forced to fly from Kilcolman, and he returned to London to die, within a few weeks, in January 1599. It must have seemed to him that the Brigants were once more ascendant, the world and the potentiality of virtue and happiness in the world more than ever precarious, order again overthrown. Is it too fanciful to suppose that the two final stanzas were written at this time, and that there is something unprecedentedly personal and passionate in the final prayer to the 'great Sabbaoth God' to graunt him 'that Sabaoths sight' and to let him

> . . . rest eternally
> With Him that is the God of Sabbaoth hight?

Index

...or people and plot alike, is the main theme of the Prologue to the whole work; that at the beginning of Book I we turn from scenes of strife and discord to consider *naturatus amor*; and that at the end of